I0580197

the blue of night

katy masuga

SPUYTEN DUYVIL
New York City

This book should be regarded partly as fiction. All elements are either products of the author's imagination or are used in a fictitious manner. Any resemblance to reality is coincidental apart from the childhood chapters, which are a reconstruction, and the figures of Jim and Susi.

ISBN 978-1-952419-12-6

Cover image: *The Book of Ahania* (1795) William Blake

Library of Congress Cataloging-in-Publication Data

Names: Masuga, Katy, 1975- author.
Title: The blue of night / Katy Masuga.
Description: New York City : Spuyten Duyvil, [2020] |
Identifiers: LCCN 2020017135 | ISBN 9781952419126 (paperback)
Classification: LCC PS3613.A81996 B58 2020 | DDC 813/.6--dc23
LC record available at https://lccn.loc.gov/2020017135

To my children,
my families

“There is no great difference, says Proust,
between the memory of a dream
and the memory of reality.”
SAMUEL BECKETT

Book I

Interlude I - The History of Henry

Interlude II - The History of My Father

Interlude III - The Last History of Mom

Book II

Book I

Chapter 1
The Great River Ouse

I was still hoping Henry would want to keep the baby when we visited Monk's House, where Virginia Woolf was living when she killed herself in the river. It was not at all how Michael Cunningham describes in *The Hours*. The river is not much of a river. Centuries ago it was naturally part of the Great River Ouse, and it still belongs to the River Ouse, but it is a small, canalized segment, leveled and straightened, out in the open without trees or even bushes. The stretch near the villages of Lewes and Rodmell, where Monk's House is located, cuts through a vast, open field, is straight and flat with a sloping, manmade embankment and is defended by a small, ugly metal fence.

There were no black silhouettes of leaf skeletons summoned up from the bottom by her pale, floating corpse, a brisk and swirling current was not bearing her along quickly, the weed was not twisting and untwisting in beautiful, thick swatches. No one in a red jacket or any jacket was fishing in the canal that day or any other.

When you arrive at the Southease train station, you cross over the modern pedestrian skyway to connect to a dirt road and then arrive shortly upon an old bridge from which a boy, it is true, may have been jabbing a stick into the water just above where Virginia's corpse rest, tangled below. But perhaps, no, the bridge is too high for a boy to jab a stick from, and even then, there would be no sticks found near a bridge traversing a barren manmade canal.

The walk to Monk's House from the Southease station is about a mile and a half, with a view of the terrain for the entire journey clear and open, and you can see the small village of Rodmell (and the larger one of Lewes in the distance) and all of its houses clustered and hidden among a little thicket of trees. Yes, there are trees in the village but not near the canal.

A few other walkers strolled along the route as we walked, and the large sky overhead was a crisp blue with billowing, plump clouds. I slipped my arm in Henry's and leaned against him, my cold cheek brushing back and forth against his pea coat with each footfall.

"Hey, darlin," he said as he always did, his deep voice reverberating in my chest, and I snuggled in tighter at the inviting sentiment. Henry was a tall, broad, ruddy mountain man from the majestic Rockies of Idaho. It was a point of connection. Both our families lived there, though his were natives and mine transplants. My three eldest sisters and oldest brother Phil moved to Idaho a couple years after mom vanished. Henry wore a tweed paddy cap that he got from his grandfather before he died a decade back, stiff, classic blue jeans, a thick, hand-knitted wool sweater and the long, blue scarf I crocheted him the Christmas before to replace the one he had lost. His jaw was sharp and striking along with his cool green eyes, his full, flat lips and pointed, short nose. He had bright, strawberry blonde hair, thick and curly and probably just about two months too long for the image he needed for his new job as a professional consultant.

I looked up into those soft and full eyes, big and wide, drooping at the corners as though perpetually expressing compassion or empathy or something to do with love. I saw through them straight into my own fear. I tried to be wary of them but it was no use. I believed those eyes, and that was dangerous. But I believe most anything, and Henry or his eyes couldn't be blamed for that. Still, there they were, inviting me to bury my head and body and fear in a large, staged, warm embrace—an embrace forced out of him that I'd unknowingly created even if I didn't create the gaze. My anxiety divided my movements into quick, segmented flashes of reality, a life patched together in uneven cinematic frames with an unreliable light source, something like a strobe light.

Absent-mindedly Henry took me in his arms for a moment and rested his chin on the top of my head. He was staring into the treetops. I leaned into the embrace, pushing my face against the scratchy wool of his coat, my cheek against a cool button. It wasn't comforting. There was a film between us. More than a film, a force field around him. I pushed in harder, but what I needed wasn't there. I felt his heartbeat in my ear as though from far away, faint and distant. The arms of guilt were around me, and I knew it. He pulled back, and I followed his eyes in their sea-green lucidity from the trees to the sky then briefly back toward me. They shifted from vacant and searching to remote and sullen.

The drooping edges and dewy-wet gloss made it hard to describe Henry's eyes without an awful sentimentality, but so it was and it was true. These were eyes you couldn't escape, that removed your knowledge, your lessons learned, your hardened spine, your clear head and plunked you right back into helpless surrender. It wasn't because they loved you or made you feel loved or made you want to love. It wasn't because you melted into them or they into you or they made you feel romantic or weak at the knees. No, it wasn't that imaginary weak-at-the-knees kind of gaze. No. It was real, and it was humanity. He held it there, held the aleph there in his eyes, and it escaped gently and cautiously through diamond angles. A refracted phosphorescence of curved and jagged marbled currents. A burning, aching wave lifted me, stuck in me, enfolding me as in a gyroscopic whirlpool. That wave crashed into oceanic silence, and I tried to breathe underwater.

My body felt foreign. My breath was quick and afraid. To make up for it, I smiled more and skid across the earth lighter than my own weight. I tried to spring ahead, to catch the sunbeams, to offer joy in my eyes, to give acceptance that was secretly an asking for acceptance. Still, my body vibrated with a turbulent frequency full of anxiety like a high-pitched tuning fork or an unsteady camera, jolting up and down up and down 32 frames a second. The anxiety sent spikes shooting into my physical heart and so I skipped across the grass or felt myself skipping. I wanted to cast something out that wasn't in me but was in him. But I couldn't cast out it. I couldn't rid us of it. I was too afraid to push hard against it and so instead kept smiling and breathing shallow and gazing deeply but gently into things. Like a skittish deer among rustling, dry leaves and unseen predators.

"This place is beautiful." Looking for a way in, I cracked open the silence.

"Sure is."

"I wonder what it was like... would be like... would have been like to live here."

Often the case, Henry was listening without responding.

"I mean, you know, with their families and friends and literary stuff and all that."

More silent listening.

"She was so tormented. They never had children because she was sick." And I wanted to add, "Leonard didn't 'let' her." And I thought about how men 'let' women do things. Even with their own bodies.

"Is that why?" By now it was clear Henry wasn't interested in what I was trying to offer, and so he gave me a question out of politeness.

"Yes, you know, she had depression and everything. But I think she wanted children."

"I see." Moments later, "probably a good decision."

It was impossible to talk about. My fear was too great. I knew that anything I said would trigger a new painful rejection. I had to watch my step. I built a variation in my mind of what I needed, and I used it to direct my gestures toward. I had to bring him back to the positive side through other means through unspoken means. I had to show him, find a way to show him through a lightness of being, an appeal to his desires and not the realness of the circumstances. It had to come through subtlety through some kind of unconscious convincing so that he would begin to feel something that he now didn't feel that he now never expected to feel that he resisted feeling.

Who was this man? Lumbering and heavy with all the appeal of a warm, inviting campfire glow, looming large over me like so many soft, gentle creatures with wild, sharp edges. It reminded me of Henry Miller's description of his relationship to his own writing: "It was like taking a cub to bed with you. Once in a while he clawed you—and then you really were frightened." My desire for safety, for his protection, for his support, to have him on my side, was set off by my acute awareness and fear of instant destruction, somehow inevitable and maybe that was the source of my happy panic. He was reflective, measured and calculated but uneven and sharp, and so frightening and unpredictable.

"It's interesting how small these English cottages feel." A long, empty pause, so I continued, "You would bump your head every day coming into the kitchen!"

"You're probably right, darlin. Good thing we don't live here."

Was he sending me a message there?

"Could you imagine, Hen? I'd have to make fluffy scones with jam in the morning, and we'd take afternoon tea in the garden! How about that?" I gestured a walk from the cottage to the gardens with my arms and hands, bouncing my body on the balls of my feet.

"That sounds nice, darlin."

He was aloof. Displaying disinterest by agreeing with my fantasy and so it stayed a fantasy. He threw me no bone and it was intentional. He would not give into what I was pursuing. The walls closed in more tightly around me. I had only myself.

"We could do something like this, you know, for real." I dropped my tone. "Like, not here obviously. But, you know, wouldn't that be great?"

"What do you mean?" Now he was listening. He would let me feel uncomfortable. He would force me to come at it directly. To confront him.

"I mean, you know, if we had a little house and all that. Friends come over and talk and write and there'd be music and, you know, have a book club or something. Or whatever."

"Sure." Henry looked at the slow moving clouds and rubbed his nose.

"Take tea in the garden!" I feigned a laugh. Henry smiled softly, glancing at me briefly.

Everything slid back into fantasy.

Who was this man? So it was that Henry's birth father married Henry's mother not long after he'd met her and not long after she'd finished college. She was 22 with a degree in Communications, and he was 25 working electrical and maintenance at the bowling alley where they met one Friday night. To everyone's surprise, a few months later, they were married, and Henry arrived half a dozen months later. Henry's birth father joined some religious sect, and the family of three rolled out of Idaho in a pick-up truck and moved into a trailer in the Arizona desert. The wife and child were left for days without warning or whereabouts of their third member, and soon the two were eating meals at the soup kitchen. Within a year, Henry's maternal grandparents drove out across Utah and Nevada in their hulking, pea green station wagon and stole the two neglected souls back to Idaho.

Henry carried the truth of his background around with him like a great weight that he hid well. I think it colored his laugh and, like the rest of us, affected him in ways he would not want to acknowledge, could not believe, did not dare want to see. It was becoming clear to me that we were edging towards the inevitable commitment to those cycles that we swear to destroy, to overcome, to not emulate.

"I'm pregnant." We lay in bed on our backs.

I felt the weight of the silence. Eyes fixed nowhere.

"How did this happen?" The deep, unfeeling voice aimed toward the ceiling.

Time passed.

"It feels really right," he said into my hair, his breath on my neck.

We turned toward each other and stared. Time suspended.

I bent my body into his and burrowed my head and arms and torso and legs linking into his. We were in his 22m2 round room apartment in one of two towers across the Seine from the Eiffel Tower.

The toilet was down the hall past the other single rooms. There was a hotplate on top of a mini fridge. It was the room for the rape scene from *Last Tango in Paris*.

He left the next day to be gone for over a month and a half, and I remained in the room alone while he was stationed around Europe. That was a month ago now.

Before I'd gotten pregnant, I hadn't any clear thoughts about having children. To find yourself young and pregnant and soon alone was common among the women in my family. I thought as you got older, you were safe from that. Nothing in my family offered any clear direction on how it should work, work well, or work for me. One night after a few months of dating, Henry told me he was going to change my mind about it. He wanted children, and he wanted me to know it and wanted me to feel it.

Soon after that night I think he forgot. Or maybe it was just me he didn't want. Or maybe it was just some random conversation that had nothing to do with me. After the beginning, after the first announcement, Henry had changed his mind. It was just a few days later. That whole first episode has been replaying in my head endlessly like a broken record since it happened.

"I'm pregnant." We lay in the quiet darkness.

"It feels really right." My long exhale against his neck.

Henry forgot a lot of things. He forgot keys and birthdays and appointments. He forgot what he said and did and how he felt. So the story changed, and there I found a crack in me, life seeping out, gray ooze seeping in.

Chapter 2
Logan Correctional Center for Women: 0 yrs

Mom was serving a two-year term at the sole penitentiary in Illinois for women when she gave birth to me, her sixth daughter and ninth child of eventually ten, at a hospital in downtown Chicago. She was taken back to prison several days later for just about another year.

When I was a newborn, I slept in a dresser drawer of one of my older sister's. This was told to me throughout my life as though it were funny.

"I remember when they brought you home. We all slid you around on the floor on a blanket as we sat in a circle, each one taking a look at you. Can you imagine? There were eight of us—well, Emma was only one, so I guess it was the seven of us passing you around. Most of us were already teenagers. I felt so sorry for you! This little baby being pulled around the floor!" Lynn said.

"Where was mom?" My question.

Lynn searched her patchwork of memories. "I don't know. I guess she was still in prison. Back in prison? I don't know. They just brought you home. That was it."

The story never varied, but depending on who was around, there were more and less details.

"I emptied out my underwear drawer so you could sleep somewhere. No one knew what to do with you. No one had thought about it." Amber's flat addition.

"There you were: this teeny, tiny baby! We didn't know what to do with you." Maybe it was Diane. Maybe it was one of the twins. Maybe an older brother.

"Amber, didn't you have a boa constrictor sleeping in your dresser drawer too?" Another addition, asked in earnest.

There was laughter.

"Yeah, that's right. I did. But I think that was later."

"You mean you didn't have Aggie in one and the snake in the other?" With a wink. Laughter.

"Did you push the drawer back in after she was in there? To sleep?"

Laughter.

When I was very small, I cried for no reason and I knew it was for no reason. Mom asked me what was the matter and I had nothing to say. She looked at me in frustration until finally she threatened, "I'm only going to ask you one more time." In the second before she asked for that last time, I panicked and knew I had to come up with something. I had to come up with something if I wanted to keep her attention, if I wanted to keep her love, keep her near me, find a reason to keep her interested in me. I searched my mind. I considered making something up. But why was I crying? I didn't know.

"What *is* the matter?"

No response. She would walk away. "I fell," I might say. It would be a lie. She would take me in her arms. But no. Mom set me down and walked away. I had no answer, and so I continued crying. She was done trying to help. She was gone.

Mom was a teenage runaway. She met a man as soon as she ran away from her small town in Michigan, hopping on the bus heading east toward any major city. She became a mother before she was 20, and she continued to become a mother ten times over the next twenty years. She had no education. No training in anything. She became a cook and she became a good cook and that is to say people liked her food. All our lives mom's jobs had her cooking nonstop. She cooked for different bars and she cooked for catering jobs. Her own heritage was American as far back as the Mayflower, but when she ran away from her Michigan childhood, she ended up in Chicago, Illinois, full of Poles and Hungarians and Eastern Europeans, billing itself as the largest Polish city outside of Warsaw. She adopted their cuisine as her own. Her first husband was Russian-Slovak, and with him she had seven of the children. When her husband died, she had three more with his Polish-German brother-in-law, which is where I come in. The first time I made a family tree to explain to friends, it came out looking like a heart, something a child would draw.

When and wherever mom was working, she cooked everything: she rolled the dough with a cracked, wooden rolling pin, thick, wrinkled knuckles kneading and folding, making steamed perogies and fried perogies with onions, fried Polish sausages with sauerkraut, sausages with beans, sausage with dumplings, spoonfuls of their doughy mass dropped into the boiling bouillon, soup with dumplings, chicken with dumplings, dumplings with sauerkraut, more flour added to the rolling pin and the dough pulled longwise for sausage with dumpling-style noodles, dumpling-style noodles with gravy, dumpling-style noodles with sauerkraut, perogies stuffed with sauerkraut and potatoes, potatoes with cheese, perogies with potatoes and cheese, potato salad, potato wedges, potato tacos, mini tacos, mini hotdogs, mini egg quiches, endless eggs cracked into large stainless steel bowls, floating sunshine yellow yolks waiting for their fate, poached egg soup, deviled eggs, scrambled eggs, fried egg sandwiches, egg salad, fruit salad with old bananas, oranges, browning apples and maraschino cherries, pork with the same fruit but jellied, pork and beans, pork chops, pigs-in-a-blanket, pulled pork sandwiches, fried ham sandwiches, fried chicken, fried corn fritters, fried apple fritters, more dough rolled out to bake apple pie, potpie, Jell-O pie, chocolate pie, chocolate cake, add water to the dough for pancakes, Polish crepes, crepes with chocolate, forget the dough for chocolate mousse, chocolate fudge, peanut butter fudge, mix and bake the sugary dough for peanut butter cookies, Polish cookies with jam, jam with ham, a side of ham, a stuffed turkey, a whole chicken, a chicken's innards, a turkey's gizzards, a chicken salad and any number of other things I don't even know how to describe because she made them up on the spot.

We went hungry as kids. By the time mom's last three kids came along, the last three of us, Emma, me and Fred, she was tired, sluggish, overburdened, and perogies, kielbasa and sauerkraut were reserved for holidays, home cooked meals becoming a rarity, and our plates altogether remaining fully empty many of the other days of the year.

Mom returned to the same Illinois prison a decade later when I was a kid, growing up in California, without her, without my father. When she was discharged that time, also just about after two years, she dropped back in to our lives for less than a year when I was thirteen, then went missing for ten years. She crossed the country to Chicago in November just before my fourteenth birthday, disappearing completely a couple months later after her father's death.

It was Mother's Day when we learned she was missing. She didn't show up for lunch with her sisters after the funeral but had just kept on driving, crossing down into Kentucky and Tennessee across Alabama into Mississippi and almost over the border into Louisiana. She was living in a small town on the Bayou an hour from New Orleans, working as a seamstress at *Le bon temps roule* and cooking at the honky-tonk jutting out on the water on stills, the whole town swallowed up by Hurricane Katrina a dozen years later. Part of that time she was homeless living out of her van, more than once robbed and beaten. She lost all her front teeth and some others besides. I don't know if that was from the beating or from drink or from something else. She never talked about her ten years away.

The police told us it's nearly impossible to find folks who don't want to be found, but we tried and, like they predicted, we never found her. We looked and looked and then waited and waited and the waiting was ten years. There was a phone call one morning at Mona's, our father's girlfriend, where he lived too.

"Hello?"

"Hello? Is Freddy there?" Mona knew it was mom. Mom in her new, tiny, fragile and uncertain voice asking to speak to her baby.

"He's not here. Who's this?"

Freddy's not *here* because he's all grown up now and in college in San Diego.

Click.

Mom said she had been trying to call for years but the phone was busy. That was my mom. That's really what she said.

When she came back after that decade, I was grown up too. She had missed our youth, but still she came back and we held our collective arms open. We found her toothless and drunk working in the kitchen of that Mississippi honky-tonk. My three oldest sisters drove across the country without stopping, bleary-eyed and breathless rescuing their mama, bringing her back to us. They took her to our sister's place in Idaho where she lived out her last decade as a short-order cook at a highway truck stop, flipping burgers, chicken fried steak and slopping gravy. To make Christmas money, she started working every November as the solitary cook for a remote hunting lodge in the middle of nowhere in the Rockies. It was dangerous, lonely and primitive, and she made a whopping $2000 in four weeks. One year she used the money to buy all ten of us certificates from the International Star Registry in Zürich.

"They were very expensive," mom explained. "But now each one of you has a star named after you—forever."

"Thanks, mom." We didn't know how to respond. And in light of how she'd earned the money. It was the strangest and maybe saddest gift I'd ever received.

She lived out there in the remote Rockies for that month in a small trailer without heat or electricity using the fur and skin of animals to keep warm, catering to the men who came out for a week a piece to hunt big game. They handed the dead beasts over to her to clean and dress, and she used some of the meat for their meals and the rest went back to their families in their million-dollar Colorado or Utah or New York homes. Marble-eyed trophies gathering dust above fireplaces. I wondered if those families had stars named after them too.

We might say it was lucky for mom and lucky for us that my sisters brought her back to their families in Idaho, and she got a job as a cook at that decrepit truck stop on the edge of town across from the bowling alley. We all visited her at least once a year in the summer and maybe winter too, everyone together again.

During those holidays with mom newly around, the scene continued as before, and no one asked any questions. She drank a bottle of vodka each day and still spent her life in the kitchen, cooking endless hours who knows why, moving her lethargic, hefty body from the table to the oven to the countertop, rolling out dough with her worn and weathered but gentle hands, pushing or pulling a casserole dish from the oven, cutting up a 5 lb. bag of onions, mixing another vodka and soda, easy on the soda. Slowly, steadily, quietly, with kids running through holding squirt guns, magazines, musical toys, baby bibs and bottles, squeaks, cries, shouts, brothers with beer bottles, sisters with mugs of wine, someone sharing shots of booze, others eating brownies, meatloaf, iceberg lettuce, leave the apple peels for the sauce, boil the milk but be careful not to burn it, pound the meat but don't trim the fat, whip the cream but don't turn it into butter, glaze the ham, slice the strawberries, pour the gravy, beat the eggs, mix the pudding, turn the stove on so Lynn can light a cigarette, and set the oven to 450° F.

Smoke that outside!

Mom spoke in such a soft voice, wearing a pair of clouded glasses not made for her, one arm held on with a paper clip and a piece of masking tape. Her eyes cartoonishly magnified through the scratched lenses.

Mom cooked anything out of nothing. I figure she improvised every single dish she ever made. We might have stuffed cabbage as we did for every holiday, delicious and filled differently each time with whatever was on hand. A combination of tomatoes, rice and meat but always made randomly each time with ketchup, leftover bread, any kind of grains, any kind of onions… *throw in that soup mix and an egg or two? What else is there? How about that old hamburger meat? And the leftover mashed potatoes can't go to waste. This can of corn will bulk it up along with those old breadcrumbs from the bottom of the toaster.*

There is an image of mom in my mind from a photograph my sister gave me some years after mom disappeared. In the image mom is smiling with those dark milky eyebrows and that perfectly but gently coifed hair, sitting on the arm of the sofa next to her man's man of a husband, who is also gentle looking, smiling, all teeth exposed and parted, drinking a beer from a can, two little girls frozen in their moment of play to the side of the photo—my two oldest sisters. Mom is wearing a short-sleeved, button up white shirt and upturned collar, pencil skirt to her calves and dark shoes with a thick inch heel. They are the picture of 1960. They are in black and white, and they are people who took turns living and were not caught in the eternity of the image but are caught in the eternity of the image in my mind.

Chapter 3
Monk's House, East Sussex

Henry and I were most of the way to Monk's House when an old farmer with a weathered face and soiled gloves holding a spade directed us along the length of his field. He pointed out the parking area at the bottom of the slight hill and indicated to turn right once at the tree grove. We took large, deliberate strides over the rows of his vegetation, and it seemed a long time before we reached the end. It was suddenly evident we were in a town or village square and that one dirt road wound back to the station while the other clearly led to the rest of the village and, ostensibly, Monk's House. We followed the second and descended the well-traveled path soon finding ourselves among parked cars that were patiently waiting along rows of 18th century cottages. These slept behind well-crafted, wooden fences.

Monk's House was a classic weatherboard, two-story home, with long, thin overlapping strips of wood painted white with white trim. The second floor of the road-facing façade had two nine-paned windows, and the downstairs had three six-paned sashed windows and a door with a small entryway. It sat perhaps six feet from a waist-high stonewall that divided it from the road. The entrance for visitors was on the backside in the garden.

The first to arrive at Monk's House that morning, we waited ten minutes at the steps and ivy-laden archway as others slowly strolled up to join us. Upon paying the admission, we were offered apples sitting in a basket taken from the tree above.

The house was kept in the same condition as by the former tenants, last occupied 1941. Visitors were invited to explore the ground floor that consisted of four small rooms and Woolf's adjacent 'writing lodge' outside, but the upper floor was off-limits, as that was where the caretaker lived. Though the 18th century weatherboard exterior felt solid and rather ancient, the walls felt as thin as a doll's house. The interior was filled with relics of the Woolfs' literary life alongside pieces of furniture and art created by the two Post-Impressionist painters and designers Vanessa Bell, Woolf's sister, and Duncan Grant, Woolf's close friend and peer. As we slowly tread across the creaking floorboards, both Henry and I noted how incredible it was that the paintings hanging in every room were personal ones. Henry got caught up examining first a somber grey-hued portrait in the passageway into the bedroom that the older sister made of the younger followed by a Manet-inspired green-nosed dog with abstract but happy children and finally a serious still life over the mantle. On the opposite wall were a series of photographs with more, this time real, children, and I wondered who they were, and if not the same children borne of pigment and oil in the previous room.

We moved through Woolf's writing lodge, where I was taken by the lighthouse Vanessa painted on the ceramic-tiled fireplace, evidently after the success of *To the Lighthouse* in 1927. The bed and room itself seemed those of a child. I had an ache to inhabit them myself or somehow watch them be inhabited by their proper tenant. Such an ache I felt, I had an involuntary need to touch my abdomen with the gently cupped palm of my hand. Catching myself, I quickly turned my body and looked out the large and wide windows onto the foliage. Not noticing my gesture at all, Henry studiously scanned Woolf's large book collection positioned over her small bed before we stepped out into the garden together.

The grounds on the backside of the house were large and contained two notably small cottages. Signs explained one was rented to travelers and the other housed a permanent museum-style exhibition of photographs of Woolf, her husband, friends and other figures from the Bloomsbury Group. I tried to identify each of them before the reading the captions... T. S. Eliot, Lytton Strachey, Vita Sackville-West, Maynard Keynes, Duncan Grant. Who was that next to Vanessa sitting in the high-backed chair? Ah, Roger Fry, of course.

The expansive green surrounded the house, including the lawns on which the Woolfs bowled with friends—many philosophers, writers and artists. There was an orchard, a pond and winding paths through yew hedges with an herbaceous area right in the center.

We walked through the gardens as though we were alone despite the twenty or thirty other visitors, mostly elderly couples. I fell into two simultaneous and conflicting fantasies: one, that the Bloomsbury Group figures were alive and walking among us, and I could be part of the excitement, the conversations, the discoveries, the aromatic teas, the English biscuits—and two, I was alone with Henry. Just that. Alone with Henry, there in that elaborate and peaceful garden. All the others had disappeared.

I imagined their afternoons playing bowls, warm evenings with tea or wine or beer or sparkling water and discussions on the philosophy of language and ancient Greek literature. What might they be saying?

Virginia, dear. What have you been working on this spring? Her sister would ask, rolling the reflective, silver ball in the palms of her hands before launching it slowly, heavily across the grass where it met with a large thump as it hit the earth and gently slid up to another polished globe, finishing its journey with the gentle clank of metal on metal.

Oh, nothing really, good Vanessa. It's not much to speak of yet. We'll see if it amounts to anything. Just some character sketches. Perhaps an essay on the side—. Woolf didn't have much confidence in herself or her writing, I don't think, or perhaps she just never wanted to jinx herself by being too bold. I imagine her being humble and reserved. It's hard to imagine anything else.

The Woolfs were childless. Many of their friends were childless, and even many of my own friends never had and didn't want children. That could be OK, couldn't it? But that didn't feel like what I wanted. Would I be inferior if I had children? Was I meant to be like Woolf? Could I not be like her if I chose children? Would I be less successful? Would I not be successful at all with children? Did it weigh on my possibility as a writer? Either actually or superstitiously? Was I only asking these questions because of a new fear? Did I need to choose no children because Henry changed his mind? Was there a way not to have to choose Henry or child? Is that the choice I was being forced to make?

"What would you like to do this evening?" Henry used the question to indicate he was ready to leave.

"We should go to the seaside before it gets dark. It's not very far."

"That's a good idea, darlin," Henry thrust his big hands in his coat pockets as though preparing for the cool air of the waterfront.

"Great. And we can get dinner at the pub."

"Do you want to walk down along the river on the way back to the station?" His large body was already shifting away from me.

"Yes, that would be nice." I spoke into Henry's back as he moved toward the exit, walking faster than me, arms now flat at his sides as though on auto-pilot.

I followed him out of Monk's House and entered the road hoping to explore the neighboring countryside and wood along the water.

"I think we can go this way." He pointed in the opposite direction from which we came.

We headed down the path. It was the same path Woolf took to get to the river. Our feet made temporary tracks in the loose sand of the dirt road, the weight of our footfalls crushing it into the unexpected patterns of our soles.

"This isn't what I expected it to look like." I broke the silence.

"What did you expect it to look like?" Henry's questions always came across as earnest and interested even if at the heart they were not. I never knew the difference between the two, only dreaded it.

"In books and things, you know, it's made out to be so beautiful. It's awfully romanticized. At least I imagined it as quite beautiful. You think of willows and green and brown grasses and a hazy, gray light gently falling between tree trunks and branches. Some kind of extraordinary forest and all that. I see her walking through it, brushing vines or boughs or something off her shoulder, crunching leaves underfoot, or even dead, silent, wet leaves underfoot, weeping willows by the water's edge, a soft embankment. She's kneeling down, the forest sort of enclosing her—all of that sense of tragic yet beautiful melancholy."

Henry was silent. He never responded to commentary, only questions.

"Know what I mean?" I added.

"Sure, darlin." He was staring straight ahead, hands in his pockets again.

He called me 'darlin' within weeks of dating. It seemed strange when I first heard it some soft, sticky night in my basement apartment in Paris, like a caricature of something, a stunted attempt at a 19th century, wild west romantic gesture. But no, it was real, just like Henry, and before that first 'darlin' dissipated through the breath between us, I recognized it as a real and natural word in his mouth, full of his Rocky Mountains and well-filled flannel shirts and beltbuckles. It could have been campy or syrupy, but that voice of Henry's was too authentic, so deep and full with rounded out edges, as full as a bear hug embrace and as delicate as a glass menagerie.

Henry kept a novel in one pocket and a journal in the other. In the summer they filled the back of his jeans, in the winter the front of his coat. His laugh was loud and boisterous and off-putting, especially since he stared at you straight in the eye when doing it. He charmed the old gals at French dinner parties, and, because he didn't try to, the young ones too. His lack of self-awareness made him a quick learner, a good consultant and a great lover. He could build a persuasive argument on thin assertions and bring a story to life that he'd heard told once. After two years, I couldn't say where his heart lay, and I don't think he ever could either.

"Look at that!" A spotted bird hung above us, suspended in the airstream, scanning the field below, drifting from side to side with wings splayed.

"What is it, darlin?"

"I think it's a hawk." We stopped walking and stared. My ears opened to the myriad sounds around us, more vivid from the renewed silence. I could feel the heat they'd been storing throb as I marched against the chill autumn air. The hawk suddenly dove in a 'U' shape toward an even plot of earth. It plunged with force and grace then returned back to the sky just as rapidly, its beak now full of the living flesh of some unlucky rodent. A momentary sliver of black quickly crossed our open vision and disappeared into the upper branches of the close.

Our vaporous breaths met the invisible atmosphere then vanished. The space around us was vibrating, humming, rustling like a thousand tiny black ants on a mound, a thousand cockroaches standing and crawling among books and shelves in a long forgotten attic, camouflaged and invisible until just one is noticed, and the entire bookcase swarms with life.

We began walking again. I slipped my hand in his pocket and held it there, and held his hand there. It was warm and made my hand warm too, and it was nice to feel his body, this small part of his body with mine walking in the cold toward the river.

"I'm pregnant." We lay next to one another on the foldout sofabed; knees, thighs and arms touching.

The silence weighed me down. Our eyes were fixed to the ceiling. Or perhaps to the searchlight of the Eiffel Tower scanning the room like a magic lantern projecting shapes through the wrought iron balcony against the walls.

"Are you sure?"

"I just found out from the doctor."

The roar of Metro Line 6 filled the spaces illuminated by the Tower.

His face was a mark on the wall.

"What do you want to do?" His voice, sucked into the open darkness.

I nuzzled my body up against his. Heart racing. Breath held. Thick city silence.

"It feels really right," he said into my hair, his breath on my neck. I exhaled.

Four or five or six cows blocked the gate we needed to pass through, and I was nervous to pass them. They did not move or seem to care that we needed to pass. They stared at us with boredom, indifference. I was afraid to project my fear on to them and had the strange sensation that they understood more than they let on. Henry was patient. I plucked up my courage, feigned ignoring them, and turned toward the gate just managing to get through.

All along, holding my breath. We carried on along the embankment, and the river offered nothing to the scene. It moved not rapidly and was a deep but flat blue, like a colorless blue. We passed a couple with a dog and then a couple with walking sticks. Each time, one of the parties had to pull off to the side to let the other pass. We reached the bridge and I looked toward the sea to the south as we crossed atop. The sea itself was not in sight, but you could feel it there above or below the horizon and I liked thinking it was there and also that we would soon be seeing it. Seeing the sea felt important now.

Henry, I thought, was a gentleman. Henry had always taken care of me, but I was frightened. Why was I always frightened? I was always frightened. I don't think I used to be frightened of Henry. I wasn't sure if there was something wrong with me or with us or with him. I sometimes thought maybe I had done something wrong. I tried to stay good to him, to stay on his good side, and now it was too late. He didn't want the baby. I was so frightened of him. I needed to not talk about it so that he would forget again and it could be like it was, like it used to be before it happened, though its happening was my greatest joy. Could I keep what was happening and keep Henry too? I was tired, though still fighting. Fighting Henry. Fighting myself as I tried to keep Henry, not knowing what I had to choose, if I had to choose.

The train south wasn't coming for 40 minutes. We were vaguely uncertain on which platform it would arrive, so we pressed the large silver button in the center of a call box attached to a solitary pole affixed to the bottom of the stairs. A crackling voice answered us.

“Is this the southbound platform?” Henry asked.

The voice at the other end was kind and reassuring. “Yes, sir. That is correct. Anything else I can help you with today?”

“Yes, thank you.” Henry was polite. We were both gazing at the call box speaker as though it were the eyes of a speaking human. “How much are the tickets? The price has eroded from the sign.”

“That would be £1.80 for the full fare. Would you like me to quote you the reduced fares for students, seniors, and the disabled? We also have a special fare for families.”

“No, none of the above here.” Henry didn’t bat an eye while my heart took a quick leap and fall. “Thank you for your help,” he said.

“You’re very welcome, sir. Have a safe and pleasant journey.”

Henry went to college but dropped out after one year, setting off for New York and then Mexico and eventually finding a path to Paris where he rediscovered his studies at the prestigious university Sciences Po in Paris, finishing with honors and a double major in sociology and finance. Afterwards he fell into one expat job after another until he finally found the new position this year as a consultant in the tech industry.

I knew it in the way he walked that something was different about Henry, arriving as we did from opposite directions for our first official date, meeting up on the quay of the Seine to swing dance. It was raining as I walked up, and he had been waiting in a café. He saw me arrive and waved, and I watched him cross the boulevard, stiff and foreign in his own body—tall, broad, full, 'a man's man', with quick, forced steps like a machine with the operator somewhere off location, perfectly replicating human fluidity and grace.

We walked over to the train platform shelter where we sat and talked about how we imagined the future. What kind of things did I want? Was it a trick question? I tiptoed around my answer. I wanted a community. Maybe have writers and artists and thinkers over once in a while, a sort of salon? Wouldn't that be neat? I wanted children. Could I say that aloud? Did I think maybe I didn't want children because I knew he didn't anymore —at least not with me? But it wouldn't be like that. It would work. It would be an open atmosphere, with intelligent people, drinks and children, laughter and philosophy. It could be. It was like a frozen scene of a good time on repeat. Everyone's faces in a joyful grin, gorgeous half-filled scotch glasses with soft, dreamy ice, children playing, intellectual jokes mixed with daily news settled in the backs of eyes, comfortable evening light coming in at the window, the scent of a warm, hearty dinner on the way. Was I trying to convince him of something?

Wasn't it already too late?

The train arrived. We took an open set of four seats with a table. There was no one else in our car, and Henry took out the book in his pocket and began to read. I stared out the window continuing to imagine I was Virginia Woolf. She had seen this landscape thousands of times.

What they said about that gap between the world and us was all true. I was staring at it out the window.

Woolf was nowhere to be found. It was a shame thinking like that, feeling like that, but I couldn't have helped it, especially in that moment.

The train sped along and the sound of the wheels on the rails together with the slight lull back and forth back and forth made the journey pleasant and numbing. I wanted to climb into the horizon and find out what was on the other side or rather what was deep within the horizon itself, but it doesn't work like that, and instead I took a long drink of water from the bottle in my bag and meticulously examined with my eyes the bent corners of Henry's book and its broken spine.

Something was gone now. I wasn't sure how to—or if I could—get it back.

Chapter 4
California, Here I Come: 4 yrs

In kindergarten they don't let you use glue. Instead you get paste with its gritty texture and homemade smell. The lid opens up to reveal a mini-spatula handle inside for scooping and spreading. You want to spread the paste slowly across the thick, colored construction paper. The texture is like a cat's tongue, rough but smooth, and it's fabulous to cut up different dark colors into shapes like triangles and squares. You press down one piece against another, bits of the paste squishing out the sides, and its sweet smell like salty Mongolian rice pudding. New school supplies.

My own supplies, the ones I got at home, only once in a while did I actually use them. These I took out gently, inspected each item one at a time then put it away. Waiting for when it was needed. Making sure nothing was ever needed. Always preserving, always using as little of something as possible. Hardly using anything. Never wanting to waste it. Waste. No waste.

The night before kindergarten began, after everyone had gone to sleep, I laid out the clothes I was going to wear in the morning. Mom had given me new packages of socks and underwear, so I would have a whole set of new pairs for the first week. She also gave Emma and me each a new bookbag. Emma's was yellow with Tweety Bird, and mine was green with Bugs Bunny. I chose my ruffled, violet skirt with matching top and lay them on the foot of my bed. It was my only outfit that had belonged just to me and no one else before. Mom bought it from Kmart for my birthday when I turned four, and it still fit, especially since it was a skirt with an elastic waist. In the morning before everyone else awoke and I discovered for the first time how I never needed an alarm but that my body had a trust in itself to wake when it was supposed to wake even if I didn't know it was happening or make it happen, I got dressed, then toasted myself two slices of stale, white bread, spread on some jam and no butter and waited for someone to take me to my first day of school.

A half an hour later, in the truck with my oldest brother Phil, I was thinking about whether I was going to be able to attend kindergarten of my own free will or not. Phil had just gotten his driver's license and sat patiently behind the wheel in the school parking lot three miles from home. He was smiling the whole time. Without a word I got out, immediately changed my mind and got back in. Phil let me come back, talked to me, convinced me to get out of the truck again and walk forward.

"You can do it."

"But I'm scared."

"Aggie, you can do it. Look, you made your own breakfast this morning! You can do anything. You're so big! You're almost five!"

"Four-and-a-half."

"That's almost five, Aggie!

I stared at him.

"Look, Mom would be so proud of you."

I grinned a little then frowned. Where was mom anyway?

"Go for it."

I took the door handle in my minuscule palm and turned it. I looked out toward the path leading to school. It looked so long.

Phil was reading my thoughts. "You can do it, Aggie. It's nothing. No sweat."

I stepped out. Two feet on the concrete. I climbed back in. Two feet off the concrete.

"Come on, Aggie. You can do it!"

I looked at Phil, back at the school, down at my hand on the door. I stepped out again. This time I got as far as the end of the parking lot before I turned back. I saw Phil staring at me through the windshield. "Go!" I saw him mouth the word but didn't hear it. I stopped. Turned and looked again. Took three more steps toward the truck. "Go on!" This time I could hear him a little. He must have gotten louder. I turned back toward the school and walked toward the door, where I turned back again. Phil was waving now with his arms, "Go! Go!" I paused, then walked back to the truck. Not running but walking as quickly as possible, hips jutting side to side. I climbed back in.

"It's fine. You can do it. No sweat, Aggie. No sweat."

I tried not to cry. I took the handle again. I stepped out again. I went through this process two more times before I made it to the school. I turned to look at grinning Phil and finally went in.

Eventually, the halfway point of the kindergarten year came, and we half-day kids switched to full-day schedules. I was ready with my lunch money for my first full day, and after leaving my bookbag in the classroom,

I went into the lunchroom to buy and eat my lunch for the first time. Where would I sit? Would I find my way back to the classroom afterwards? It had been explained to us and we had practiced, but doing it on my own was something else. I was overwhelmed in the large, open room by myself, full of the long, slick tables with their attached benches. The lunchroom was outside under an open roof in a courtyard, enclosed by four walls with open, adjoining walkways. Everything was bathing in sun. I was scared, alone finally and truly five. Just the state of things. Not questionable. Not debatable. Just the state of the universe.

A student was working the lunch cart, learning the procedure. I reached up my hand and struggled to set down my money on the cart without it dispersing across the floor.

"Does she want a full lunch or just a carton of milk?"

The supervising teacher stared down at me, so far down. She looked me up and down as though trying to locate the answer.

"Do you want milk?" She asked.

"Yes."

Yes, I want milk with my lunch, I thought.

"OK, she just wants milk."

Nothing to be done. The girl handed me a carton of milk and my change. I slinked away to an empty long table with its smooth matching bench. I watched the others eat. My belly grumbled. I didn't say anything to anyone. Was it my fault? She did something wrong or I did something wrong. How could I fix that? I said the truth but it didn't work right.

When the bell rang, I followed the others back to the classroom. I sat on my carpet dot in front of the chalkboard as instructed. The dots were many different colors. Mine was red. I did what I was told usually before I was told. That afternoon there was an eye exam. Dark and mysterious, in some unfamiliar area of the school. I held up the blinder to one eye and called out what images and letters I saw. The nurse mistook me for my older sister. There were so many of us, they were always getting us mixed up. Emma was only a year older and had also had the same teacher for kindergarten.

We handed mom the notes from the eye doctor when we got home. Emma's said she needed glasses. Emma cried and mom threw away the notes.

A week later, a group of children visited our classroom from another school. I was assigned a girl with a name just like mine. She sat next to me next to my dot, she in a pretty dress, I in old shorts worn by most of my older siblings. She was only my friend for her one-day visit. A week later I was transferred to the neighboring class. The bully said it was because I was too small. I wasn't and I knew I wasn't but I was worried and ashamed. I still knew I qualified to be in school, and that was all there was to it. My birthday was in late November, and I squeaked into the deadline. I wasn't too little. I had starting kindergarten officially at 4 years old just like Emma before me, and I was special for it, just like her. It meant I was smarter just like her, and I would be smarter. They would see.

At the end of the year, on the night of open house, the parents came to our classroom. Phil and Charlie, who was just one year younger than Phil, Emma and Baby Freddy came with me. My teacher wore a handsome floor-length skirt with pieces of our art pinned to it. I admired her. I wished I also had such a dress—no, I didn't wish I had such a dress. I wished for her to wear her dress and to be my mom. I understood her dress. Her dress was full of care, of attention to each of us, of kindness, of an interest in our abilities, an interest in our names and bodies, our smiles and tears and laughter and fears.

I was proud of my work and excited to share it with Phil and Charlie and even Emma and Baby Freddy. On one of the classroom walls at the open house were the paper silhouettes of our classmates. In the last month we had learned how to draw and have drawn of us a silhouette:

Sitting perfectly still, you let your proper real self out, you let the other kindergartner outline your dark, shadowy shape projected on the wall. You were patient and calm, and the process was soothing and gentle, as you sat near the wall, becoming your own image, your silhouette, which you couldn't look at while it was being constructed, and your image was projected from you like that against the wall and it was your lips and eyes and the shape of your large growing head and your chin looking wise and yet young and innocent and unknowing and having some other child make a piece of art out of you—her foreignness becoming you, becoming one of you, taking you from you but not taking it but becoming part of it, almost like suddenly that child knew you better than you knew yourself because she had made you. She had made you into something, a permanent outline, a dark aura that could be traced, that could be found, that could be made into paper, cut out of black construction paper and glued with the magical paste onto a deep blue or green or bright yellow background. It was for you to take home and keep, your shadow, like Peter Pan's, an eternal best friend but now cut away, now separate, your own version of your classmate belonging to her now, and hers became yours, though it wasn't you but more you than ever.

Before I had even started going to school, sometime in the dirty, cold spring of the Midwest, we all piled in a used RV and left Chicago in the middle of the night during a big snowstorm and traveled across the country to find a new life in California. It was random, and it had something to do with "bad checks" mom had been writing around town.

The journey was a fantasy. The sun came out, and we visited National Parks and watched too many horizons to count, as they grew closer and again further, for days on end. Amber, three years older than Phil and so seventeen on the cross-country trip, made Wonder Woman paper dolls out of the thin cardboard packaging from our greasy supermarket doughnut box, tracing their bodies and outfits with a blue ink pen found at a truck stop. At the Grand Canyon Amber glued a pinecone to a piece of paper and sprinkled cigarette tobacco over it all, showing us what Christmas was going to be like in dry, sunny California. Before we got there, though, we broke down right at the bottom tip of Nevada and lived in the parking lot of a Las Vegas casino for a month.

"There's been flooding in California. We have to wait out the storm anyway," mom said.

Maybe it was true. Maybe it wasn't. Maybe mom suddenly thought her lucky number had come up. All we had to do was wait around for a while. I do remember there was a lot of flooding in the mountains a few years later when I was in the third grade, and a girl and her sister got swept away and died. They were the only black kids in town. I envisioned them sliding down the unpaved gutter on the long road up to the ski resort that always filled with water whenever it rained. The girls in my imagination were whisked away on their backs in a horrendous rush as they lay helpless in the current, hands folded across their bodies or arms flat against their sides, frightened but serene faces with eyes closed pointing upward out of the water. Much in the way we lost our muffler in that same storm crossing over the intersection at the ski resort. The car dipping down into the shoulder and re-ascending, with a low scrape and without our muffler, out of the swimming pool-sized puddle. We watched it carry on down the muddy stream.

The Vegas casino had an intangible magic that felt like we were living in an amusement park of the imagination. Emma and I, five and four years old, wandered on our own across the children's level, playing games, staring at the people, the costumes, the prizes, mesmerized by the endless flashing lights, the cocktail waitresses, the circus music from every corner, the sudden bursts of high-pitched laughter and the *ching-ching-ching!* of the slot machines above and below. Mom bought us beads and feathers strung together at the end of a strip of leather for hanging in our hair by means of a small, jagged clip that my brothers called a 'roach clip' they used for smoking dope. We were at the only casino with a dedicated section, a whole floor even, to children's games. We played tic-tac-toe, tossing softballs into small, adjoined boxes. Winning horizontally was best, as indicated by the boxes lined with red paint. Next, we played the bowling game where you push a bowling ball over a small slope but just barely enough to keep it from rolling back. I won a few times.

Finally, we played my least favorite game because it had a clown that lived on bursts of violence. With good aim, competitors fired a steady squirt-gun stream into the clown's mouth, activating a balloon that blew and blew and blew up to explode if you shot it straight and fast. The popping balloon exploded in my head like the white violence of my father who I saw chase and beat my mom and follow us to the mountains but didn't live with us after the beach and so was sometimes around and most of the time not around. At the casino, I preferred the game of tossing a quarter on a collection of 50 small plates dispersed across the booth. All you had to do was make one little old quarter land on the plate and you won a stuffed animal as big as you. I never did win at that one, but all those clinking, clacking, clacking, dinging, crispy, light, electric, chiming, bouncing, singing sounds of millions of bits of metal against glass were soothing, like the rain must be at the rainbow connection. Somehow Emma, Baby Freddy and I came away with so many prizes, and Phil and Charlie had no more pocket change.

Charlie, a year younger than Phil, was a joker who tried to hide our hardship from us with antics and surprise. Phil was also shielding and gracious and was Paul Bunyan. A high school dropout, semi-literate construction worker, accidental outsider artist without any knowledge or help or means or even a sense to know what he was up to—

now living in his van gone missing in the woods with bears and eagles and mountain lions for days and weeks and months and even years. Charlie dropped out at the same time and was up to no good until his twenties when he apprenticed in electrical work to pay our rent after mom left. Twelve and thirteen years older than me, Charlie and Phil often took care of me, Emma and Baby Freddy—feeding us, making us laugh, taking us places, metamorphosing privation into scouts' fun and games.

They taught us how to catch a lizard, catch a moth to feed a snake, shoot a gun, make a potato gun, show your guns, pitch a tent, chop a log, swim in whitewater, swim underwater, do a back flip, jump off a bridge, a cliff, a rooftop, strum a tune, sing a tune, tune a guitar, carve a guitar pick or part, carve a pumpkin, carve an arrow, carve a ski mogul, ski like fire, build a fire, build a clubhouse, build a snow figure, build a milkshake with banana and barley malt, shake an apple tree, climb a tree, climb a rock, skip a rock, ride a motorcycle, ride a bike, hike a mountain, climb a mountain, climb a rope, train a dog, bury a dog and whistle through your hands cupped like you're in *The Good, the Bad and the Ugly.*

We were waiting out something before mom could take us to California. Why were we going to California in the first place? There was a tension we were used to and so didn't call it a tension. It's like when your belly rumbles with hunger and you know nothing is coming, but you think mom might come home with some old sandwiches or she might not come home at all, and you just carry on either way. Everything always shifting. Always shifty. Mom's ways were strange maybe, always scheming to strike gold, how she thought or wanted or wanted to think and maybe didn't want to accept to realize or maybe didn't actually know that good things only come the long way.

When we finally crossed into the Golden State, mom hid our four pieces of softening fruit at the bottom of the trash bag between the bucket seats at the head of the RV. I knew even then we were built on being deceivers, we were getting away with something, but not only that, we were doing something wrong because we had to and that was that. Or was it because we could get away with it? You didn't like it but you did it or she did it and you were it and you were her and she was you and that was that. Dirty and wrong and so live with it. Pretending to know nothing, say nothing, we waited stiff, erect, patiently, breath held hard and short for the border patrol to let us through.

After we arrived in California, we lived in a motel somewhere near the beach, before we got our first house down there and I went to kindergarten and Emma first grade. There was a pool with a chalky, dry patio and thrumming dragonflies. We tried to keep our heads under the water until they flew away, but the trouble was we couldn't see when they left until we resurfaced. Success was always a gamble.

We lived in a handful more than twenty different houses after leaving the beach town when I was five and moved up to the mountains, before mom went to jail again and Charlie took over taking care of us until we finished school. It was lucky we moved to that small town in the mountains for no good reason, because there was only one set of schools for the 10,000 residents, so Emma, little Freddy and I never lost our friends, like our older seven siblings did, growing up and moving 20 times all around Chicago the previous decade when they were little. When mom was still around with us, we lived with different men usually but sometimes on our own and once or twice in a trailer and a couple times in motels.

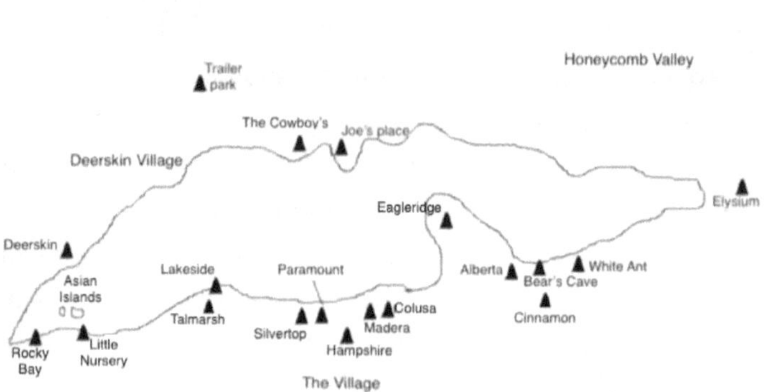

Our first home in the mountains in California after the beach was at the Paramount Lodge. It was called a lodge, but it was just a short row of little, white, one-room cabins. The eight of us lived in one. At the Paramount Lodge there was mom, all my older brothers Phil, Charlie, John, my younger brother, little baby Freddy and two of my five older sisters, Sarah and Emma. We ate pretzels with mustard and red licorice ropes for dinner the first night we arrived. The snow was falling fast and it was freezing outside and in.

There were only eight and not eleven (counting mom) because my three oldest sisters were grown. Diane was in Chicago with her husband (the oldest at 22), Lynn was also in Chicago, about to have her first baby with her boyfriend fresh out of prison (she was 20), and Amber (21) lived in the flatlands of Orange County with her new baby and husband, school buddy of Lynn's freshly-sprung boyfriend.

Mom and Sarah made up for rent as the lodge's cleaning ladies. Sometimes Emma and I helped. We learned how to turn the corners of sheets under the mattress to make the bed look clean and smooth and fresh. In two-months' time, mom got us a place of our own: a small, empty greenhouse we called the Little Nursery. We had no electricity so we used kerosene lamps. We had no heat so we slept by the fire downstairs and used it to roast hot dogs and marshmallows for dinner. In the morning Emma, Fred and I played outside where it was warmer, in the dirt near the junkyard next-door. We sang *Buffalo Bill* and danced around an old ox cart. We pretended to eat fried chicken with the drumstick-shaped cores of pinecones, the seed scales eaten off by the squirrels.

We lived at the Little Nursery until we got our first real house before the deep winter set in. Each place where we lived mostly took its name from the street it was on, but like the Little Nursery being an actual greenhouse, the Deerskin House also got its name in an unusual way. It was in a part of town called Deerskin, on the north side of the lake, the oldest village in the mountains, without even a gas station or post office, just the pizzeria run by an old Italian, the penny arcade, the North Side Tavern and the grand, red and white Deer Lodge, the latter built in 1919, combining New Orleans ornate colonnades and Wild West wrap-around balconies, sitting at the three-way crossroads of Deerskin Lane, the forestry road to Honeycomb Valley and the Boulevard encircling the lake. In its day the Deer Lodge was an impressive hotel, saloon and restaurant with ground floor arcades under archways populated by small businesses including a barbershop, a lunch service and a ladies' dance club. Legend has it that it once served as a whorehouse. The Deer Lodge closed down in 1985 and never reopened but it still looms ancient and mysterious over the small village, taking up nearly the entire north end of the main street.

Like I said, one road encircles the lake, and both the Little Nursery and the Deerskin House were on it, though miles and miles of windy lake and mountain apart. To us, the Deerskin House was magnificent. Mom tried to live as though we could afford something like that, always pretending we weren't poor, buying kitschy housewares with whatever last bits of money including what she'd swindled from someone back in the Midwest before we made our hillbilly caravan escape.

The Deerskin House was three stories high—if you included the attic and basement—with a long, windy driveway that we sledded down in winter. To us it was majestic, and it sat high on a hill. The wide east-facing windows were so vast and clear that birds committed accidental suicide. Phil and Charlie shared the bottom floor with heat lamps in the bathroom to grow plants for smoking and to warm pet lizards and snakes that we caught, fed by moths that I helped Phil catch, proud of myself for not flinching or letting go as their delicate and gently dusted wings flittered and fluttered back and forth against my thumb and forefinger in the cool light of the moon. The twins Sarah and John had the loft upstairs, and Emma and I shared the attic. Baby Fred slept with mom in the one bedroom on the main floor. There was a church pew in place of dining chairs next to the kitchen. It didn't belong to us and we weren't religious, although Mom sometimes took us to the community center church on Easter for the songs and free breakfast.

I get the sense now that the Deerskin House is bigger and nicer in my memory. It was just an old cabin on the north side of the lake, in that small village built during the Gold Rush that still gets boarded up for harsh winters and opens for easy summers. Little, boxy rooms with lots of windows in the front to face the lake. All the same, compared to the many other places we lived, Deerskin was practically a mansion.

The day before Thanksgiving, Sarah went skiing with her freshman class on a ticket bought by the school, which they did once a year for all the kids—including kids like us. Sarah went back to Chicago after Christmas and lived with Diane, but for now she went skiing with her class at school, and she went snow blind and had to wear bandages over her eyes for at least a week. My brothers teased her at dinner all the days of her bandages. They directed her the wrong way to find her food. Peas rolled delicately off her fork, and she set her bread slice down in her applesauce. Sarah had three older sisters and three older brothers, if you count her twin John coming out first, and so she took the brunt of most jokes and pranks.

The Deerskin house was built into the side of a colossal mountain, the summit of which we never reached although we tried. Mostly we roamed around lengthwise and across it creating little worlds where it was inhabitable. We once discovered a very large and flat, triangular rock, and Emma soon had a piano bar. I gave my best dance atop it trying to emulate a jazz-singing, leg-kicking Josephine Baker, driving home after the show on a VW Beetle rock located a short ways off. We had homes in the bushes and trees. We crawled around inside, designating which room belonged to the maid, which to the children, which was the bathroom and the kitchen and den.

Then there was the Big Rock, which perched over the entire world from a ledge not too far from our house. We knew, however, that the minor valley that separated us from home surely contained at least a thousand species of birds and reptiles and tunnel-digging mammals. It was worlds away. We could see our house from the Big Rock, and we also saw the lake across the road and the esoteric, impenetrable mountains beyond the obscured valley behind the lake. On the backside of the Big Rock was another dip so that the rock felt perched between valleys: the one before it leading to our house, the other leading to the remote neighboring house—an empty cabin hidden out of view, 50 yards away tucked behind trees and bushes and little rolling mountain desert hills. The Big Rock had a short platform for the three of us to stand on side by side. The rock was shaped like a ball that must have rolled from the top of the mountain eons ago, but it was only three-quarters full as though a quarter pie-shaped segment had been cut away or broken away when it crashed into place. Our bodies occupied the empty space of the missing fourth wedge, and we leaned over the top with our chins on the ledge peering at our world below.

Chapter 5
Dinner on the Ile St. Louis

When I first met Henry, one of his favorite possessions was a discounts pass for an art-house collection of the some 100 cinemas in Paris, where he often went by himself. He took in whatever was on whenever he found himself wandering the city looking for a destination. The cinemas were everywhere. In one of those small, independent film houses days before meeting me, Henry met an old native Parisian called Edith. It was a screening of *The Dead*. Henry came in ten minutes late and had sat just behind her. Naturally, she had been graciously presumptuous and invasive enough to fill him in on the missed scenes right then and there. She took an immediate liking to the real-life Gary Cooper, and, after the screening, their equally gregarious and amicable personalities shared a lively film analysis after which they exchanged calling cards.

The first time Edith invited Henry to dinner, he got the call while sitting with me over a plate of homemade perogies on one of our first dates. I was promptly invited too and since that time, Edith regularly included us in her dinner party rotation when the table called for other young couples, particularly if one partner (or both) was another foreigner living in Paris. Every few months we shared intense and superfluous conversations with Edith and company on the state of the EU, American culture and medical advances in Asia over sparkling wine and boiled potatoes. Edith adored Henry with a schoolgirl crush and jumped on all opportunities to praise him.

"*Mon chéri!* Henri, your French is impeccable!" Edith exclaimed at every dinner party. Henry politely tried to shake off the compliment. Edith always persisted. "I've never heard such perfect French on the tongue of a foreigner. *Mon dieu!*" She adored me too but not in the same way, not with such passion and affection. It was almost an afterthought. If she loved Henry, she would love what he loved too. I could never work out if I lamented how she gave Henry love and not me, or how she took love from Henry that I wanted for myself or simply that some old maternal gal was giving out love but not giving the motherly love to me.

The last time we saw Edith was just before Henry was sent across Europe and London and the situation with the pregnancy had begun. Edith sent Henry a vintage greeting card with undecipherable writing, as she often did, and invited us over for the following Friday. We hadn't seen her in a short while but she looked the same, which is to say she was still a thick-bespectacled eccentric French woman in her late 70s with severely arthritic hands like the contorted knobs of a pruned sycamore. She had, as we soon learned, encyclopedic knowledge of American westerns.

"I've seen every John Ford film—twice," she boasted the first time I met her.

"Can that really be true, Edith? John Ford directed over 100 films!" I was in disbelief.

"Agnès, when you get to be my age, you will have done a lot of things at least twice."

Edith lived on the Ile St. Louis in a petite second and third floor Haussmannian apartment, where she had been throwing frequent dinner parties alone for the past 25 years. When her two kids left the nest, Edith took the irregular one-bedroom rental with the uneven floors and inner courtyard view, and her husband Michel retired from his law firm in Paris, moving permanently back to the family home in Brest. Edith went out to Brittany to see him once a month.

"*Bonjour, mes enfants!*" She greeted us with a passionate kiss on each cheek. "You can hang your coats behind you." We turned around and found the hooks completely hidden by a gross assortment of other coats, scarves, hats, shawls, sweaters and bags immediately to the right of the door and next to the boxy kitchen. She had a classic Parisian apartment that favors sitting rooms, relegating utilitarian spaces like kitchens and bathrooms to the faraway corners, behind pressboard, left purely functional and bare.

We handed Edith a bottle of wine, and made our way to the back end of the lower level of her modest two-story *pied à terre*, to where she had fashioned her lounge. Henry sat in a Louis XIV upholstered chair in red velvet, while Edith offered me the matching Louis XV settee. On the neighboring table was a three-tiered cake stand filled with assorted crackers on one level, pickles and onions on another, and chocolates on the top. Several small crystal dishes holding olives and other snacks sat on a neighboring glasstop.

"Would you like a *crémant*, my dear?"

"That would be fine. Thank you."

Edith handed me a tall, slim crystal flute glass containing the bubbly, pink liquid.

"*Henri, qu'est-ce que tu veux? La même chose ou un whiskey pour mon grand homme américain?* The same thing, or a strong whiskey for my great, big American man?"

"*La même chose.* The same as Aggie, please. *Le crémant. Merci*, Edith." Henry's voice was gentle but insistent, dismissing the rouge but respectful. He smiled politely.

Edith offered Henry the small dishes of olives and crackers as I gazed past them to the floor-to-ceiling and wall-to-wall mahogany bookshelves in the dining part of the room. I imagined living there. I imagined a life there with Henry—with a family. With the books and chairs and pictures and antique tables. Tucked in as we were in the corner of the room, I examined the two open sides of the sitting room, as they led back to the front door and toward the hidden stairwell leading up to Edith's low-ceilinged private quarters. The only toilet was upstairs and placed modestly behind a folding partition, similar to the rough, temporary-looking style of the kitchen. She jokingly called the upstairs her 'motorhome'. It reminded me nothing of my childhood motorhome days, but I never would have said that to Edith. The disjunction between my life growing up in a large, poor family in a small town and dinner at Edith's was vast. Her so-called 'motorhome' bedroom was nothing short of exotic and chic even if modest. It was never more unbelievable to me that I lived so far removed from my upbringing than at friends' unassuming homes that nevertheless took my breath away.

Edith knew many of the writers on her walls. She knew lawyers, politicians, revered musicians and all of their circles and took great care of her library and of the combinations of guests that she entertained regularly. Edith herself could indeed be considered eccentric, but she was an esteemed retired lawyer. Her true love however was cinema, particularly John Huston.

"You two!" Edith's voice was enthusiastic and mischievous. "You two! My little American couple, when are you going to have beautiful children and bring them to see me?"

I glanced at Henry and quickly looked away. My eyes glued themselves to the dark, hardwood floor. My mouth emitted a quiet, awkward laugh. Henry met my eyes for that half second and smiled before answering.

"*O la la, Edith. On ne sait pas. On ne sait pas encore… mais… on verra!* Who knows. We will see. We will see."

Edith couldn't leave it at that. "Henri and Agnès! I demand to know!"

"Don't worry, Edith, we'll see."

She stared at him still waiting for more of an answer. The pause became awkward. The three of us were looking around, with Henry and me avoiding eye contact.

"Oh, Edith! There'll be some kind of news before you're gone, I assure you." Henry laughed and winked at her. "Don't worry."

Henry's jokes were sometimes accidentally tasteless, but Edith was satisfied.

"So, Edith, who is joining us tonight?" Henry readjusted his body, shifting his weight as a gesture toward the new topic.

"Ahmed and Bill, of course, and also Dora with her niece from Dublin. She's playing a cello concert at the Embassy this weekend—part of the annual Franco-Scottish Cultural Festival. Remember, she won that extraordinary scholarship last year? She is quite accomplished. And such a refined young lady. You're going to love her, Henri."

"I look forward to seeing Dora again," Henry's voice offered a combination of enthusiasm and control that I knew only too well. At that moment the doorbell rang.

"Oh!" Edith rose with a slight start from her seat. "Perhaps that's them now."

Dora had been in Paris since the 1950s. She had married a *fonctionnaire* of the highest and most prestigious class, *Les Grands corps de l'Etat.* Monsieur Bellard was a decorated engineering professor groomed and recruited for an executive position from which he was effectively permanently on leave, making his fortune in the private sector while retaining all rights and benefits of his governmental appointment. Dora herself was from Clan Murray of Scotland, whose family still possessed one of the largest private property holdings in the UK. Dora's father, one of the six Murray brothers, invested in coal mining in Scotland leaving his family with less of a fortune than his brothers' heirs in Leicester but a fortune nonetheless. Knowing Dora was another one of those oddities in my Parisian life. How did I come to have such a woman in my circle? My clothes felt shabby. My conversation stilted. My manners awkward. What was it like to be in Dora's family? What would it be like to have Dora for a mother? As usual, I briefly gave myself another parallel life, but they always slipped through my fingers, granular and loose, and I was left once again with nothing but my own old shoes.

Dora's expansive apartment, across from the Seine, was halfway between Edith's place and the Bastille. Her husband died eleven years ago, and they had no children, but Dora retained a regular servant.

"He keeps me from feeling lonely," Dora causally admitted the night Henry and I were invited to her home for dinner. "His name is Pakshi," she continued. "I adore his cooking."

Pakshi was Indian, and he cooked great Indian food. Dora took advantage at her dinner parties. His oddly stiff white chef's smock delicately brushed against my shoulder as he served me with a soup for the first course, his hands inside stark white gloves. He dressed immaculately like an early 20th servant and existed mostly behind the wallpapered partition that divided Dora's luxurious apartment into its entertaining quarters, private quarters and 'invisible' servants' quarters.

After the soup I excused myself to the toilet, which was similarly hidden as at Edith's. As I exited, I encountered Pakshi right outside the door, making eye contact and not knowing how to end the exchange either with a smile or hello or perhaps nothing at all. I felt sheepish around servants, feeling myself more identifiable with them, yet accidentally socially connected with the bourgeoisie feeding me dinner, dessert and wine over disconnected political conversations.

"I'm frightfully sorry we're late, Edith darling. I normally would have walked, as you know, but we decided last minute on a taxi due to the rain, and the driver was held up by a traffic incident crossing the river! Can you imagine?" Dora waved her arm in the air as though dismissing the event, sending it and its irrational existence into the ether.

"Never mind, Dora. It is a pleasure to see your lovely niece again. Hello dear! *Bienvenue à Paris!* Allow me to present to you Henri. Henri is a wonderful pianist. And he's hoping to write a fantastic book on Scotland."

"Oh, Edith. *Ce n'est pas vrai.* It's not true." Henry contested.

The girl politely though awkwardly stepped in for the French cheek kiss, nudged forward from behind by Edith, but was instead promptly greeted by Henry's firm handshake.

"My parents forced lessons on me when I was growing up," Henry added apologetically, leaning toward Dora. "I haven't played in twenty years."

The girl blushed. "*Enchantée*," she said with a thick Scottish accent.

"This is Aggie, my partner. Now she is the real musician!"

"Nice to meet you." I said. "But, no, I don't play. Just a little guitar, but really it's nothing. It's actually my brother and sister who are the musical geniuses." Emma was an elementary school music teacher, and Fred was a struggling guitarist of singular talent.

"I can agree with that, but darlin, your musical skills are great too. You're a natural."

I was sure that I blushed too, and I was embarrassed for being embarrassed. Henry did that to me—made me feel like a goofy child.

"In any case, it's also Aggie who is the writer. Not me. I'm just a consultant. Aggie has published several books."

"Oh, stop." I said politely though very self-conscious and uncomfortable. I wanted it to end. Henry looked in my eyes and gently touched my shoulder.

Edith broke the confessional by bringing us back to French traditions. "How are you, Dora?" she asked. Everyone gave one another the standard French cheek kiss, *les bises*.

"Hi, Dora. How have you been?" asked Henry.

"Why hello, Henry! Lovely to see you. Have you been following the elections?"

"You know, I've been waiting all week to talk to someone about this!"

"Well, fantastic. I look forward to hearing your point of view. How is your book coming along?"

"Dora, *un crémant*?" Edith interrupted.

The niece stood awkwardly in the archway possibly looking for a place to sit. I was hoping I would not get stuck with her. I took the chance to squeeze in my hello to Dora and rose from the two-seater. "Hi, Dora. How are you?"

"You're looking well, Aggie. Thank you. Have you met my niece?" Dora was smooth.

"Yes, yes. We were just introduced. I'm sorry. What was your name again?"

"Aggie, this is Fiona. Fiona is at the *Conservatoire*, a young cellist playing a concert this weekend at the Embassy."

We all made slight nods of agreement at the news we had already heard while Edith busily filled glasses and distributed the uneaten canned olives and pretzel sticks from the table.

"Nice to meet you, Fiona." I dutifully popped an olive into my mouth. "Excuse me, I'm just headed upstairs to the toilet for a moment. Pardon me, thank you." I quickly moved past her and opened the minute, almost hidden door to the second floor. Ascending, I could overhear Dora and Henry's conversation on the Scottish political climate. By the time I returned, Ahmed and Bill had arrived and were sipping *crémant* as well with the others and eating peanuts covered in a reddish-orange powder.

It was a wonderful and horrible feeling to be at a French dinner party. The light was soft and inviting. The champagne was cool and warming. I was embraced by the laughter and intimate sounds of glasses being lifted and returned to tabletops, cushions compressed by sitting bodies, gentle breaths moving in and out of lungs. It was an excruciating feeling of belonging and of not belonging at all. I didn't actually want to be there—be forced to interact, share stories too loudly, interrupt points of view—it's that I wanted to be part of the experience from a distance, to watch its happening but for it also to belong to me, to log it into my life:

Yes, I did that.

Yes, I'm worth that.

Yes, I matter.

It wasn't so much that I wanted the dinner party to last longer but that I wanted to bottle up the moment and hold it there, untouched, unmoving, reliably pleasurable, and without any expectation of me. I could be part of it, without worry, without fear of being an inadequate guest, without fear of it being taken away.

Ahmed and Bill spent half their time in London where Bill was a high-end art dealer. He was from Kansas but left for Paris as a young man. That was 40 years ago. Ahmed was his much younger partner, and when we visited them at their home in London Henry's first weekend there, we had no idea of the extent of Bill's ventures and wealth while also realizing Ahmed was what can be called a kept man. What would it look like, I wondered, to have everything you needed and wanted, but to have procured none of it yourself and to be wholly indebted to someone for it? Could you buy security with your freedom? What was the tradeoff?

Across the street from a home of a Saudi prince in Knightsbridge, Bill's enormous flat was more remarkable than Dora's and in a significantly different way. It occupied the ground floor of a red brick, Victorian conversion, where the rooms were meticulously adorned in priceless Middle Eastern and Asian artifacts and exclusive works of art hand-selected by Bill. His office was nearly as massive as the salon where we had tea and cake, I noted, as I passed it on my way to the toilet and thought I may have accidentally entered a neighboring business or law office. The bathroom had underfloor digital touch controlled heating with a secondary, double-door exit onto a private garden patio. Ahmed's own work space was awkwardly positioned in a sort of hallway between the master bedroom and two other sitting rooms, where accordion doors revealed inlaid woodwork in the panels behind it with a computer set-up. Ahmed was Paris-born, but his family came from Algeria. His voice was rich and mellifluous, like a warm soap bubble on the verge of rupturing.

Edith insisted on seating everyone by gender and never next to their own partner. This put me between Ahmed and Bill, followed by Dora and then Henry who was always seated next to Edith, while the young prodigy sat next to Edith on the other side, stretching the limit of the hostess's rule.

Edith never forgot I was vegetarian, which meant I was given boiled eggs and boiled potatoes after the salad, while the others usually had a pre-cooked, store-bought, rotisserie chicken or baked ham with their potatoes and mustard. The barbarity was excused in its being followed by a fantastic dessert of extraordinary artisanal pastry from the neighborhood and famous handmade ice cream from the corner *glacier*. Edith offered coffee and tea and port or whiskey, replacing the constantly full wine glasses at dinner of white or red based on the course and selection.

It seemed that the moment the goodbyes were shared, we were back in the cold night air on the sidewalk with Notre Dame on the water as our backdrop. I threw my arms around Henry with relief and let out an exaggerated sigh as though I'd been suffocating. And that was the real moment I was finally free to enjoy the dinner—once it was over.

"Ah! I can't wait for our little trip to Italy tomorrow!"

"Me too, darlin." There was a cool and sweet space lingering in the air. "Let's take another short trip too before the big one to America. There's just enough time. I'll be working so much at the new job after that. We have to get in as much traveling now as possible."

I pushed up against him and his body responded.

"Where would you like to go?" Henry was staring ahead, walking slowly.

"The Pyrenees! *I've always wanted to wander in the Pyrenees!*" I pulled away, skipping next to him, shouting my absurdist message out sideways.

"That sounds like a great idea, darlin. And let's walk home tonight. I know it's far, but it's a fine evening. It will take 50 minutes."

"That's a lovely idea. These are some great plans."

"Yes, they are good plans, darlin. I'm glad you thought of them."

"You were so good to think of them too, Hen."

Chapter 6
The Christmas That Wasn't: 5 yrs

It was in the summer before first grade started that we moved into the Deerskin House, out there in the oldest community around the lake, named by the first pioneers trespassing on the Native Americans inhabitants. Searching for gold, white settlers came upon a native camp with deer skins hanging and drying from trees. I don't know why Deerskin or the Little Nursery were not named after the street like all our other houses. I think it's because those two houses were on the long nameless Boulevard that encircled the lake. At the Deerskin House, a lot of new things happened including:

1. Before going back to Chicago a few months later to live with Diane, John built a fort, a clubhouse kind of a kid getaway up in the mountains behind the house.
2. Phil dug a grave for our dog Bugle-Boy killed by the UPS truck. It was a shallow grave and his fur was level with the earth so that a tuft stood above even after the last shovelful was laid. After the winter, we never found the marker Emma had made out of ice cream sticks.
3. Mom showed Emma and me how to make dolls out of an empty shampoo bottle and a dried apple core. You first eat an apple then carve away her face with your fingernails before the apple withers up, and you set it on the mantle for some days. Once it's dried, you paint on some blue eye shadow and some ruby red lips with a

wet jellybean. Mom sewed or crocheted a little dress and showed us how to put together a bonnet and shawl from scrap material, and we filled up the doll bodies with water for weight and strength. That way they could stand up straight and be carried around. Mom learned it from her mom, before she died in childbirth when Mom was six.

4. Mom caught a baby raccoon she hoped to domesticate. Then she'd sell the offspring or the pelts or something. She locked the raccoon in the bathroom, and before the first day was out, the space was destroyed. When Mom opened the door to shoo it out for good, the poor creature flew through the rooms, tearing its claws into any object that supported its flight. Finally, it jumped right off the second story balcony and landed halfway down the stairs to the long, steep driveway leading to the road and to the lake. I was quietly glad the raccoon had made its daring escape.

We spent our first Christmas in the mountains at the Deerskin House, but it might not count so much as Christmas, not in the usual sense, but that comes later.

I didn't finish kindergarten at our house near the beach, but I was still advanced to the first grade. The bus didn't come out to where we lived because we were too remote. We had to get a ride several miles into town and wait at the Deerskin General Store. At the general store we'd get one cookie a piece or a package of old fashioned peanut butter bars: two in a pack, a set of three rectangle-shaped wafers as long as a cigar, stacked up with peanut butter in between and coated in chocolate. Emma had a little can of pineapple juice, so I chose what I thought the opposite: a little can of tomato juice. Fred did what I did.

If Mom took us to the general store, we got breakfast while waiting for the bus. If we got a different ride, we'd have to wait until the free lunch for poor kids at school. That fall Mom had all of us except the three older sisters to look after: Phil, Charlie, the twins John and Sarah (until John left soon after) and then the last three of us, from the second litter of her ten kids—our father her brother-in-law.

The road back home from the Deerskin General Store, where the bus left us, was long and full of endless turns, winding along the lakeside with the mountain woods on the other side. Circuitous and picturesque with views across the horizon to the neighboring peaks, it was used more than once in a car commercial to depict both technical precision and an exhilarating experience. We were there when a helicopter flew overhead, and we tried to imagine the fancy car driving on our old road. It seemed impossible that something so fancy and important would be driving on our road—us poor, unguided, irrelevant rascals.

We lived near the dam on the far end of Deerskin and, since Mom was usually not around to pick us up after school, we'd drop off our roller skates at the penny arcade in the morning and skate back home those three miles on the curved waterfront. Some days Phil and Charlie stole quarters from the pinball machines, and we'd eat snacks from the General Store while we skated home.

The arrangement at Deerskin didn't last too long. No house lasted long while Mom was around. Some years later, when Charlie took over because Mom went missing, things stabilized. With mom though, each house lasted less than a year, maybe even just three or four or five months, about twenty-five in that ten-year period before Charlie took us in. The Deerskin House was probably the nicest house we ever had.

There was an enormous snowstorm that first year in the mountains. When the propane truck came to deliver the winter fuel supply, it nearly turned over on the long and windy and steep driveway. We stood at the window watching it stuck in the storm, one wheel hanging off the edge in the ditch that led into the large ravine next to our house. It was like seeing a movie with the monstrous vehicle precariously leaning towards its side. Mom screamed. We'd never heard her scream. We were scared, and I remember chewing on the wrapper of the beef jerky Phil had brought home. I was like the raccoon, a petrified wild animal wishing for a way out. I tried to get back the flavor of food, pretending nothing horrible was happening. In perverted Proustian form, the aroma would linger in my head every time I had that memory.

A week later, I got a black eye hitting my head on the corner of the giant, boxy television affixed inside a wooden case while the boys were out arranging with Santa on a mission for a special tree, tall and dignified. Phil and Charlie went up with the chainsaw in the delicately falling snow, while the three of us little ones entertained ourselves with the newly self-installed cable programming, courtesy of Phil shimmying up the electrical pole on the street corner. Mom was gone somewhere. We watched music videos all that night on the new music-only station called MTV.

The next day, Christmas eve, Phil told stories as the three of us youngest kids lay in Mom's bed. He sang all the songs from the TV specials we had never seen, and made gestures to go along with them.

"*There once was a Christmas that almost wasn't! Almost wasn't!*"

We giggled and bounced around with excitement. We tried not to fall asleep. It was the first time we'd heard of the disgruntled Heat Miser and his brother the Snow Miser. The first time we heard of Rudolf and the Abominable Snow Monster and the Misfit Toys and about the possibility of Christmas being cancelled.

"Once upon a time," Phil began, "the Heat Miser and his brother the Snow Miser were sitting in their houses waiting for Christmas. The Snow Miser said to his brother, 'Well, I guess it's almost time for Christmas! I guess I'd better make a snowstorm.' This made the Heat Miser even angrier than he already was. He hated Christmas and he hated winter. He said to his brother, 'If you make a snowstorm, I'm going to make it melt and cancel Christmas!' This made the Snow Miser very angry, and so he went to Santa Claus to ask for help. It turns out that Santa had gone to find one of his reindeer who went missing in Mississippi, and Mrs. Claus was the only one home. Mrs. Claus said, 'Mr. Heat Miser and Mr. Snow Miser! If you two do not behave, I'm going to have to call your mother!' That's Mother Nature," Phil explained. "The Heat Miser complained and said the Snow Miser was trying to make it snow when it wasn't supposed to snow yet, but the Snow Miser said, 'But Mrs. Claus, I need to make it snow otherwise no one will know it's Christmas, and Christmas will be cancelled!' 'We will just have to wait for Santa,' Mrs. Claus said. And that's what they did.

So by the morning, all the children learned that Santa had come, and Mother Nature told the Snow Miser to make it snow as planned, and Christmas was saved. Now to bed!" Phil ended the story there, and we went to bed wishing for snow.

When we awoke the next morning, we discovered it was all true. What hadn't happened to them happened to us. Santa didn't come. We ran down to the living room to find nothing. Nothing different. No presents. Not even any parents. Just a bright beam of sunshine coming in from those tricky bird windows. And I wondered if Santa would have come if the snow had fallen like it was supposed to.

We milled about the cold house looking for things to eat, sitting around, feeling aimless, indifferent. Someone said something about Mom being in Vegas. My brother told us not to complain, and me especially since I had just had my birthday in November and got a Strawberry Shortcake low rider tricycle. Mom had Fred hide in a large pile of laundry, and on cue he rode it out to surprise me. That inadvertently meant it was his bike too. Emma made me a puppet out of a used tan sock adorned with a sewed-on face: a blue button eye and a brown button eye, a nose made of black thread and a red yarn tongue. It was magical and precious, but not precious enough to not be lost. Everything was always lost when we moved to the next house. It always happened that we were unable to pay the rent and bills and would have to move somewhere else, squatting as long as possible with candles, a fire, marshmallows maybe hot dogs and always kerosene lamps, and suddenly one night leaving with what we could each fit in a suitcase or, more likely, a couple of plastic garbage bags.

That Christmas we all slept in the living room in front of the fire. I had a nightmare and woke up in the middle of the night. Lying there with my eyes wide open staring at nothing, I thought I saw little worms crawling on the carpet.

Phil was sleeping on the couch, so I climbed up there with him. He was dead asleep, but he sensed me coming with my fear and held on to me, kept me safe.

Those brothers took us on hikes and on treks to Dee's, the small diner near the dam with the horseshoe-shaped counter. They bought us one-cent lollipops, and we walked over through the trees and brush down by the lake. It was our secret spot, there in the trees and bushes by the lake. We ate our lollipops, two a piece, not a care between us.

Those brothers took me and Emma and Fred to Grey's Landing just a short distance down the shore, where we'd watch folks launch or tie up their boats, other men fishing, poking worms onto hooks, casting their lines into the water. Walking up the dock and out overtop the water, it was almost as though we were in a boat ourselves. The end of the dock wobbled and gave way a bit, the smell of fish mixing with the crackling sound of the sloshy waves against the mossy, algae-covered wooden plank that separated the space between our feet and the depths of the water.

Grey's shack sat at the point of the dock edged against the water. It sold tackle and candy bars and chips. Charlie bought a soda in a glass bottle to share, popping off the top with the rusty opener screwed into the side of the shed.

Pffp!

The cap bounced off with a mini explosion, a little vapor rolling out of the bottle.

Ping!

The cap ricocheted back and forth into the metal bucket below. The sunshine streaming down, the licking little laps of the waves, announcing themselves as they splashed up against the dock and our feet.

Near the Deerskin General Store, at the other end of the sweeping road that circled around the lake's north shore, was a small bridge over a creek, where folks did a little fishing on land. It was a different sort of fishing because the trout were making their way upstream from there to breed, so plenty of fish were swimming in that small stream, and early and late winters the banks were covered with opportunists. Fred and I played there when Mom was cooking dinners down the road at the Moose Lodge. It was late winter. We tried to catch the fish with our bare hands. The water was freezing. Our hands were turning blue. I succeeded once, but it turned out my fish was already on a line with many others that had been left like steeping tea bags over the rocks. The cool rippling current kept them as fresh as possible until their owners were ready to take them home, gut them and eat them. The slithering, slimy thing in my hands flip-flopped back and forth smacking against my palms. Mortified, I learned you can't get a grip on a fish, especially someone else's fish.

Chapter 7
Cinque Terre

We flew to Pisa the day after Edith's dinner party and took the train to La Spezia where we switched trains for Romaggoire. I knew that morning before we left that something was happening to my body. A cheap test confirmed it. I decided to wait on telling Henry until we returned so that I could have the official word from a doctor. It was only the two-week mark, but the sensations flooded upon me, emotionally, physically—exciting and frightening. I supressed my fear of sharing the surprise and dove instead with the speeding train into the endless bright blue horizon. On either side of our carriage were rolling sandy hills peppered with green patches of farmland. The closer we moved toward the sea, the more the landscape flattened out, and irregular rock formations began to appear on the hillsides.

It had rained an hour outside of Pisa, and we were worried the trip would be wet, but it was gone by the time we got to Cinque Terre. The seagulls were overhead and the tourists were afoot. We climbed out of the cavernous tunnel leading to the main road composed of large stones. The path ascended straight up the mountain speckled on both sides with tourist restaurants and trinket shops, pubs and hotels. Even though it was only March, the road was awash with languages from all corners of the earth. We walked halfway up and entered an ancient, crooked door into a narrow hall that was the reception of a modest hotel.

"*Buongiorno*," Henry addressed the receptionist.

"*Buongiorno!*" she replied. "Are you Henry and Aggie?"

We nodded.

"We can speak English. I'm Canadian."

We nodded again.

The Canadian wore a sweater dress that hugged the natural curves of her body. A matte layer of watery, nude powder disguised her pretty face. Her hair was long and dry as though it had been dyed too often. "I'm Suzette," she continued with a big smile. "I'll take you to your room." She was perceptibly professional and extra friendly. I wondered if it had something to do with being Canadian or with being a Canadian who'd spent many years in Italy. The two of us Americans and the lone Canadian exited the lobby and continued to ascend the steep road until we turned up a set of irregular stone stairs and through an elaborate network of small alleys and more stairs and archways over and under passes that I was sure we'd never remember once our guide left us on our own.

"Here we are!" Suzette announced as she slipped the skeleton key into the accepting slot in the door. "Don't mind the workers downstairs. They'll be gone in an hour or two." She gestured us into the holiday apartment while she remained standing in the doorway. "This is one of our newest rooms. It has just been renovated, but I'm assured it's been made ready." Suzette paused. "We offer breakfast from 7AM to 10AM. If you arrive where we first met, someone will direct you to the café."

She looked at Henry and me for eye contact confirmation then continued. "OK, let me know if you have any questions, and enjoy your stay!" She spun around quickly, flinging her mass of straw-like chestnut hair to one side then descended the stairs into the labyrinth beyond.

We set down our bags and glanced around. There were no curtains, no bedclothes and various builders' materials were strewn about the floor. A fine white powder covered everything, and we could hear the machines of the workers below the window methodically destroying some old portion of the structure.

"I don't know about this," I frowned. "I guess we can make do?"

We sat down side by side. I slipped my shoulder in his. Henry took a drink of water. We took stock of things while the sharp grinding sounds of the workers' machines penetrated the air.

"No, this is not what we paid for," Henry declared. "You wait here, and I'll go settle it."

I carefully lay down on a narrow strip of the bed looking at the stock wall posters of New York and Paris. Fifteen minutes later he returned.

"They don't have another room for what we've paid for so they're giving us their larger apartment for the same price. The only problem is that it's right on the central road across from the pub.

"Well, if that's all there is, then we have to take it."

We picked up our bags and walked back through the compressed circuitous route to the main road, turning left seaward and down to the hotel lobby entrance. Suzette looked like she had added another layer of make-up. Her newly applied mascara had left minute flecks of black in the deep pockets just below her eyes.

"I'm so sorry for the trouble." She was waiting for us.

"Thanks," Henry replied. The word briefly hung alone and lonely in the air then swiftly fell flat with nothing to hold it up, leaving a blank awkward space around the three of us. We didn't know what else to say. I absently looked through brochures on the table for land and sea tours. Unfazed, Henry stared at Suzette while she rummaged around for keys and other items before walking out from behind the counter.

"Please, follow me." She gestured.

We turned in behind her as she walked through the archway to the street. Suzette directed us to the new room in another brightly colored and irregularly rectangular building three doors down on the left, just across the main, old stone road. She examined the room herself this time.

"Everything seems to be in place here." She looked over the bed, passing the palm of her hand across comforter folded up at its foot. Moving into the bathroom, her voice came back to us muffled. "Towels, tissue, soap, and everything's clean."

I nodded in approval. Henry was looking out the window.

"I'm so sorry again for the trouble." She frowned, avoiding eye contact. She looked embarrassed. "Do let me know if you need anything. Just a reminder, breakfast is from 7AM to 10AM in the adjoining café to where we just came from. Have a great evening."

Again, I nodded.

"Thanks," Henry turned from the window and gave a half-hearted wave.

From our new window now facing the main drag, the two of us peered down upon the hostel-style pub. Bob Marley gently wafted up as did the other sounds and scents from below, the early evening laughter and cries and calls of the hundreds of passersby drifting up and down with bags, children, animals, hats, luggage, bread, fish and pasta. It was Good Friday. As the sun went down, a procession began crawling up the road led by a holy man carrying a holy cross as large as himself. Someone had painted it in white with gold ornamented tips. The holy man was followed by a long string of locals, children and animals, carrying candles alight, musical instruments gently sounding and voices singing along to his chanting as it came piped in through a cheap megaphone. A holy assistant was pulling along the crackling amplifier attached to a small and broken, rolling luggage cart. Four young men dressed in robes, also holy, carried an enormous icon of The Way of the Cross on a sedan chair. Unsteady and lopsided, it cruised along peacefully among the crowd.

I lay down on the large bed. I was already feeling the new and strange sensations taking over my body. Physical exhaustion. Emotional volatility and melancholia with an illogical urge to cry. I found my interactions with Henry to be too extreme, dramatic. I was afraid of irritating him but for some reason I couldn't control myself and I also couldn't tell him yet why it was happening. Would he ever forgive me once he knew? Would he be able to look back and know I had a reason, that I was justified, that I was driven by something inside me that wasn't me but that dictated my behavior without me? No. Henry didn't work that way. He couldn't be retroactively placated. He never forgot his primary feelings and so never forgave. Instead he set his pain to one side, eventually letting it fester and remount itself when least expected. It was my worst fear, and so I tried to suppress myself, my irrational behavior, but it was futile. I ached and felt painfully 'hormonal'. Perhaps when the truth came out, that itself would override or at least diminish all the minor conflicts, but as much as I tried to believe it were possible, I couldn't let go of the fear, Henry's response would be, if nothing else, unpredictable—not just his ability to rationalize retroactively but also to accept what was now undeniably happening. I hoped he would embrace it.

"I want to see where the procession is going," Henry said and moved toward the door. I lay there melancholy with a headache and nodded my understanding. After he left, I missed him instantly and desperately and jumped up to see him float into the mix of bodies and beings walking north toward somewhere I would never see. He passed out of view and I lay back down. Days and weeks and months and years passed and I cried in love and in pain for missing him and for the coming baby and for being alone and also being left behind and betrayed and being caught in the middle of a new life and a world without knowing if support would come in the fear of not knowing if it would ever come.

I lay down. I stood up. I went to the window. I lay down. I stood up. I went to the window. I wept and many thoughts passed through my head—how he left me is leaving me has forgotten me forgets me loved me and loves me no more but stays with me in guilt in some strange form of guilt that is a kind of love.

I tried to fall asleep over and over, but my pain was wide and wild and strangely great and lost in a swirl of unrelenting anxiety. How can you convey the passage of time without the passage of time? Waiting long nights for Mom to come home and her never coming home or maybe finally coming home at 4AM or 8AM when you are already so far into sleep that you forgot the depth of the heartache of waiting and of falling asleep without the wish for Mom ever being fulfilled. The fear and emptiness of waiting for what might never come, though you know in reason it must come at some point but not before you're swallowed by such an alone emptiness. *Night is longing, longing, longing beyond all endurance.* How do the hours pass without the hours passing? Finally the door opened and Henry returned as peaceful and peacefully as he had left.

"Why did you just leave me here?!"

He stared at me, first surprised then disgusted.

"Why did you just leave like that? You were gone for so long! Why did you stay away for so long? How was I supposed to know?" I began crying. I felt like a child.

Henry stood there, staring at me.

"How was I supposed to know something didn't happen? Did you not think of me? You just left me like that. What was I supposed to do?" I was behaving like a child, and yet I couldn't stop. I thrashed and cried. "Don't you see? Don't you understand? The wrongness? Of not knowing? Of you not saying, not saying a word, not a word of my not knowing where you where and when you'd be back and—?"

"You are overreacting," he calmly stated. "I just

followed it to the end. To the top of the hill." And then as though an afterthought, "It was beautiful," he added.

"Can you please just at least say sorry? Why did you leave me?"

He sat down, shaking his head. "Darlin—" He began but didn't know where to go. "No, I'm not going to apologize."

"What? Why? Why did you just leave for so long like that? What was I supposed to do? I was just here! Here by myself!" I was becoming hysterical. He would not apologize. He would never apologize. He never did and never would. Never for anything.

He was right, but I couldn't say so. Caught again now in the desperate moment of wanting to retract what I had displayed toward him, the show I had made, had poorly made, I saw the two unfurled paths open to me—begging in agony and begging for forgiveness. I could stay stubborn because I felt sheepish or I could let myself be wrong and not care and that way make peace. Always make peace in doubt and love. Perhaps I could apologize and undo the damage, but that was impossible too, impossible for him. I would have liked to try to do it but it didn't matter anyway because it would never have been undone for him. Nothing could ever be undone with him. And I couldn't apologize anyway because my body didn't let me, so I went to him and held him, buried myself in him and allowed him to bury himself in me, and so he held me in return, in pity and guilt and antipathy and finally the next hour passed, and we shared chocolate and tomatoes and bread and water and made love and fell asleep.

The following morning I planned to run but couldn't bare the separation again and so walked with Henry to the castle ruins, reminding him with a false lightness, hoping to express my independence and respect his, that I would break away and let him wander alone and that we would meet again in the afternoon.

"I'd like to get a run in after this hike. Is that OK?"

"Sounds good. Whatever you'd like."

But I couldn't break away, and together we hiked a strenuous steep path to the top of the mountain. Henry was unhappy but enjoyed himself and I tried not to notice, continuing instead to transmit a sense of joy. Once at the top, the only thing I could give him then was solitude.

"Is it OK if we split up now?" I asked in bad faith.

"That's a fine idea, darlin. I'll see you in a little bit. Have a great run."

When he said yes, I ran to the north and he walked along the road to the south. I looked back until I saw him disappear into the foliage.

The villages and vineyards were spread out below me with the endless sea just beyond, filling the horizon lengthwise and crosswise. I ran along the cliff passing an apparatus that resembled a miniature rollercoaster and was bright yellow with small, connected carts on a double iron rod track and looked to be for transporting something through the vines and bramble to the bottom of the tremendous slope. Paths swooped and curved and cut among cliffs and between gardens and fences and piles of rocks and old doors and flowerbeds and wood for fires. I didn't pass many hikers but when I did, we stopped to share the precariously narrow way. The houses and rooftops were a rainbow of colors and reminded me of Bosch with their haphazard, irregular and almost playful construction, like a deliberate malfunctioning, the way a child or grown man might wear two different colored socks or build a sandcastle too close to the water's edge using the molds of buckets and boxes and cupped hands.

I ran long and steady and hoped my heart rate wasn't too high. It was difficult then to know what was safe. It was the infancy of newness. I ran gently and quietly and didn't run beyond myself because I was new in my body. And when I reached the bottom of the mountain, there were couples with dogs and groups of people wandering looking waiting eating. The rain during the winter had brought horrible mudslides that closed the trails from one village to another so that it was necessary to take the train to get back to the village where we were staying. I had a bill in my shoe that I kept there on runs, and I bought a one-way ticket for 1,40€ and walked up to the platform to await the train and lay down on my back atop the concrete, eyes closed, lids penetrated by deep sunlight.

I could hear the sounds of the sea just next to the station a few meters away and the sounds of the birds flying over me and over the sea and back again. The concrete was warm and soothing after my run and I felt myself wrapped in it as in a blanket. The heat rose up around me. The newness that was me escaped into an empty space floating between the sea, the station and the sky.

Chapter 8
Captain Ahab: 6 yrs

I was six and in first grade when we moved from Deerskin to the Talmarsh House, between the neighborhoods of Lakeside and Fire Ant Hill. There were the five of us: Mom, Sarah, Emma, Fred and me, and Mom was always at the bar. Phil and Charlie had gone back to Chicago. Mom had a new boyfriend who looked like Santa but rough around the edges, an old sailor or miner or both. We lived in a little cottage next to his, which was full of old sailing and mining memorabilia. An aged door from a whaling ship that he had sanded, shellacked, and mounted was his living room table. He was Captain Ahab, old enough to be as old as the vengeful leader and with a grizzly beard, a check shirt, suspenders older than him and big black boots that could bust through a wall physically as imposing. Behind his cottage, alongside random, rusty and ancient objects that you could build a 19th century horse carriage from or an outhouse or a sawmill, there were tons of long-forgotten doors. Some of the sailing doors were notably small. I never asked why —they were my size and they captivated me.

"You take one a' yer choosin' out back and I'll show ya to sand it and shellac it and give ya a mini-version for yer own," he said, limping back to his workbench like his left leg was made of whalebone. I was now first mate.

The mystique of that door, of the smell of the shellac, of the experience of living on the tip of the woods in Fire Ant

Hill with rough-and-tumble sailing and mining gear from an imaginary century all over the yard belongs always to a story that doesn't feel like mine though something in there is mine. It fueled in me a desire to climb into the past, into old ships, into old woods, not just into fairytales but into history itself where a man who made those boots worked. The man who blew the glass for the port windows that were now lying around a hillbilly drunk's backyard while he's courting his neighbor, and the woman who darned that man's socks who maybe died from tuberculosis and had eight children and never smiled once in her life, and the man who made their mead who perhaps slept with his wife's sister, and the cows who gave them milk who lived and died and mooed and swished their tails and do the same thing now somewhere else, standing stock on their heavy feet in the deep soil.

These small elements gave me a passageway into a world that existed around me but was left in pieces to be deciphered, wood and iron that smelled like somebody old, a world that I wanted to be part of it, that was magical and separate from this other one, even though the present itself was something in its own way. It wasn't a complaint about where I really lived and who I really was. I never longed to be elsewhere. I wanted to dive into the richness that surrounded me but that I didn't know how to penetrate. I didn't have the tools yet nor anyone to show me.

Playing catch in the road with Emma and Fred, I let my mind wander to thoughts of our family and our big brothers and the magical worlds they opened for us. At that very moment when I was wishing Phil or Charlie would come back, walking over the bend with a little pack slung over his shoulder was a grinning, dusty Phil, fresh from the 2,000-mile trek from Chicago to California. Two weeks later, with Fred and Emma standing by, cheering me on, I mounted an old bike Mom's boyfriend had around back. Again and again I mounted while Phil pushed me up the road. I got more confident coming down and pedaled faster, feeling secure that I could have ridden across town with Phil holding on the back. When I turned around to check he was there, I found him still way back up the other end of the street. I immediately crashed into a chain link fence and got a purple gash end-to-end on my cheek. That was my lesson, and now I was a real-life pirate. Phil taught me to ride a bike. Ten years later that same big brother taught me to drive a car.

After that grand arrival, Emma and I began to play hobo, each putting on one of Phil's flannel shirts with one of his printed handkerchiefs that was carefully used to enclose picnic goods (apples, bread, candy cigarettes). We knotted up the corners and slipped the top of the kerchief through the end of a perfect stick to carry over each of our right shoulders. We walked down the street, plucked a few crab apples from the old lady's tree and set off into the bushes on our lonesome trek.

In the summer Mom split up with the old timer and the six of us moved to the Lakeside House, which was a few blocks from the old Talmarsh House but on the lakeshore, a big house with a basement where Phil put a pool table. I started second grade and turned seven some months into the school year. At school we learned two- and three-digit addition and subtraction, and I had a pretty good grasp of the times table thanks to Emma. My schoolmate Jeremiah lived right across the street. The first weekend we moved in, we played G. I. Joe, watched *Tron* and went roller-skating. His mom was nice, and they both had red hair. At the Lakeside House a lot of things happened:

1. I had the worst nightmare of my life and wet the bed, changing my sheets silently in the lightening dark of morning, that space when the night is blue.
2. Mom taught Emma and me how to crochet.
3. Sarah, our only teenaged sister, showed Emma and me how to apply makeup and feather our hair.
4. Fred and I got our first pair of unused winter boots with red laces like real mountaineers.
5. We lost our kitten for three days behind the sofa. (She was OK.)

When Lakeside expired the following spring, first thing Mom had to do before leaving was to get rid of the dogs. She had gotten two breed dogs off someone for free, thinking they were worth an ever-elusive fortune. Unfortunately, the St. Bernard was not too fond of the Collie and used to fight with it until blood was all over its coat. In witnessing that, the violence would rise up white before me, like the kind that happened when my father was raging, like a calm static thing in the rabid dog, and you'd have to pour water on them to make it stop. The awful sounds they made and the attack of a beast one on another shot the white flash of fear and violence in my eyes and the hate and the hatred of the dog one towards the other.

The St. Bernard didn't like the Collie and didn't want her to have any food, it was like Mom and my father fighting scary violent loud, the white violence in my eyes. The loud noises, the violence and its strange glowing seeping white energy everywhere, where I had to walk through in the room to get to some destination to play to sleep to find familiarity to go to school to all of it, always crossing scary thresholds of the thick but airy invasive but expected white violence to get there. You watched it happen blankly, intensely frightened and cowering. When we moved out of Lakeside, Mom left the bloody Collie behind on the side of the road, and Phil took the St. Bernard as his own. There was something the same with our father: he didn't live with us, but he was around here and there sometimes, and then there was the fighting, and then we were moving again. He'd show up again and we'd be afraid again. And we'd move on again.

Interlude I
The History of Henry

I met him at a party. Hen, my Idahoan. I had been in Paris only a few months. I had arrived for a teaching job a couple years out from my Ph.D. I spotted him immediately upon arriving, standing in the kitchen of a fourth floor flat off the Brady Passage in the 10th arrondissement surrounded by grungy outdoor Indian restaurants, voices buzzing, glasses clanking, spices floating through the air. The apartment was dark, irregular, multiple centuries old with low, wood beams across the rooms, the toilet tucked away in the corner of the kitchen through a kind of hidden door less than five-feet high. The place was owned by a 65-year-old retired lawyer and Ox-bridge divorcé. Musty corners overflowed with art, magazines, clothes, treasures of lives past. Thirty minutes later, I was dancing with Henry in the main lounge, its sole occupants.

"Tell that good-looking guy in the other room I want to dance!" I had told my party companion on a whim, and so it went.

Henry was classically handsome. His tallness disguised and enhanced by broad Rocky Mountain shoulders, angular jaw, enormous, icy, almond eyes, full, round lips, straight white teeth, thick blondish hair with fairytale curls styled without a thought like Burt Lancaster, steady baritone voice.

He came through the doorway from the kitchen to the lounge with a solid and earnest grin and took his partner, took me, without hesitation. The first thing I noticed, apart from his staggering good looks, was his laugh. He laughed not only completely without inhibition, but he laughed at and with everyone. He laughed as though the laughter itself was a form of his communicating, of him being intimate with me, with everyone. He laughed directly, unabashedly right into my eyes, and the more he felt himself connecting or maybe disconnecting, the more he laughed, and the more he gazed at me, I shared in the experience that was suddenly growing at high speeds between us.

He was in tech. A consultant. He worked at home when we met. Eight floors up, modestly challenging the height of the Eiffel Tower outside. Little by little I learned that he spoke at least ten languages—he never let on—but I got hints here and there, from books lying around, from phone calls. He was writing that damned book on Scotland. He was a consultant. He was a writer. He was a poet too. A good poet. I only found out much later. The first thing he published was a bit of poetry in friends' journals. He went to readings. He took part. Then he wrote stories. He found a job as a freelance consultant and later got a permanent contract with a tech firm. Everything else seemed to be protected inside him. He was humble and direct. He answered questions without hesitation and without flourish. He was honest, I think, and straightforward and said to people, "I am a consultant." He was never a poet or a writer or someone who wandered dusty roads next to wild tigers in Africa or someone who spent a year meditating and cooking in a Buddhist monastery in New York or someone who spent a year in Mexico caring for street children in an orphanage. He was never the young man who read every book of literature and poetry in sight and studied sociology and finance because he wanted to know more about how to save the world in a real way. But he was all of these, which I found out by chance. If I talked about what year I went to graduate school, what year my mom died, what year I lived in Berlin or England or somewhere else, I reflected on him and asked him where he was then and was startled into a new universe each time.

The guy was true. Tall, handsome, good job—but something was odd about him. He dressed a bit strange? Was that it? Was his hair too tall? His shirts too big? His pants pulled up too high? His body tight, stiff, unnatural. Maybe it was just a question of me trying to find things wrong. Henry wore thick t-shirts bought from JC Penny by his mom. They matched his eyes whether they were bright red, sky blue, brown or green. They were too bulky. Excessive stitching. Excessive stitching? Old man shirts? Kid shirts? Shirts someone's mom bought. They reminded me of the shirts some boy wore in the sixth grade. Slightly off. Somehow too chunky. That one kid who wore surfer shorts a bit too low or long or wide or wrongly patterned—or something plain 'wrong' about them, and all the other kids knew. Right? Too new and fresh. Shoes similar enough to the other kids' but bought from a department store favored by a mom or grandma or aunt. Things unnoticeable or absurd to notice. How can a t-shirt be chunky? I was looking for excuses. Henry wore the kind of glasses a pharmacist in an advertisement would wear: thin, metal rims, clear nosepieces and they made me nervous.

There was something strange in the straightness of his neck and back when he walked. An unfamiliarity, a discomfort with his own body that made me uncomfortable. It signified something. It signaled a detachment.

I knew it would end badly. I tumbled in despite it all. I tumbled in, and we got drinks near the Pantheon when the waterfront dance session got rained out. His

French was impressive. Already in Paris a decade. Had gone to college at Sciences Po. Clung on with odd jobs until things picked up. Made his way through. What were we talking about? Everything. Literature, art, tech, pop culture, music, wine, family. He was smart, interesting, nice to look at, but I was trying to find a way to escape the date. Uneasy and that incongruity about him. I decided before I sat down it was a no-go. I can't get close. I'm nervous, afraid, aloof. Why couldn't I just say I wanted to go? We were finally leaving. He said he'd walk me home. I didn't want him to walk me home but didn't know how to refuse, how to explain. He walked me home, a long walk, it was taking too long. I didn't know how to lose him. It was my fault. I feared encroaching intimacy.

When we got to my gate, he asked to kiss me at the end, diving right in for it. I dodged him and blushed deliberately.

"A raincheck on that."

"A raincheck!" He laughed, beginning momentarily with embarrassment and ending in acquiescence.

The more time I spent with him, the more I fell and unfell. I wasn't sure why I was sticking around. Perhaps it was a kind of politeness. It wasn't politeness. It was inaction. He asked me out again, so I went out again. I was sure I couldn't go through with it, but I kept going out anyway. That's what my sisters said to do, so I did.

When I first met Henry, he was living there at the top of a tower across the river from the Eiffel Tower, with windows all around. The second time I visited his apartment, I found a record player on the sidewalk. I brought it inside with me.

"Where did you get that?" He asked.

"I found it while running over here." Henry looked at me surprised. "Like I said I would," I added.

"That's true. You did say you were going to find a record player last week. You have all those old records you found and no way to play them. That's amazing. How did you find a record player? Your life always falls into place, I see." Henry looked out the window toward the Tower waiting for the strangeness of the story to sink in. The metro rattled by. "That's pretty extraordinary you found a record player."

"Let's see if it works." It didn't, and I spent the next hour repairing it. Henry and I had lunch sitting on his floor. Warm baguette, soft, sun-dried tomatoes in olive oil, goat cheese and bunches of arugula; peeling grapefruits and clementines after. We lamented not having a record nearby to test my handiwork. "I'm going to go home now and try this out," I said triumphantly. "And tonight I'm going to watch *Last Tango in Paris*. Do you want to come over?"

"I can't. I have other plans. I'll watch it tomorrow though. I've never seen it, even though I live in the apartment."

"I've never seen it either. Let's compare notes."

I went home that night and watched Maria Schneider bring a broken record player over to Marlon Brando's apartment, which was Henry's apartment. Then I watched him rape her. I was glad we did not watch the film together for our next date.

In those early days, the two of us slept at night in a bed that we pulled out from the wall toward the center of the room, because the room was too small for it to be anywhere else. Our heads poked out into the night air. I always imagined seeing the two of us through the window from the outside. Two little bodies, small in the world. The lights of the tower sparkled on the walls inside. The riverboats cast incredible patterns through the thin, watery glass and the balcony's iron grating like a magic lantern. Blue, pale orange, green. We were suspended above the world, side by side, breathing into each other's eyes closed, the metro rattling by every fifteen minutes until one o'clock in the morning, two on weekends. We curled in an enclosure. This life that seemed to surprise me constantly then because there are so many ways to go about it.

We were suspended in the world, eight stories up, the river below, the bright sliver of a moon gazing in from the east. Two bodies under a blue blanket on a blue sheet in a round room. Two little bodies side by side, perpetually human and innocent in the falling-asleep. Prone. A strange vulnerability. Lying there, waiting, breathing, exhaling. Skin to skin. Eyelashes, knees bent, socks, soft pillows, scraped knuckles, the must of living bodies in the sheets. And then eventually, spreading out, waiting for sleep, and it coming.

Mornings at 7AM, Henry got up to start working. I lay there a while longer. A solid, bright red sun shone in on me, on the bed, him in the chair in front of the desk. It slowly rose. Complete redness, but as it ascended it became lighter, orange, filling the sky, then yellow finally. I fell asleep once more for a handful of minutes and then got up, feeling guilty in the decadence of my longer repose. I didn't have to work immediately. I made a cup of tea. He drank cold coffee. Sketches I'd done of him for fun littered the corner of the room. I ate jam and bread and cream cheese. He ate yogurt and banana, but never really ate it. It sat there for hours while he worked, eyes transfixed ahead. I was generously silent. When I left, I remembered to take the old grapefruit rinds from the night before with me down to the garbage.

Dinners were simple and thoughtful. We had warm mushrooms and cream and quinoa. He took the bottle of red wine from the cabinet. I never knew what the wine was he chose, but I loved them all.

"Look at us: two writers in exile," he said.

"What do you mean?" I asked.

"Here we are, both wishing to be something, living somewhere that chose us."

He set the wine on the table, folded up a small square of cardboard and slid it under a leg to stabilize the wobble. I felt the cool night air through the thin glass of the window behind my back.

Slowly over our evenings together, I found out Henry's story. He came from a prosperous family in the state capitol, adopted when he was nine by "Papa", his mom's new husband. Papa was a widower once over with four children a bit older and a bit younger and from two previous marriages, one adopted from the Fort Hall Indian Reservation. Papa and Henry's mom had a daughter of their own a decade later. "*Yours, Mine and Ours*!" his mom laughed with straight prom queen teeth, singing the old film title that now told of her own family but on a smaller scale. Papa was a solid but gentle self-made man and entrepreneur, a do-gooder of sorts from Montpelier, Idaho who, when left parentless at an early age, lifted himself, and his siblings too, by his thick bootstraps.

As I cycled back home from Henry's apartment, I was thinking about his stories, how entirely opposite to my own they were. We had been spending time together for four months and had officially passed into love. That night before falling asleep together we had talked about his father.

"How did you feel about your mom getting married?"

"I was jealous." His voice was direct but warm. "Papa took my place. Sure, I was only nine, but I knew what was happening. Before him, I had my mom all to myself. It was just the two of us. I wasn't too excited to have some one replace me at home," Henry confessed and after a pause added, "I didn't complain."

"How do you feel about Papa now?"

"Oh, he's huge." Henry's eyes softened and moved past me. "He's a great man. Successful. Did what he wanted in life. Hard act to follow."

"What was it like when they had your little sister?"

"They were trying for years to have a baby. It was difficult. When my little sister was born, I think mom felt complete. She had everything organized."

"Yeah, but how did you feel about it, Hen?" Henry either didn't understand the question or didn't want to answer.

"My parents were happy. It was good."

"Were you happy? Were you happy to have a baby sister?"

"I was 20. Sure, she was cute."

"Did you take care of her?"

"No, I moved away pretty soon after she was born." Henry was playing with a piece of paper, turning it over and over in his hands, folding and unfolding it. "But my mom has one story she likes to tell where I think she left my sister home with me once early on—just to go to the store or something, and I didn't know what to do when she got a dirty diaper. I was terrified I would break her. I finally had mom paged at the supermarket. She didn't know whether to laugh or cry when she got home. Mom didn't leave her with me again after that." His hangdog smile was well-worn.

In the early days my apartment was a few miles away from Henry's, across the length of the city and to the south. I had decided to go home along the river because I didn't want to ride through the city center. I was glad I'd made that choice. It was beautiful. It was cold.

I was made to stop on my bike at the light next to the Hôtel de Ville. An old woman, surrounded by others of all ages, crossed the road. She stood out somehow. I knew I would make eye contact, and I did. She stopped walking when she was directly in front of me.

"*C'est bien de faire du vélo!* Going by bike is a great!"

"*Oui!*" I replied with a too-excited grin.

"I myself only just gave up my bicycle a couple years ago. I gave it to my children. They told me I was getting too old to ride, and so I did what they told me."

She whispered to me, as if she were being watched, "But… I miss it!"

She looked around and leaned in again, ever more cautiously. "But… don't tell: *j'avais peur!* —I was afraid!"

"Ah!" I wanted to speak to her, to talk about the traffic, to talk about something. To know about her. To wonder what her children would think if they knew she walked up to random strangers but how her children are just people and think and don't think and have a right or none to think anything. To wonder what her children are doing with their ancient mother's old bicycle. She's their mother, and she was and is also just a woman of the world. And she talks. She lives. And talks to strangers. She wasn't my mother but I extended my bond and my body to her and wished to share in her life.

What I began to know was that you learned new universes at each and every turn. Nothing was as you thought it was. You're 25 or 30 or 35 or 40 and beyond, and the world is as fresh and mysterious as when you're fourteen or nineteen or any other time—all those years not quite meshing together but somehow existing in their own private universes according to city to family to relationship to graduate school or graduate school search or job or job search or life or life search. And somehow that reality changes and begins to turn back into what it was when you were young. That suddenly, yes, the world really is new and strange. The humility before it allowed me to take into account the nuances of the unexpected experiences.

The light changed with so much left still to be said to the woman. I was frozen, paralyzed in front of her waiting for it all to continue.

She shook herself from the strange slumber I seemed to have put upon her, and suddenly, she urged me excitedly, nearly shouting, "*Allez-y! Allez-y!* Get going!" She excitedly waved me away.

And I was off.

Chapter 9
Raisin Bran with Ants: 7 yrs

After Lakeside me, Mom, Emma, Fred, Sarah and Phil moved into a small house on Hampshire Boulevard at the corner of the big turn right before the Village. It was a cheap, stucco house with an adjoining one-room cabin next door, where Phil stayed. Sarah slept on the sofa. Emma, Fred and I shared a room since Mom wanted her room to herself with her new boyfriends who seemed to be coming and going more quickly during this time. Was Mom selling herself? We were disconnected. She did what she did and we did what we did. We were lonely without her but we had each other and we also knew you had to let Mom do what she was going to do. And so the loneliness was struck down and you turned hard from it instead.

It was not yet spring, and I was in second grade. Little Freddy was only four and not in school yet, so Mom usually left him with a friend for the day. It didn't make any difference. Whoever it was, they would drop him off as soon as Sarah, Emma and I got home from school, and the three of us would work out what to eat if there was anything around. Sometimes Phil would come home early from long days working construction and we'd go to McDonald's. Sometimes we went to bed with empty bellies.

For a few weeks at the end of March, our second eldest sister Amber, her son and new baby daughter broke away from her husband for long enough to come up to the mountains from their dingy beach city three hours away. We built snow figures in the woods next to our house. Amber was also doing construction and was trying to build a side business of airbrush-painting: fiery skulls, sexy figures and whatnot on motorcycles. She taught us how to build snow sculptures like a giant Smurf and Garfield that were both as big as we were. Phil built an enormous dragon snow figure that we all rode like a beast flying to a far-off land.

A few weeks later Phil left (again). Amber reconciled with her husband (again) and went back to the ramshackle city, so it was just the five of us (again), but Mom was never there, and it was getting harder to find things to eat. Sarah discovered an old box of peanut butter wafer cookies at the top of a cupboard. She slid the table against the counter and slowly climbed on top. Steadily, she reached up and grabbed the package before dropping it down on the table. We stood looking at the torn open package and saw worms crawling on the cookies. Luckily, Fred had unearthed a bucket of fake bacon bits under the sink, taken from the kitchen of the Moose Lodge. We ate them for three days.

When Mom turned up that spring with a new boyfriend, an old cowboy, and told us we were moving to his place back in Deerskin, Sarah returned to Chicago and lived with Diane to finish high school.

Deerskin was old and beautiful but very uncool for kids and far away from everything. Mom hung around the North Side Tavern a lot, before it was lost in a fire less than two years later. Built in 1917, North Side Tavern burnt down seven times over the course of the century and was always rebuilt. Maybe it was cursed. My schoolteacher played piano there every second night, and we used to go in with Mom once in a while. We kept ourselves amused with shuffleboard or the jukebox, ordering a Shirley Temple or a Roy Rogers, waiting for Mom to get her fill of the place before heading home, always the strong smell of vodka or whiskey on her breath.

The old cowboy was a widower, and his sister didn't like Mom too much. He had a kind house built in the early days of the valley, on a short hill about a mile east of the Deerskin village, and maybe half a mile from the North Side Tavern. His house was rooted and nice, a deep wagon-red, with three bedrooms. The three of us kids slept on the various sofas and love seats in the stuffy and cluttered living room, over-decorated with tassel lamps, afghans, ruffles and bed skirts on the sofas. Everywhere you looked were nameless knickknacks, corks and their screws, backscratchers, broken clocks, ceramic whiskey bottles shaped like old miners, Western belles and outhouses. One of the bedrooms was for Mom and the cowboy, one was kept perfectly in order for his heaven-resting wife with her earrings quietly awaiting nothing in open, musical jewelry boxes, gloves, bracelets and perfumes still lying on doilies, her clothes neatly folded in the bureau, the soft light penetrating the delicate curtains, shoes lined against the closet door, and the other room, attached to the main bedroom, was full of indecipherable junk.

Mom didn't love the cowboy. (Who did she love?) I heard her yell that at him sometimes, and I heard her having sex with him upstairs too.

"There are bugs and white flakes all over your body! It's disgusting being in bed with you! Why don't you ever wash?"

She was angry with him when I heard her say things like that. She only had sex with him because it gave us a free roof. That part she didn't have to tell us because we knew it was true each time we lived with someone new. What we did hear her say, along with the grunts and moans through the wall, was how much she disliked him. I learned through that wall that certain needs demand tolerance.

We never had somewhere to live that ever felt like our own place, and it was acutely evident at the cowboy's place with a dead wife who still had her own room and two dirty poodles both simply called 'Baby'. Cleaning up the dogs' frequent diarrhea was somehow our duty. We didn't like the things he did for us because he was an old-timer in a strange house that we had to live in, but he bought us food, and so we knew he was a nice man and did these things for us because he was a nice man. We didn't like the things he bought though because he always bought the same three things on repeat that we didn't find so nice: Kellogg's Raisin Bran, 7UP and Chips Ahoy! He thought we liked those things because the first time he bought them we quickly shoveled it all in, so he always bought the same ones. He was old, real old, 80 or more. He cupped his hand around the back of our necks as a gesture of intimacy and gentleness. To us, it felt like he was holding us steady like an animal, controlling us by the neck, firm and precise, maybe about to brand us on with an iron. Like something from another century, from black-and-white TV. We hated it and tried not to let him stand behind us whenever we saw him coming.

And there were ants in the raisin bran.

"They can't hurt you," he said, but he didn't eat them. They were for us.

Fred ate the raisin bran and ate the ants. He had just turned five, a whole two and a half years younger than me. For his birthday, he had a gotten yellow, electric-motored, four-wheeler about the size of a moving box that went two miles an hour, slower than the pace of walking. The three of us took it for a spin down to the lake across the street. It was a struggle to walk so slowly alongside it. We took turns, watching it barely able to support the weight of the smallest of us. At the lake we tried to catch fish using marshmallows for bait and rainbow-colored sewing thread for the line. We surmised our lack of success was due to the thread. Fish are not attracted to rainbows.

At the cowboy's house, we had a game called Emma's Bar where we had our own imaginary families and places to be. Emma was oldest and so the game was named after her and her bar. On the other side of town, on my sofa, was my family. I had seven children, the eldest was Anna at twelve years old, a homemade doll bigger hence older than all the others, then there was Sadda, a Cabbage Patch Doll, followed by an Outerspace Kid (a Cabbage Patch knockoff) and a handful of other dolls down to a small, plastic newborn. I left Anna to babysit while I spent the day at Emma's Bar where Emma, the magnificent bartender, worked. Leaning one elbow up on the imaginary bar, a roll-around cabinet full of liquor bottles and glasses, drinking something imaginary "on the rocks," and smoking from a straw, I shared my woes. My sister, the imaginary bartending Emma, listened and shared back woes of her dangerous and sad life.

After a full day compressed into fifteen minutes of wiling away the time with Emma the Magnificent Bartender, I staggered home across the room to my sofa to find most of my children asleep. I felt hollow and angry, because that's what happens after a day of drinking, and reprimanded Anna for something pointless followed by a big squeeze and a few tears from my make-believe eyes.

Chapter 10
Last Tango in Paris

Henry and I arrived back in Paris from five days in Italy at the Gare Montparnasse on Wednesday evening. We walked down Boulevard Raspail to an inexpensive buffet serving homemade soup, quiche and pastries. We drank cool water from wax-coated cups and ate a warm dinner on recycled paperboard plates, quietly brushing buttery crumbs from our chins and cheeks, then pulled our small bags back to the station and took the line 6 to Passy, riding over the Pont de Bir-Hakeim. I loved the Pont de Bir-Hakeim. Passing over it on the metro gave a true sensation of really living in Paris. The views all around were unapologetically vast and carefully designed. The train atop the bridge ran east-west. The station itself was on the eastside, so as you traveled across, you saw the river below and the Eiffel Tower to the immediate north. Beyond that was Sacre Coeur far off in the distance, and nearer and to the west, the spires of the Paroisse Saint-Pierre de Chaillot and L'église orthodoxe grecque. Directly ahead to the west was the Palais de Chaillot and the impressive fountains of the Trocadero. Out the south side of the train was the Isle aux Cygnes, the long, slender island which held the 1889 Statue of Liberty at Pont de Grenelle on the south end, given by the Americans at the centenary of the French Revolution. Also directly to the south were the perimeter of the city and the alluring forests of Meudon and St. Cloud in the distance on the hills above.

The sun set slowly and widely to the southwest out of the train's left windows. Out of the right where the raucous rattle of tracks abrasively entered, the Eiffel Tower was tall and blue and flickering in light. The water below looked cold and still and mesmerizing, and on either of its banks were the long houseboats rocking gently against the tides.

The train hissed and slowed and pulled into the Passy station. We pushed through the metal shutter doors and descended the long flights of stairs under the bridge to the door of the bottom of our turret. Henry entered the code and leaned against the heavy, wrought iron gate that towered eight feet above us. The magnificent entryway was dark, and I pressed the button on the wall to activate the timed chandelier illuminating our arrival. Henry entered the second code, and we squeezed into the cramped elevator with our bags until reaching the eighth floor where we entered the minuscule circular room. That night as we fell into bed without any words, content to be home yet bodies still vibrating from the recent trip, I felt a new throbbing silence envelope us.

The next morning I slipped away, and an early doctor's visit confirmed what I knew. I waited until the safety of bedtime to tell Henry.

"I'm pregnant." We lay in bed on our backs. My heart racing.

I felt the weight of the silence. Eyes still fixed on the ceiling or the river or the Tower or the mark on the wall.

"How did that happen?" Flat line deep voice.

"I don't know." The voice of a mouse.

"I thought we were careful." He looked out the window.

I stared at him while he stared away. Heart pumping.

He looked back towards me.

"How did you find out?" Still flat on his back, now looking at the ceiling. His voice was calm, as though he were asking questions for a news story.

"I had a feeling." The metro rattled by. "But I just found out from the doctor this morning."

A long silence followed.

"What do you want to do?" He asked.

The fridge condenser came on and overtook the silence. My body turned towards him. I burrowed my head and arms and torso and legs into his and pushed my face against the side of his chest hiding it from myself and from the expectation to respond, to be forced to have something to say. The hotplate coil on top of a mini fridge made its peculiar and random ping sound.

"It feels really right," he whispered. I breathed out and into his chest.

We fell asleep like that, in the round room of the apartment for the rape scene in *Last Tango in Paris.*

Chapter 11
A Broken Eardrum: 8 yrs

Mom carried on with her usual, smalltime catering business at the cowboy's. That was between cooking at the Moose Lodge and the American Legion or the Pine Sap Saloon. Each summer she tried to win the annual chili cook-off, and each summer she lost.

"The judges conspire against me," she insisted. She also entered us in the chili cook-off Showmanship Contest, which we always won. We were the only kid act among various drunks performing skits or singing off-key.

That summer at the cowboy's house in Deerskin, Mom also entered Emma and me in the Little Miss American West pageant. She made our floor-length Victorian dresses from cheap material she got at the dime store and got us vintage accessories from the thriftshop or from the stash in the immaculate room of the old cowboy's wife. Brown suede boots with a small heel and eyelets all the way up came to my knees. I wore a cream-colored lace bonnet Mom made that tied under my chin and had an ivory cameo pinned to my neck-high, lace collar. I was seven and a half years old, and I won second place. Emma won third. First prize went to a girl from L.A. who had gotten her sunshine yellow satin dress at a costume shop.

For our debut Showmanship performance, Emma and I were given faded garter belts with stockings, bloomers, and pioneer-style sleeping bonnets. Mom dolled us up like lucky ladies from a 19th century brothel, and we feigned cooking chili with large pots and spoons while singing our song. Set to the tune of *Jingle Bells*, the song transformed the title lyrics year by year based on Mom's employment: Budding Pines Trailer Park, the American Legion, the Moose Lodge, the Bear's Cave, but the rest of the lyrics stayed the same.

"First put in the meat / Then the sauce and spice / Stir and stir and taste / And yummy it's so nice!"

"Louder!" Mom was standing in front and off to the side helping remind us of the exaggerated motions.

We danced along, made gestures, poked giant spoons into the oversized, empty pots, winked at the audience, grinned at one another, flashed our baby teeth smiles, all on cue all according to Mom's plan. "Add a lot of love... and then a little beer!" Emma mimicked a big swig off a bottle of ale, I shook a finger in disapproval. "Stir it once again / The best chili is here!" To finish off the number, Emma prompted me to deliver the last sticky-sweet, heel-clicking, dimple-bearing Shirley Temple line, leaning in towards me, her giant blue eyes anticipating my response: "It's so good..." She sang, and I responded with a jovial squeak: "Oh! So good!" We ended it together: "And better than the rest!"

We went home with a plastic, gold trophy christened with the cheap beer residue of some honky-tonk wisecrack.

I don't know why Mom left the cowboy. Maybe it was the pressure from his sister who hated Mom's gold digging ways, maybe it was the bad sex, maybe he was too old, maybe he told us to leave or maybe Mom just couldn't stand it anymore for some other reason, and so we set off to find a place of our own again at the end of the summer. We had already lived in six places in the two years in town. We moved from Deerskin to the Eagleridge House on the Eagleridge peninsula near Prairie Park halfway between the Village and the ski resort.

I started third grade in the fall and turned eight a couple months later. At the start of winter, I awoke in the middle of the night with a pain in my head and ear that was unbearable. I climbed into bed with Mom and she got me an old rag doused in warm water. I lay next to her falling in and out of sleep all night for the pain. Soon the rag was cool and just wet and scratchy, bunching up on my pillow. When the sun came up, it was covered in blood and wax. My eardrum was broken. It was before Christmas and from that day I missed three weeks of school and didn't go back until after the new year. I lay on the couch each day by myself as I watched Emma and Fred finish off classes two weeks later with Christmas parties and cheer. Eventually I watched them decorate the tree lying there in the same spot on the sofa. Mom washed out my rag with warm water once in a while, and we'd start the process over. I finally got to go to the doctor when it was clear that it wasn't going to get better on its own.

"Well, your worthless father is never going to show up and take you."

"Did you tell him?" We rarely saw our father and when we did there was shouting and hitting involved and always alcohol.

"Yes, he knows. I made sure he found out. We'd better go before it's too late." It had been two weeks of bloody wax misery. Unsteadily I slid someone's snow boots on over my feet pajamas, and Mom wrapped me in a blanket.

"How did it happen?" They asked at the hospital.

I shrugged.

Who knows. Who cares. I felt special to be at the hospital, to belong to the hospital, to be there with a purpose with something about me that was special that warranted being at the hospital, and now someone was going to take care of me. They cared about me and what happened to me.

I watched them pull the dividing sheet between my examination bed and the others around me, and it belonged to me. They gave me antibiotics, and they were mine, and I was special and meant something to have to take them—the flavor still lingering in my mouth, like a pink bitter sweetness, like the edges of little triangles tumbling across my tongue, tickling it with a soft aroma that feels like what pink itself would taste like.

The doctor said I'd be lucky if my ear healed and I didn't go deaf and I'd better keep it from getting wet and stop eating hard things like apples off the core. On the way out, he opened a big jar of lollipops and reached his hand inside, pausing.

"How many brothers and sisters do you have?"

I couldn't tell him the truth. He'd never believe me and think I was a thieving kid.

"There's Emma and there's Freddy and there's me. Three." I was sorry for all the others, but they were big enough not to mind, and they didn't live with us anyway.

That Christmas Mom took us to the dime store next to the supermarket. I held the cooling rag against my head, awkwardly trying to keep it tilted sideways. While two of us three kids waited outside, Mom took one of us inside to pick out things we wanted.

"Anything. Anything you want," she said.

Anything that could fit in her purse.

"Aggie, you come with me first."

"But I want to go first! Why does she get to go?" Fred was five.

"She broke her eardrum, Freddy. You'll be next."

"Let's go, Aggie." She led me by the arm into the store. "When you see something you want, you tell me quietly but not too quietly. Just act normal. Be normal. And don't make a scene. And don't look around you."

I spied the toys and tried to choose quickly. My first choice was a stuffed raccoon with a pink hat and matching sweater that read "I♥U."

"More stuff, Aggie. More stuff. Faster." I didn't know what to take. I pointed at some Barbies and then Hot Wheels. "You stay here. I'll be right back. Browse around. Don't look suspicious." Mom left the store to empty her purse. I wandered around the candles and greeting cards. When she came back in, I was ready to point at the coloring books with markers and packages of glittery stickers and Scratch'n'Sniffs.

Mom went outside three or four times just for my stuff. My Little Ponies, SuperBalls, He-Man figures including Teela, card games, two puzzles, and a random handful of old toys like jacks, marbles, a jump rope and the ball with paddle game.

A strange dream come true. Each time, she dumped the stolen loot right out front of the store into the shopping cart on the sidewalk where the others waited their turn.

She did this with each of us. When everyone was finished, we took turns pushing the overloaded cart home.

That new dime store came in handy more than once, but the time after my eardrum broke was the only time Mom loaded the shopping cart like that. Usually it was one purse full of more essential items, and that was it. Going to get dinner in another instance about a year later, Mom discovered with dismay that she had forgotten her purse altogether. Her solution was right next door, and she found a replacement in the dime store itself, the right shape and size: a dull faux leather brown and big enough to fit a pound of hamburger meat and a quart of milk but subtle and flat enough not to show it. She took the purse just like that from the dime store, casually walked right out with it hanging over her shoulder like it was already her own, then we went to the supermarket next door and she took the meat and the rice and the tomatoes the same way. She paid for the powdered milk with food stamps.

We did the same thing with winter coats more than once.

"Act normal. Don't look suspicious. Just walk right out."

We did as we were told.

Chapter 12
Romani

In that first year together, Henry proposed dates in the park or by the side of the river. I'd pack a lunch, or rather, the two of us would spontaneously decide to take a walk and stop off at the corner market to pick up an instant picnic. I always had in my bag a few pieces of fruit, perhaps a morning pastry as well as napkins, water, and utensils. Nevertheless, such events regularly turned into much more of complicated affairs than anticipated. We had to get bread, cheese, what else? And which cheese? So many to choose from. Henry favored the soft cheeses like Camembert and chèvre, whereas I preferred Comté and the *tommes*. Next was deciding if any vegetables could be squeezed into these makeshift sandwiches. I carried my pocketknife, but that never helped keep the tomato from becoming a pulpy mess. It soaked everything it touched coloring the sandwiches in a thin, watery pinkness.

These details have minute significance in their happening and are afterwards lost and forgotten. We live in the moment and if we try to talk about it later, it comes out poorly, like a thin, watery pinkness. Do we have an ability to balance, to permit, to separate to intertwine our lives from those of others? To become part of the lives of others or to let theirs become part of ours in a way that is accepting, open, varied? I was gushing love. I did not want to be afraid to say it.

But it is not enough to say love or not love.

We took a walk along the river in the afternoon, watching the barges slowly move through the heavy water like lumbering but graceful giants. I often tried to run at their speed when I was alone, cutting through the throngs of tourists and booksellers along the banks, making my way across the city, my effort exceeded by the power of my heart, the engine of the machines, the push and rush of the small furling white waves all around their edges. And the riverboats continued to light up the banks and a warbling sound droned through the air, of a voice, a voice giving an explanation to the passengers, telling some story, explaining some architecture, mesmerizing the silhouetted figures, men, women, children, babies. Their eyes were transfixed here and there, all around. Looking and blinking, enjoying without enjoying, relaxing both deliberately and unconsciously.

Other walkers strolled on the bank. Most had cameras in that neighborhood. There were a few beggars. There were secret Romani beggars. They were slaves, but everyone hated them for other reasons: they were deceitful, they were dirty, they were uneducated. But mostly because they were deceitful and unassimilated. They had small children whom they'd hit and cradle and drag along in extreme poverty and neglect amidst elements of the world that most people abhor and judge and condemn even when they don't understand where it comes from or how it happens or how to keep it from happening.

The next morning on my way back to my own place, I went in a shop to buy a banana. Two Romanies and their two children were just ahead of me in line. No one else was around. The women looked barely beyond their teenage years yet their skin was thick and flat and shining with grime and the unspeakable. Their skirts were long, dragging on the floor, strings hanging, covering tough bare feet. Their hair was pulled back in long ponytails the full length of their backs, the soft down of new hair curling gently flat upon their foreheads. The children jumped and shouted in shabby, oversized clothes. They were all dirty, small hands holding out piles of change for someone—for me—to count out the cost of a large bottle of soda that I saw them sharing ten minutes later several blocks down against the black gates of a closed building as if it were nourishment, as if it were the only nourishment they'd had all week. They didn't know how to count or understand the change that they begged from the passersby all day long. They cheated the tourists. They trusted the bored, angry clerk of the cheap grocery store to take the correct amount. She picked out 39 cents piece by piece. She was not invested. She did her job. They left and passed the bottle around.

In those early days with Henry, my eyes saw everything through love and detachment. An anthropologist in my own life. I wondered about the relationship between the girl and her mother. The Romanies violated all codes. It was destabilizing but I continued to love. They had each other and that was something. Wasn't it?

In Paris the Romani men jumped the gate of the metro station and played accordion on the trains to the tourists and angry residents. They played the same song for years. They had a small luggage cart, which they strapped to an amplifier that produced the hiss and cackle of electronic percussion. For an unknown reason, they were told or they found it enhanced their accordion playing. I don't know if they got more money because of it but I found the accompaniment unbearable. Sometimes a child was with them instead, though not often. When he was, he shook a tambourine with indifference. He was too indifferent to be unhappy; he was too hungry to be thirsty. He was too young to be ashamed.

Several days later I was on a metro train to the suburbs. A Romani girl was there alone. Her father with the accordion was working the track at a different interval. I saw him first, then ten minutes later, I saw her. She was setting cards on every seat. There were hardly any passengers. The card explained she was deaf, in a large family, needed help. The first claim is never true and frequently told. The other claims are always true. I was on my way to work. My backpack had a mesh pouch where I had put the shiny, silver inner bag from a box of tea, with just two teabags left inside. When I did not give the Romani girl a second or first glance with her cards, she pointed to the silvery thing in my bag. She wanted my attention. She wanted something. She would get something from me. She said with her eyes I needed to give her the silver tea bag.

"Can I have it? I want it!" Said her eyes.

"*Ce n'est que du thé.*" I spoke aloud. *It's just tea.*

It made no sense to her. She didn't understand French though she was born in Paris. She does not understand not wanting shiny things even if they were nothing.

And again—

"Can I have it?"

"It's tea. Tea."

"Tea? This?" She spoke. She pointed.

"Yes, tea. Nothing but tea."

She walked away shrunken, without understanding, but knowing I gave her nothing. She wanted it anyway and I think still I should have given it it her. She never knew she didn't really want it.

And this child on the train, and the other child on the other train, I imagined them as someone's children, as part of my own family, and that was frightening. More than that, I imagined myself as that child. I identified and was ashamed to identify. I was humbled. Her life, her poverty, her prison was larger than mine ever had been or could be. The Romanies I could not tame in my mind. I thought of myself as having my own brand of independence, of love, of morality even—but I could not assimilate it with the Romanies. They opened a new darkness, a new place of sorrow to me.

That night after work I took the metro to Henry's. Nearly there, the train was crossing the Bir Hakeim bridge. A woman who had been tumbled through the world stepped on the train at the last moment. She was wearing a dark skirt to her calves, a black sweater that made her large body more shapeless. Her hair and face were dark. She had been tumbled. She was younger than she looked, she was probably younger than me even, but she was probably still a grandmother. Her dark hair was long and thick. She was unafraid, she was unafraid out of an old obedience. The doors closed, and she began singing with a full, rich, broken voice from somewhere in eastern Europe. No one paid attention. They were too dulled to be annoyed. It was better than the accordion. The song was beautiful. She had no amplifier. When the woman sang and had the amplifier, the song was not beautiful. She probably got the same money either way. She probably did not get much money. I don't know why they buy the amplifier.

The woman was beautiful and she was an object. I couldn't complain, but I was dulled and insensitive. Not always but often, especially with the electronically-accompanied accordion. I felt violated and jumped off at the next stop and ran into the adjacent car. People sometimes do this. Then I remembered I was nothing better. I went back. I listened to the woman. She brought tears to my eyes. But then I remembered if you speak of love, you are a sap.

In the early days with Henry, before the pregnancy, Henry met me on Tuesdays and Thursdays in the Jardin du Luxembourg near the gazebo. I always arrived before him. I was listening to an old jazz number as he approached. I gave him one of the headphones without sharing words and he took it the same way. I soaked in the atmosphere of Paris, the park, the tall, big man from Idaho meeting me under the gazebo at sunset. He held me close and danced me across the sand, between the chairs, his breath in my hair, his humming, my fingers clasped, held up, held together.

"I know this one." He started singing the tune. *Mood Indigo.* His body was bent down upon me, next to me, drinking me, his breath on my neck, this old song trickling large in the world in my ear, the vibration of his rich voice in my chest. Turning me slowly, shuffling dirt under the gazebo in the Luxembourg Gardens at sunset.

We got shooed out of the park. They were locking up the gates for the night. The guards came through herding out the stragglers toward the closest exit. Henry knew a bistro close by, and he wanted to take me to dinner, but I refused. I always refused.

"We should go to the market and make dinner at home."

I wish I had let him take me to dinner. I never let anyone take me to dinner. I've almost learned that I'm worth being taken to dinner.

We got a baguette first and went into the market for peppers, mushrooms, cheese, radishes, apples. I picked carefully. I was always worried about the cost. Henry never thought of the cost. He chose what he wanted. It was how he grew up. In Paris he had a decent-paying job and continued to live as was comfortable for him.

"Do you want anything else? What are we having?" Henry asked our plan.

"How about you make that Greek salad you always do so well? And you can get some feta and pita bread from the shop on the corner. We need olives."

We finished off the basket with a bottle of wine and we packed everything into our backpacks.

I couldn't wait to get home. It's always an eternity between choosing to eat, to recognize the desire to eat and then finally to get to the point of eating. With Henry it never mattered. It was slow and cool and every moment was full with our presence together and his careful, meaningful gestures. Washing the vegetables, opening the wine. I turned on the record player. Chet Baker. It was always Chet Baker. *It could happen to you.*

The room was round, and the little table was round, pulled into the middle of the room as we sat centered in space on the 8th floor with the Eiffel Tower directly out of the window and across the river below. We faced each other with a little tea light off to the right on the big desk next to the little table. I liked the sounds of forks hitting plates, pushing and lifting food, sparkling mustard jars serving as clinking wine glasses that slide in small jerks across the marble top surface, lifting and setting, landing safely next to an unused knife. We both sat in great big office chairs with wheels, the only chairs in the room. They made the round room shrink around them. The plates were nicked, the forks mismatched.

"A couple of friends of mine had a baby today."

"That's fantastic news! How exciting for them."

"I suppose so." Henry was holding a corner of pita bread in one hand and was spreading tapenade across it with the other. "I imagine having children one day, but I don't know when that might be." He put the bite in his mouth. "I enjoy my freedom. Control of the things I do, when I do them." The lights on the Eiffel Tower flickered. "I like to travel."

"I know what you mean." I picked up my wine glass. Henry snickered, pointing at my wine glass. "Oh! I didn't mean that." I laughed. "But, yeah, that too." I took a sip. Thick purple geometric shapes tickled my tongue as the wine slid warm and slow down my throat.

"Do you want children some day, Aggie?"

"I'm not sure. It's one of those things I kind of defaulted to thinking 'yeah, of course.' You know, 'yeah, sure. It's what you do.' But I haven't planned it into my life or anything. I don't even know. When I start to think about it, I wonder if it's what I want at all. That's kind of strange."

I wasn't quite sure what I was saying, and it was partly disingenuous. I knew that it was safer to say and think and believe I didn't want children, both for me and for my relationship with Henry. I didn't want to frighten him. I didn't want to frighten—or disappoint—myself.

"Maybe I'll have to convince you then." Henry grinned. I wasn't sure what he meant. We hadn't been dating that long. Maybe it was just a challenge for the fun of it, but I liked it.

"I know I want children, but, like I said, I just don't know when." He repeated.

"You've got a piece of red pepper in your teeth."

"That's because I can't stop eating when I'm trying to talk to you. The food is good. You're good."

"That's what I like about you, Hen." I raised my wine glass. "You're good too," I added.

"To being good." The red wine sloshed around as our glasses came together in a toast.

We laughed, told stories, drank the wine, picked olives with our fingers, scooped torn pita with hummus, crunched apples and radishes, sipped sparkling water, absorbed, familiar, moving quickly, moving slowly.

The wine bottle was empty and translucent dark green. The crackling, vibrant sound of a woman's voice from a *bateau mouche* passing by lofted into the room. The lights of the boat cast shadows into mesmerizing shapes through the iron grating outside the three windows. The walls were transformed into fleeting fairy worlds, palm desert mirages, Bauhaus machinery, carrousels without circus music. The wavering single pane glass along with the movement of the boat across the water produced color effects in pastel greens and pinks, suddenly blues, oranges, yellows. Slivers of light beamed side by side passing around 360°. The plates were empty. Speckles of pepper and olive oil, a few grains of couscous, the remnants of olives. He looked at me. Eyebeams full and clear diving in, refractive, pulling and darting back out through my chest.

Chapter 13
The Miners' Jubilee: 8.5 yrs

From Eagleridge we moved to the White Ant House, not named after any street but after the state of affairs inside the walls. It was at the three-way junction between two villages and another area called Mooncliff with cabins and the ski resort. There was just one small house there at that junction, right in the parking lot between Circle Market and the Coral Saloon. I was eight and in the middle of third grade. Emma was nine, and Fred was turning six and in the middle of his first year at school. It was January, the height of winter. My eardrum had mostly healed, and I finally got my first pair of glasses.

The White Ant House had two bedrooms and two living rooms and two kitchens because really it was two adjoined cottages, each about 200 square feet. Except that one was only for sleeping though, since its bath and kitchen were out of order for one reason or another. Emma and I had bunkbeds on that side, and Fred slept on Mom's side. When the real cold nights came and since Mom left our side unheated, we moved over and Emma slept on the sofa and I slept on the floor. The first time I saw the white ants, also known as termites, I was on the toilet and noticed a messy pile of them crawling all over the floor between my feet. Then I saw the bathtub was full of them. I wondered where they were when I was sleeping, but since I didn't have a choice where to sleep, the answer to my question didn't really matter.

At the end of winter when the days weren't too cold, we played behind the White Ant House near the creek that ran between two rows of tall trees. It really was a brook that dipped and gurgled and sang and babbled and plunged over the glossy rocks and stones on its way out of one and into another forest. It was a great discovery especially when you're eight. I had no idea how I got that lucky to have such a creek or even a crick, knowing what I knew about who I was and was going to be and where I came from and what I deserved coming from where I did. I felt worthless, without knowing it was being built into me day after day, house after house. Any moment of magic lifted me up also without knowing the good it was doing. I felt unloved without actually knowing what love was or how to miss not having it. Emma and Fred and I could cherish each other also without knowing the good we gave and did for one another. We lived in a parking lot, but the brook gave us three an escape, this time with fairies and gnomes and trees that spoke and whispered the great secrets of the universe and fragile promises of enchanted days.

From the White Ant House that spring, we moved to another small lodge in the Village again, called Silvertop. Set up back-to-back with the old Paramount Lodge but not as nice, it was designed like a campground, with the cabins populating a small forest and their inhabitants, the kind of folk like us. Each cabin was constructed like a square donut. There were four rooms in total, and you could walk around the entire cabin back to the front door without ever turning around. The entry opened into a small living room. If you turned left, you were in the kitchen; if you turned right, you were in the bedroom, and between the bedroom and the kitchen was the bathroom. Mom and Fred shared the bedroom like in the old days, and Emma and I had our bunk beds in the living room by the front door.

We played hopscotch and four-square out front and jumped rope to the different rhymes we'd learned at school.

Not last night but the night before, 24 robbers came knocking at my door. As I ran out, they ran in. Hit me on the head with a rolling pin! Asked them what they wanted. This is what they said: Chinese dancers turn around. Chinese dancers touch the ground. Chinese dancers do the splits. Chinese dancers get out of town!

The jumper performed the tricks of the 'Chinese dancers': run in, run out, spin, crouch, quasi splits, run out. As I sang, I envisioned myself inside in my bed, laying there in my bunk right by the front door, when the 24 robbers came in like a troop of the Sea Hags clone-like Goons, and I chased them out with Mom's big wooden rolling pin that she used to make all those thousands of cheese and potato perogies she sold to restaurants.

We had to leave Silvertop a few months later because its housing code violations were finally discovered, and it was permanently shut down and then torn down, replaced by a public parking lot for the growing tourist industry. So at the end of the summer, before fourth grade when I was eight, we moved from Silvertop to a new condo by the ski resort, called the Cinnamon House on Cinnamon

Lane. All the streets of that neighborhood were named after spices. I thought we were lucky to have the best one.

Mom was running a food stand at the Loggers' Faire, one of the big events of the annual Miners' Jubilee. Every summer the festival of the Miners' Jubilee commemorated the town's historical roots with a month-long celebration including the Miss American West contest, the Burro Derby and the Red Rouge Race. Events opened with the Chili Cook-off and wrapped up with the DooDee Parade. For the Burro Derby each male entrant pulled one of the Mexican stubborn beasts around the lake. That took about a week. The women pulled their own Mexican stubborn beast around town for an afternoon in the Red Rouge Race. I never understood the need for the gender division. There were dances, dinners and bowl-a-thons and the bars and restaurants in town had deals and events too.

The Loggers' Faire was like a county fair without rides. As a traditional loggers' competition, it had axe-throwing, pole-climbing, tug-o-warring and log-sawing. The kid section included nail-hammering and seed-spitting. Emma, Fred and I wandered around looking at the different stands and all they had to offer: homemade fudge, pulled taffy, cotton candy, ice cream with chocolate and rainbow sprinkles, chicken on a stick, plump hot dogs, sodas with crushed ice, snow cones bright blue and red, warm puffed-up pretzels, caramel apples, frozen bananas coated in chocolate. Our bellies rumbled. Lips parched. Once we snuck one of Mom's $1 teriyaki sticks to share.

Cinnamon House was a condo that we called a house. For the first month, I had a bedroom of my own. Mom shared the big bedroom with Fred, and Emma had the attic room; then Mom rented out the attic room to a gal who smelled badly and was large with curly, orange hair and a cigarette voice. She was scary but kind and gave us each a stuffed raccoon toy with a built-in music box that played *You Are My Sunshine.* When she moved in, Emma and I joined up in the big bedroom with the big bed to share, and Fred slept in my old room, which was actually Mom's room, but Mom was never there.

The three other units of the new building connected together in the middle via a communal room with a hot tub. Two of the units weren't occupied and we played hide-and-seek in the one with a broken lock. The fourth one had a couple in it with an angry little pug called Fuyu. They were part of Mom's scene, the low-down bar-scene, but they were younger and flamboyant. The woman had a long, black wig, low-cut blouses and dresses, tall leather boots, flashing eyes and bright red lips. She was called Bobbie and looked like Elvira with curls.

During the Miners' Jubilee, things were hectic at the Cinnamon House, with Mom getting her stand ready for the Loggers' Faire while also taking care of a big catering job. She was just about ready to speed over to the location of the party in time to get back to her $1 teriyaki beef sticks for the Jubilee in Deerskin. She put the appetizers for the party in the car, mounds of cream cheese, shaped like pinecone cylinders with toasted almonds up and down the sides. The nuts were the scales that the squirrels would eat if it had been a real pinecone, or the scales that we could pretend to eat if we had been squirrels who had real pinecones or if we had been patrons at Mom's party, squirrels or not. She set them in the car and dashed back in the house for another tray, meanwhile transferring the teriyaki sticks from the broiler to the chaffing dish to smother in the sauce. By the time Mom got back out to the car fifteen minutes later, that Elvira lady and her curly wig along with her handlebar-mustached boyfriend and another honky-tonk friend with glazed, red eyes had polished off both massive, edible pinecones. That was the only time I ever saw Mom cry.

Living at the Cinnamon House, Emma, Fred and I used our lucky pennies at the gas station next to the ski rental shop to buy strawberry-flavored hard candies, gumdrops and malt balls from the 1¢ jar. I got my first bicycle at Cinnamon that was just for me with no sharing. It was sky blue and had a banana seat. It was used and beat up and from another generation and I chased the other kids around the neighborhood under the guise of my identical twin cousin who wore green overalls and was from the countryside. At night I made toys out of white paper and clear tape, matchbox-sized cars with paper dolls and a white paper town that had streetlights so the paper dolls could see at night.

A truant officer came looking for one of my older brothers at Cinnamon. Since it was just Emma, Fred and me, the officer asked if he could come inside and look around. Emma said yes but the officer didn't find my brother though he even looked in the pantry to find him there.

"Where's your mom?"

Emma shrugged.

"What are you three eating for meals?" He asked after

checking all the cupboards for my brother and finding nobody and no food.

We stared at the floor. I looked at Emma. She shrugged.

"Chips!" Fred blurted out with a grin. The officer looked at Emma. Fred was still five.

"You're the oldest?"

Emma nodded. "I'm nine. I have some chips and candy upstairs."

The officer nodded his head in approval. Emma returned the gesture. Satisfied, he tenderly touched the top of her head and walked to the door. "Get some sleep, you kids." We three stood there until we saw his car pull out of sight from our window then went upstairs for our make-believe dinner.

Chapter 14
Lourdes

Just a week on the heels of Italy, Henry and I took the train down to the Pyrenees, first to Lourdes where we spent the night and picked up a rental car in the morning. The freedom to travel was part of the joy Henry and I had built into our relationship. Something about both being expats, being open to newness, exploration, culture and nature. Thinking about the baby, I began to realize I had perhaps taken that for granted, and fear crept up in the place where I felt uncertain about how our lives would change. I had hoped he would be open, continuing that vast sense of wanderlust and learning, but it would come at a price and it would not be easy.

We had planned to book just one day in advance from each previous hotel so that we could choose our hiking destinations as it suited us for the five-day trip in the French and Spanish mountains. The hotel was quaint and across the street from the train station where we would also get the car. The first thing we did was walk down to the Domain and the Grotto, and Henry decided to drink from the taps because we were there in Lourdes. I refused, carefully checking everything that went into my body now—no unpasteurized cheese, no alcohol, low sugar and definitely no random, unfiltered water seeping out of a rock.

On that beautiful sunny afternoon the Domain and Grotto were full of the sick. They came in wheelchairs and on crutches. They were disfigured and crippled, small and large, young and old. They came in groups of children and groups of the elderly, groups of nuns and groups carried on carts like flat wheelbarrows pushed by the grounds people. There were conferences and pilgrimages, masses in Latin and English and French and Catalan. Spanish and German and Dutch and Russian tourists. Events and dinners, and long lines to pass along the holy stone wall where the water trickled down, and no lines for the fifty taps installed just next to where the water fell naturally. Vendors sold empty water bottles at three times their normal price as well as keychains and palm-sized religious icons.

To my American eyes the Notre Dame du Rosaire de Lourdes looked like the castle from Disneyland where Mom had taken us when we first moved to California. I took a pamphlet as we passed an information booth and read about its history while Henry took a few pictures.

Consecrated in 1901 it is one of multiple churches in the Domain, all of them clustered together above and below ground, fighting for the space surrounding the site of Saint Bernadette Soubirous' alleged visions in 1858 of aqueró, or "that" in Gascon Occitan, the former language of the region. The object of her vision was later elucidated to *uo petito damizelo*, "a little lady" who expressed the holiness of the water and instructed the fourteen-year-old Bernadette and her village to build a chapel there where the old garbage dump lay.

We momentarily sat down on a bench and watched the crowds in silence for several minutes. I continued reading.

The Notre Dame du Rosaire de Lourdes however was not the first basilica and so it was positioned somehow in front of and slightly below the minor Basilique de Notre Dame de l'Immaculée Conception de Lourdes of 1876, which also was not the first. That honor went to the basilica known as the Crypt of 1866, which directly supported the structure of the Notre Dame du Rosaire de Lourdes on its back. There was also the Basilique Saint Pie X, colloquially known as the Underground Basilica, built in 1958 and likened to a parking garage in its lack of aesthetic appeal.

After a drink of water from my own source, I wandered with Henry in and out of the churches and over the grounds, and we eventually made our way back up the steep hill through the village. We gazed at the various souvenir shops, kebab stands, cafes and eventually took pictures of the enormous *Palais du Rosaire* that looked like a cheap toy store but sold millions of miniature religious icons in all shapes and sizes. Four massive open-wall doors exposed the store's entire contents, with large bins full of junk located inside and out. You could choose from plastic containers for holy water in massive five-liters or 5 centiliters with images of the basilica or Jesus or Lourdes or Mary on them. Inside hung busts of Mary from the walls, life-sized to fingernail-sized. Clustered icons of Mary stood in the corners, life-sized to palm-sized. There were pill containers of plastic or porcelain with images of Lourdes or Mary or Jesus on top. You could get dizzy from choice: cards, fake flowers, dolls, cuckoo clocks, bags, handkerchiefs, mugs, bowls, bells, posters, ashtrays, candles, pendants all emblazoned with images of Jesus, Mary or some cathedral of the Domain.

I walked between two rows of the large bins and picked up one of the small bottles used for holy water. The lid was attached to a faux gold necklace chain. The bottle itself was glass and shaped like a heart. It resembled the magic bubble containers my friends and I wore in high school with the wand inside the top to dip in the soapy water and blow bubbles at parties and football games.

I continued browsing around the shop. There were so many objects. It was impossible to take it all in. The faces of the icons were worn and tired. They were mostly of Mary with her child or of the crucified Jesus. Why were there no candles or canvas grocery bags with Joseph? As soon as the thought crossed my mind, all I could see were all of the Marys with baby. Mother and child. Mother and child. Mary with baby on a kitchen apron. Mary with baby on a lampshade. Mary with baby on shoelaces. Mary with baby on food leftover containers. Mary with baby on baby clothes on women's clothes on bed clothes.

I shook my gaze away from the menagerie of icons and spotted Henry a half dozen rows away watching an affectionate pregnant couple choose among a series of large colorful candles. His thoughtful but stone-faced expression gave no indication how he felt about the scene. A knot grew in my stomach.

He looked up and caught my eye, making a motion that he was ready to leave. We walked out of the shop in parallel and met back up on the sidewalk. We slowly began ascending the busy road in our own silence.

"We shouldn't be having a baby together," he abruptly said.

In an instant I went from shock to despair to anger to desperation.

"What do you mean? What does that even mean?" A large, suffocating weight descended from unknown heights and rested upon my sagging shoulders. I suddenly felt excruciatingly tired.

"We don't get along. We should have split up long ago."

Could he really be saying this? Where did it come from? How was it possible? Just days ago he loved me, joyous, radiating happiness. I wanted to cry and run and bury my body, my entire self in the hard earth. That would cancel out the words, the noise, the universe, reverse it, silence it, but instead I turned on my happy no-wait-let-me-show-you-how-we-can-save-the-whole-world-with-love face.

We were still walking slowly and hadn't yet reached the top of the main street. We were like any other tourist couple, casually having our conversation. I watched others enter businesses, buy ice cream, drinks, wait in line, walk into and out of their hotels, push wheelchairs, strollers, cross streets, read restaurant menus. My head was getting cloudy. It felt strange to be in the world, in the normal world and to be having this conversation.

"But you wanted this. I don't understand. Maybe we didn't plan it right now, but it's happening to both of us."

"I don't like being forced into this. You never asked me. I didn't choose this."

"But it's happening to us, Hen. I didn't choose it right now either, but it happened. What do you want me to say? Is it my fault?"

"Look, Aggie, I don't like being forced into this. You're forcing. I don't like being forced." He wasn't looking at me. We were nearly at the top of the road. We didn't know where we were going but just carried on walking. An anxiety was increasing, and I felt like I couldn't stop moving forward. Though I wanted to stop walking, I couldn't stop my body. It was as though I had to plow through, physically, and bring Henry with me. I lost a sense of the outside world and tried to face Henry directly as I walked, my body moving perpendicularly. I could smell grease and garlic from the nearby pizzeria as we passed. The air was warm and bright, but I was hardly aware any longer of the people around us. For all I knew, they were listening.

"Don't think of it like that!" I was skipping sideways next to him as we ascended. "Don't think of it like that!" I repeated, looking hard inwards for my next piece of advice.

Taking broad strides, Henry was silent, aloof, brooding, angry but calm as always.

I needed to find a way to help him, bring him around. It wasn't working. My spirit dragged behind me. I wanted him to understand, to see the joy, the great challenge in himself to recognize the beauty in it, the significance of it, the undeniable life-changing value.

I mustered my strength as I always knew I would and would have to, as I denied in bad faith knowing that I always would, as though imagining a big change coming. I knew I wanted the baby because I loved Henry even if I feared his abandonment and felt almost sure of it.

I changed my tone. "You have to choose it—like you said. I'm choosing it! We can choose it together. It's all just in the way you imagine it." I dipped my body towards him, rubbing my head against his warm broad shoulder. "Show yourself that you can do it, that it is a choice you can make, that you want to affirm for yourself so that you can believe it in and begin to recognize the enormity, the beauty of it. How it will transform you, re-define you, give you something you never realized you wanted or could have but learning along the way that it is the meaning of everything, so much more than you could imagine."

It was all hogwash. It was all true. I didn't know why I had to spill my guts out like this endlessly, to bring him around to something that he couldn't do himself. And why couldn't he? I felt he was a coward, self-involved, disconnected, I was afraid, and I hated him for it, for doing this, for rejecting something that was incredible and, most importantly, for blaming me for screwing up his life as he saw it—his life, not ours. But I guess he was just rejecting me. I wished it were different. I wished he were different. I wished I were with someone different. I didn't want to fight like this. I didn't want to engage in this kind of discourse. The way he pulled me down on his path, as though it were common, understandable, acceptable. And maybe he thought the same: the way I was pulling him down my path? But it wasn't 'my' path. It was beyond me.

I was in this relationship with him, which meant I had to meet him on the ground he stood. There was no way about it. That's just how it worked, and I had already learned it the hard way. I thought I would never be in such a situation again, engaged in such a numbing, obstinate track of mind, appalled with myself to find I was there now and using the tools against it that I carved myself.

"You have to choose it! Then it can be so beautiful!"

"I'm angry." He said in that flat voice of his. He stared straight ahead as he walked. "I don't want to be forced," he added again, now with a stronger edge.

He didn't want to be forced. Henry got away with whatever he wanted, but it wasn't so much a matter of getting away with it for me as it was of having to live on eggshells around him. It was impossible to ask him to do anything. He refused to be controlled, as he put it. He would not do the dishes if you wanted him to, but he would do them on his own accord.

"Let's find somewhere for dinner." I changed the subject.

"OK."

The afternoon sun forced its way between the blackened buildings creeping up the hillside. An old woman was walking a small dog across the street on the downslope. She wore a green and purple scarf over her head tied under her chin. The dog was a dirty white with brown, wet fur hanging from its chin, ears and eyes and covering its paws. I felt like vomiting.

We looked around.

"Let's embrace this, and these experiences. It's an amazing opportunity. You have to choose it. You know? You have to choose it now. See?"

I heard nothing but the weary repetition of my phrases. I heard myself repeating them over and over. I was disgusted. I meant all those words, and I hated every second of saying them.

We found an Indian place across the street from our hotel. There was no one inside, and we knocked on the door until the woman came out. She didn't understand what we wanted. She went back into the kitchen, and the man came out and gestured us inside. We were catered to with personalized care and a delicious meal with cold Indian beer to wash down the spice. It was before 6:30PM and we were the only customers.

When we got back to our hotel, Henry picked up the guitar he had brought and sat against the pillows on the bed to play. I slid up next to him and looked over the map thinking about our next destination.

"Tomorrow we'll drive to Cauterets and hike to *Pont d'Espagne* where we will be able to see Spain."

"Sounds good, darlin."

Chapter 15
Rattlesnake for Dinner: 9 yrs

We passed a winter at the Cinnamon House. By the springtime of the year I was nine and in fourth grade, Mom had found another new boyfriend back in Deerskin, so we were able to ditch the Cinnamon condo for the new guy's big waterfront property with a view of the ski resort on the other side of the lake. It was a stone's throw from the cowboy's old house. The new guy wasn't around very often, and we explored his house with its porcelain sculptures and African masks in the dark hallways like cultural anthropologists. We never gave it a real name but always just called it Joe's Place. We dipped eggs in dye and vinegar for Easter, and the next morning Emma, Fred and I followed individual trails of hard-boiled and brightly-painted eggs with our names. Each of us found an Easter basket full of goodies awaiting us somewhere in the house. The rooms were clean and brightly lit and my Easter basket was in the dining room with sliding doors out on to the deck overlooking the lake.

On Mom's birthday after Easter, we went skiing for the first time. Almost all our brothers and sisters showed up for the party. Charlie and Phil helped us layer up with their big, thick socks, long johns and jeans, too many sizes too big. I had grey earmuffs, and Emma had pink that we'd gotten for Christmas the year before. They still worked. I was nervous because we had just gotten our ears pierced, but it turned out that the earmuffs made me feel safer sliding down the mountain for the first time on my 145's. Emma bent her rental ski pole. Diane helped her fix it. Phil and Charlie showed us how to snowplow and how to get across the flat run called Cowpatty by pushing with your poles and skating on your skis. The two wild boys skied around us, doing tricks flying out of the trees, sailing off jumps fit to impress their audience. We glowed from early morning hot cider and cool mountain air on warm skin. Our cheeks burnt just a little from the sun and the breeze was on our faces and our warm hands in big gloves clutching the bar of the chairlift, beams of light shining down on the slowly melting snow.

Mom didn't last as long with the second Deerskin boyfriend. That May after Mom's birthday when I was still nine and in fourth grade, we moved into our own rented house on Elysium Street, which was out east on the other side of town where most of the kids we went to school with lived. Elysium House was small with one bedroom and a loft that was more like an attic. You reached it by ladder that I fell out of once but didn't get too hurt. That was my second lucky accident. The first was at Talmarsh House, sleeping in our homemade bunk beds that Mom fashioned by simply stacking two ordinary beds with tall bedframes. Mom and Fred were in Emma's bed on top when it came crashing down on me. I didn't wake up but I screamed in my sleep, they told me, and I had another one of those end-to-end gashes across my face. I woke up as always at the regular time for the start of school, never needing an alarm clock, trusting my body to wake itself for the right time, as though it was a separate mechanism inside me; kept me on schedule, kept me structured and moving forward regardless of my own state of mind or being, impairment or otherwise. As always, Mom repaired my wounds herself. She used papertowels and tape, usually electrical tape since that is what we had, sometimes a few bobby pins as reinforcement, like the several times I split the back of my head open when I was a toddler.

At Elysium I practiced my lines for the spring school play *Orphan Annie.* I missed the tryouts but later got the role of Molly, Annie's puny and forgotten companion in the orphanage, who opens the play with sleeping screams, suffering a recurrent nightmare where she loses her mom. Even punier than my character, my little voice did not impress the schoolteacher director at rehearsal and so, when the curtain opened, he instead had me yell as loud as I could, "Mommy! Mommy! Mommy!" as the seven of us orphans lay on our collective plywood bed on the stage. Annie comforted me as I recounted my nightmare and expressed my wish for a real mom, one like Annie confidently always claimed to have.

The play was a success, the school year ended, and we were evicted from the Elysium House by summer. We found ourselves at a trailer park on the north shore with no electricity or water, just a place to sleep. Most of the time we went down to the desert that summer where Mom had a new temporary boyfriend. Phil also took us for long stretches to Honeycomb Valley where we camped, swam in the river, caught lizards, and shot guns. In one instance, as the four of us followed a trail back to our camp from a swimming hole, we each stepped over a rattlesnake without knowing it, until Emma—the last one in line—saw it before stepping.

"Phil… Phil…" She said, mostly in a slow whisper.

Phil looked over to see the culprit between Emma's legs.

"Don't move, Emma!" Phil yelled out. We all stood still, every eye on Emma, then on the snake, then on Emma. Her arms were raised midair as though softly resting on a countertop, one knee bent in full stride, the heel of her foot lifted ready to push off to the next step. Chin down toward the earth in front of her, she was quiet and calm, staring at the snake, not moving an inch, lifting her eyes briefly to look at us, head remaining fixed.

"Aggie," Phil motioned to me next. "Give me the bag." I wordlessly handed him the canvas shoulder bag containing our water and lunch. Phil kneeled under a nearby tree and hurriedly but calmly removed everything from it. He slowly moved back down the trail toward Emma without making a sound, and with one quick gesture, he grabbed the snake by the head, pressing his thumb between its eyes, and swinging his arm around and around, as the snake coiled its body around his elbow and forearm. While his right arm was moving in rapid circles, his left hand held the lunch bag open out toward the center of his body. Emma slid up next to me and Fred, and the three of us cowered near the tree where our food lay, holding our breath and periodically covering our eyes. With a violent jerk, Phil threw the snake into the bag, and without skipping a beat, tied the loose handles twice together and began spinning it around as he had previously been doing with just his arm on which the snake had been entwined. After a few minutes he lightly tossed the bag not far from us in the opposite direction, turned and poised himself, took a deep breath, ran his hand through his hair and walked the few paces over to where we stood. Soundlessly, Phil picked up the water bottle and took a long, slow drink, his body covered in a thin layer of sweat, beads dripping down his forehead and the sides of his face. That night we had rattlesnake and potatoes for dinner with roasted marshmallows for dessert.

When it was time to go back to school, Mom and Emma and I got the trailer ready to live in properly, and Phil and Charlie, who were living nearby with friends, fixed the electricity. Mom also got back her cooking gig a couple nights at the Moose Lodge, near the Tavern, making the move to the trailer park rather convenient.

The trailer itself was dilapidated, beaten down and very small. It had two parts: a bed in the back, and a kitchen with table in the front. The bathroom was in the middle, but the plumbing remained broken, so we used the outhouse bathroom a few rows over like at a campground. Mom slept in the bed with Fred, and Emma and I slept on the plywood that made up the bench around the table in the front. There was nowhere to play.

"Can I draw a dollhouse on the other side of my piece of wood?" I asked when we moved in.

She didn't care, and I used a red marker.

It was like a red blueprint. Thick lines setting off each room, rectangles to indicate the beds and sofa, circle for the dining room table, squares for the chairs and sinks. I had that remarkable feeling any child has from acquiring a magnificent dollhouse.

For the 4th of July we walked down to the shore of the lake to watch the fireworks. I felt many things that I didn't know how to express like missing Christmas that first year we'd arrived in the mountains or feeling cold not having a blanket sitting at the edge of the water watching the spectacle in the sky. Something in the way that things happen or don't happen, and they stick with you in your memory, and when they come back you remember why they stuck. Like when Mr. Ramsay in *To the Lighthouse* tells his youngest son James the weather will not be fine for going to the lighthouse next day. Mrs. Ramsay hears him and is sad and thinks of poor, young James, He will remember that all his life.

Children never forget. What one says and what one does is so important.

I felt that then and feel that still. I remember some things that I don't know how to share but that are in me and that have made me and are a part of the way I live and breathe and make decisions whether I know it or not.

Chapter 16
Cauterets

The village of Cauterets was a ski destination, abandoned in the late spring with hardly any visitors. Our hotel room was rectangular and cold and it faced onto the street where the two-star sign hung in front of our window. In one direction I could see the bridge we'd crossed to arrive and in the other I saw the snow-capped mountains. There was a soft, grey storm hanging in the distance. Henry and I had seen a frowning couple with a discontented baby having breakfast the next morning in the barren hotel café and not a soul otherwise. It was a gloomy sight, so we decided to find pastries elsewhere on our way out of town for a hike. Henry left the key at the desk as requested and we headed out onto the long quiet road.

We first walked through the abandoned town square, occupied by a large puddle the size of a swimming pool and a carousel with a well-fitting, leathery beige cover. A bandstand stood in the center against the foot of the mountainside, and the open central space was itself the size of a baseball diamond, surrounded by cafes and restaurants all shuttered that late spring. We moved slowly, walking up toward the modest church. Henry always liked to go in the churches. Inside was cold and empty and one corner by the door contained odds and ends with a charity donation box. For sale was a large variety of books, used toys, linens and worn household items. Henry wanted to buy the whole 19th-century encyclopedia set. Adverse to spending money frivolously, I tried to talk him out of it. While Henry didn't share my frugality, he kept himself from buying it, though with difficulty. Not due to my nudging—Henry usually did precisely the opposite of my suggestion—but because it would have been cumbersome to transport.

We moved through the petite village in a scant fraction of time and began ascending the hiking trail up to the mountain peak.

I found him by the railroad track this morning
I could see that he was nearly dead
I knelt down beside him, and I listened
Just to hear the words the dying fellow said

The whole way on the ascent, Henry sang in his baritone voice the song he had recently been teaching himself on guitar.

He said they let me out of prison down in Frisco
For ten long years I've paid for what I've done
I was trying to get back to Louisiana
To see my Rose and get to know my son

Henry's heavy and forthright voice was comforting despite the somber tale the song wove. We walked through the miraculous forest reminiscent of California and Idaho woods, a babbling brook, mossy stones, and damp leaves slick against glazed rocks.

Give my love to Rose, please won't you, mister
Take her all my money; tell her to buy some pretty clothes
Tell my boy his daddy's so proud of him
And don't forget to give my love to Rose

We trod over bridges of stone and wood, and it began to snow. I handed him a stocking cap as we shared a drink of water.

Won't you tell them I said thanks for waiting for me
Tell my boy to help his mom at home
Tell my Rose to try to find another
'Cause it ain't right that she should live alone

I wondered about the distress of the man in the song—dying in a stranger's arms, sending his Rose to a stranger's arms. And why did he leave them? Henry handed me the water bottle, and I put it in the backpack. His hands were cold to the touch.

"Do you want your gloves?" I began rummaging around for them in the sack. Or maybe his distress was knowing they didn't wait? They couldn't wait? He could only feign a truth to disguise his guilt for leaving.

"I'm OK." He was looking at the snowy peaks through the high mountain mist. I looked at his dark profile against the bright light of the March morning. His sharp jaw was pink from the cold and covered in several days' stubble. I instinctively leaned onto his arm and closed my eyes. Each endless tangible moment built itself one upon the other, and yet they were not coming together as a whole. The whole was frayed, amorphic, falling apart with every step. It was peculiar to feel such beauty and happiness in each fleeting instant, then watch it slip away before the sensation itself was complete. There was joy and immediately there was dread.

"Your hands are cold."

"It's OK. I'm fine." He thrust his hands in his pockets.

Don't ever ask Henry twice if he wants something. He knows himself the first time. I had forgotten that.

We began walking again and passed two hikers descending who told us the summit was not far off where we would be rewarded with a glacial lake. When we reached the top, the snow was falling thick and steady, and for a long time we stood in peaceful silence under the awning of a solitary shed in view of the glorious water.

Everything might be OK. A tremendous ache in my heart drove me again and again to project only love, to outdo the pain, to overcome the space between what he might be feeling and what I hoped he could learn to feel.

We laughed and kissed and took nice pictures. The flakes landed in our eyebrows and eyelashes. The tips of our noses were rosy.

"You look like a snowman."

"A-hem. That's a snowperson, if you please."

"Pardon me, madame! In that case, a snowlady. May I have this dance, m'lady?" Henry put out his hand, which I accepted, and he twirled me around on the edge of the lake, his head buried in my hair and neck, humming his tune in that deep baritone voice.

We decided to make our descent on a parallel mountain path, a disused ski slope, in order to avoid the slippery stones and creek on the primary path that we had already taken. With squeals and a new sense of play, we launched ourselves down the vast and wide mountainside covered both in new flowers and patches of white snow, abandoning ourselves to the winter-like spring weather and the expanse of the slope so different from the narrow and treacherous path going up.

"How's the new story about your mother coming along?" Henry took my hand in his. My first short story had just been published, and I had been encouraged to follow-up with something about my childhood. It was proving more daring and more difficult.

"It's hard to write about my mother."

"Tell me what you mean, darlin."

"Readers want conflict, to hear about the struggle, the abandonment, the inner torment, but I don't really feel those things. It isn't so much that I have forgiven my mother, not in any direct sense, but that perhaps there is nothing to forgive, perhaps it just isn't the way I understand the world." I looked off toward the striking fog-enshrouded mountain in front of us. "It's hard to explain."

"Tell me, darlin," he repeated. It touched me that Henry cared, that he asked me, that he wanted to talk and to learn about what was I doing.

"Well, I don't feel like I hold a position or whatever that gives me the authority to 'forgive'. Who am I to judge my mother?"

"She was harmful to you. And your family," Henry said bluntly. "She abandoned you. She was a raging alcoholic. She didn't take care of you." Henry knew my whole story.

We spent hours sharing stories about our families during those riverside picnics and the strolls in the Jardin du Luxembourg. He asked questions. His inquiries were never judgmental. They were collective. He seemed to absorb what I said, somehow store it away in himself, information he would process or use later.

"Yeah, I guess that's true," I conceded. "But… I don't know. I just don't know if I need to hold on to the bad feelings."

"But that's what you need to write about. It's up to you to tell the story so your readers can understand where you've come from, what you've gone through, where you are." He paused, and I heard the delicate fullness of the wind as it encircled the trees and deep crevasses among the peaks. "It's a great accomplishment what you've overcome." Henry always seemed so honest in everything he said. This validated his support all the more, and of course it attracted me to him, made me love him deeply and even blindly. I never knew myself to be so vulnerable, so persuaded without persuasion.

"Ah… well, thank you," I mumbled.

His words were neither flat nor foolish. And they weren't polite. They were genuine and I wanted to hide from them. I hated all the compliments I got about my supposed success. I felt embarrassed and small and eager to get away from the praise. I didn't think myself anything extraordinary. I had survived a difficult childhood, but so have many other people.

"Anyway," I continued, looking into the distance in an impossible effort to make Henry look away from me. I methodically slipped off my hat and slid it back on again, then pulled at the bottom edge of my coat in readjustment. I breathed in, wiped the snow from my cheek and gave the landscape a quick survey, breathing out. "Yeah, I guess that makes sense. I would like to write something bigger than the struggle though, but it feels so… it feels so… well, it feels like that is not what writing is for—conventionally. But that's just it—I want to explore why it feels that way, why writing seems to be constructed as something from A to B, and then how I might experiment with possibility. Perhaps I can write something unexpected? Perhaps I can write how I feel, what I need to write without falling back into the old patterns we always see: conflict, climax, resolution. And so on. Like Katherine Mansfield or Faulkner in *As I Lay Dying*, where 'being' is it. Like Djuna Barnes who wrote one of the greatest novels of the 20th Century that no one's heard of."

I had caught a good train of thought. The defiance and excitement rose in my voice. "What about love, you know? In the sense of a kind of deeper spiritual understanding?" I continued.

"Everyone wants to read a good story," Henry reminded me, my questions dismissed.

"Yeah, that's just it. That takes me back to the beginning. Maybe what I want to write isn't a 'story'." Running with my defiance, "Besides, why do I have to write a story? Why does writing have to be a story anyway? I mean, in the sense of beginning, middle, end, conflict, climax, etc. Sure, quite a lot of things don't resolve or that have a series of conflicts, and so on. I just mean, in general. You know, what people expect and so on."

"Right. Depends if you want to sell any books."

I looked at him. "Yeah, exactly. Reminds me of a line in Antonya Nelson I'm reading, where she says something like, 'The problem with life was that it often did not feel obligated to play by the rules of literature.'"

Henry pursed his lips and nodded slowly as I watched him digest the phrase. "I get it. I get it that everything doesn't need a beginning, middle and end. Conflict and climax and all that. Not all good reading has to resolve, has to have a Greek format. I'm just saying, folks want to read something compelling."

I reset my gaze far off again. I surrendered. "Oh, I don't know. Whatever. Maybe I do have loads of baggage from my mother. Maybe I'm just totally blind to it. Maybe I just need to write that and see what comes out."

"I think that's a great idea, darlin."

Large wet flakes descended upon us, as we curled around under the ski lift. We eventually crossed back again over the stones and stream toward the bottom of the mountain, laughing and stumbling and tasting the coldness of the snow. That night we ate *tartiflette* and *fondu* in front of a fire at the only open restaurant and talked to the woman behind the bar about her two children and I felt safe and warm and happy. Funny how all conversations lead back to family. Mother and child. Mother and child. Afterwards, we walked through the town now on the other side of the river and watched the sun disappear into a crevasse, into a valley between two peaks and all the tall but modest hotels and houses turned a pale shade of themselves and the cold air fell down into the slender alleyways and between parked cars and into our pockets.

The next morning we hiked to the Cirque de Gavarnie where it was snowing again, and the glacial mountains formed a circle around us. At the top was a closed pension and we took shelter in its overhang to rest, seeing the same two hikers as on the previous day. We laughed and smiled and waved at one another as they passed us descending near the summit just as they had done yesterday.

On the path back to the village there was a calico cat on a raised field of green held aloft against the road by a low, stone wall. It reminded me of my own tuxedo cat, who had traveled with me from America to Paris on his own passport. There was another babbling brook with an ancient well nearby and a dirt path for animals that led to a grey stable. Ancient cottages speckled the hillside. An open pension was set back some meters from the brook where a small handful of hikers with cups of tea and lemonade sat at picnic tables enjoying the newness of the sun as it broke through the nada of the grayness. The air was cool and the earth wet. Horse and dog and cow prints marked up the path. I found a public toilet while Henry wandered into the only shop, where fresh milk, cheese curds and leather sacks were sold. That afternoon we drove to Luchon.

INTERLUDE II
The History of My Father

My father grew up in an orphanage because his parents were too poor, too drunk to care for him and his younger sister. There's a photograph frayed and missing a corner that looks like a snapshot from the 19th Century though it's not that old of course but anything old, older than me, seems old enough to be from another century. Maybe it's because I never lived with the families of my family, the families of my parents' families, and so they seem old in that untouchable, historical way like Emily Dickinson but not too far away like Shakespeare.

Written in the soft, tattered margin on the bottom is "Christmas 1950". My young father, in a kind of a scout's uniform, stands squarely in front of his mother and father with his little sister doing the same right at his side. He has a silly expression across his wide, Polish face, head slightly tilted, totally oblivious as a child feels in his heart that was born in him when he was born that knows what it is to know the heart. His mom looks like a living version of Olive Oyle. His dad looks like a 1950s, belt-wielding father. Starched shirt, icy eyes, tight lips, arms at his sides, body rigid. Next to the perfect little family is a Charlie Brown Christmas tree: diminutive, cheerless, neglected, hardly any ornaments, hardly any life to give, life given and taken and squandered in 1950 that has its own heart that was born and it knows and is squandered. The upper left corner of the photo has been overexposed and is flashed out and makes the viewer think of the heart of the picture, its heart and the flash that shows it's old, proudly old, and bearing the weight of its age. The tip of the old man's head succumbs to that absent space.

Another corner is torn, but it doesn't affect the little girl's smile that seems to know something pleasant the others do not know. The two children, my father and his baby sister, were sent away the following year.

My father tells the story of how he had to drive to Pittsburgh from Chicago in the stormy winter white to get legal permission from his mother to marry his high school sweetheart. His parents had left him at the orphanage when he was thirteen and his sister ten. He was still forced to ask their permission to marry. His alcoholic father, however, had died of a heart attack three years prior. His mother had remarried and moved out of state. She remained a drunk too, gave her permission and died two years later, also at age 50, also from a heart attack, outliving the belt-wielding man in the photo by five years. My father would tell that story with good humor. I used to wonder why he told that story and how it felt to tell it and how it felt to feel it. And I used to wonder how much it hurt him until he hurt me enough to stop looking for answers.

When his parents were still together, they would take the car to visit his Polish paternal grandparents. They would fight the whole way. He saw his own white violence as a kid and maybe that's what made him pass it on to us, but I know I'll never pass it on. The violence is white for me because I see a flash of white lightening behind my eyes when it happens. A form of synesthesia, the whiteness of the violence changes colors with its mood and depth and pain.

My father's father watched his own father get killed by lightning. That means my great-grandfather was killed by lightning. I don't really have a great-grandfather or even a grandfather. I don't have them because I never knew them, and they were long gone before I was even born. When my own father would speak of them, he'd speak as though they were outside of my world, my life, my very family. I was named after a woman who was my grandmother, but my father only ever said "my mom" and not "your grandma".

My father, the orphan, had his best friend bite off his nose after a drunken fight when they were twenty years old. My father was a rookie policeman at the time. He wore his face bandaged for months as the doctors miraculously took skin from behind his ear and stitched it to his face, then managed to make it grow so that eventually a new flap of skin was secured over the gaping wound. Anyone looking at him afterwards was never able to tell. When I asked him to share the whole story with me once, finally when I asked, he told how humiliated he was that year when he had his face either bandaged or in a state of transformation. Anyone looking at him probably wasn't be able to tell that either.

My father would wear a smile like the best of them or at least the best of the romantics. He would dip his toast in his wine and put ketchup on his eggs. He would sing a tune like he had cartoon bluebirds on his shoulder and would tear up watching a sunrise or a sunset or a ballgame or a wedding or when someone who loved him said I love you or when someone loved someone at all or said I love you to someone anyone at all. He cursed and judged, was charming and persuasive and an expert victim.

The last time I saw him the white violence roared up

like it does when you don't expect it but you know it's coming.

Get the fuck out of my house!

It was the last time. I didn't leave because he told me to but because what he said exposed a toxicity I suddenly knew I didn't have to accept any longer. Never again crumble from that white violence.

When I imagine my great-grandfather being killed by lightning, I also imagine Benjamin Franklin standing out there with a key on a kite. A cartoon figure with that pince-nez on his nose, well, really I think he wore glasses with a coiled wire frame, all dressed up to sign the Declaration of Independence, but first he's discovering electricity on a golf course with a kite and a key on the string of the kite in the rain. Brave man! Brave American! Ruffled white shirt, powder-blue jacket with tails in that 18th century way. Stockings up to his knees where the velvet, grey culottes leave off. Leather shoes with big buckles. Is it possible such a man was real? Like Walt Whitman. Figments.

As the story goes, my grandfather's family, Polish immigrants, lived on a farm in the middle of Indiana. Without warning a big storm quickly moved in and my great-grandfather went out to put away the cows, his young son watching him through the big front window. Suddenly he was struck. Just like that. His son looking on, nothing to be done. He was dead. I don't know that he was ever real.

Chapter 17
Snowboots with Bread Bag Liners: 9.5 yrs

Emma, Fred and I ordered Velcro sneakers and underwear from the Montgomery Ward catalogue, choosing our colors, sitting on a picnic table outside the door of the trailer. It was exciting when the package finally arrived. We had waited forever, but it still came in time before school started. Emma's shoes were pink. Fred's were dark blue, and, as usual, opposite of Emma's, mine were light blue. For the first time, we all went to different schools. I was still nine but in fifth grade now. Emma was ten, in sixth, and Fred was seven, in second.

More and more folks were flooding to town, and a bigger high school was needed. It was built far out on the edge of the valley up in Sweetloaf. Grades K-5 were split into two schools, so that the old middle school in the Village had third through fifth grade, and the elementary at North Side had kindergarten through second. The old high school in the center of town became the middle school. Because the trailer park was even more remote than the original Deerskin house, the bus didn't come anywhere near us. Mom drove all of us into the Village every morning even though Emma started school an hour earlier than Fred and I did.

We piled into the back of the white pick-up truck with the camper shell and drove around to the other side of the lake first to Emma's middle school. The trip was ten miles.

Someone was bound to get carsick on the way. We passed Fred's school after five miles, but since he wasn't starting until 9AM, he had to go with us for the whole trip into the Village. After we dropped off Emma, Mom took Fred and me to Jack-in-the-Box or McDonald's for a breakfast that we ate in the parking lot of the Pine Sap Saloon, Mom's regular hangout where she spent the mornings preparing sandwiches for the lunch service then spent her earnings on the bar in the afternoon.

Mom said good-bye to us and went inside, and Fred and I sat in the car for that hour before school, playing tanks with our Styrofoam breakfast containers, straws jammed in the top. Afterwards we walked up two blocks from the Pine Sap to my school where Fred caught the bus back to North Side. I watched the big yellow slug pull out and drive away as we waved to each other, then I went in my own school right behind me and back out through the rear door into the playground toward my detached classroom that stood on the old tetherball court.

Emma went in her school earlier and so came out earlier, which meant she walked into the Village and met me as I was getting out. We played imaginary supermarket in the parking lot across from the Pine Sap until Fred's bus dropped him back off at my school and we fetched him up the two blocks. We walked back to the Village and fantasized about buying cookies at the Village Confectionary for 25¢ and playing games at the Mountain Bear Arcade for 10¢ and then decided whose turn it was to go into the Pine Sap to get Mom or at least ask her for a quarter or two. We did our homework on the curb or sometimes in the car if it was raining or snowing.

After Mom finally came out, we got leftover sandwiches from the lunch crowd, a hard roll with mayonnaise and bologna or ham, and headed back to the trailer, the drive long and silent and dark.

When hard winter came, we moved to the Rocky Bay House. Fred and I went snow blind there like Sarah had at the Deerskin House years before, but for us it wasn't from skiing. I just turned ten. Fred was seven and a half, and school was cancelled because of a big storm, so we played out in the snow sledding in the woods behind our house without eye protection from the sun. When we went in the house, everything looked dark, and it stayed dark. We also got pretty bad sunburns on our faces. Later on after dinner, Fred went into a delirious flu, knocking and crying to get out of the bathroom where he had wandered in his sleep. I felt jealous since I was only snow blind and not sick with the flu. No one paid attention to me. You only got love when you were sick and not just hurting.

We lived at Rocky Bay through a winter that wasn't easy, but Phil and Charlie were back with us. We didn't have heat or electricity so we slept in the living room by the fireplace. There was a big room downstairs just like at Deerskin, but it had flooded straight away from the snow and frozen pipes and had turned into ice like the floor of an ice skating rink, only irregular and dirty. No one went down there after that. The Rocky Bay House also had mice that Slinky the cat used to catch. We put them in an empty fish tank with a screen door lying across the top. They knew how to escape and did it often.

It was snow boots time again, and we shared year after year based on foot size. The boots were always worn and old and leaked and we had a trick for that. We slipped each foot first into a long, plastic bread bag before putting them on. Taking those leaky boots off and exposing old bread bags while we changed into normal shoes at the door of the classroom was embarrassing, but not as embarrassing as arriving at school in the Dial-A-Lift van because we couldn't get our car started in the cold when the school buses weren't running from too much snow. The Dial-A-Lift, which the school kids called Dial-A-Joke, meant you were so poor you didn't have a car, or you were so poor your car was broken, or what seemed to be the worst, you were so poor you couldn't stay home from school in a blizzard because there was no heat in your house.

The Rocky Bay House was in Rocky Bay, full of large rocks and boulders that made up the mountainsides surrounding it. There were two little islands composed of enormous boulders in the lake. In high school the kids who worked at the docks took everyone on boats onto the lake and we headed over to the islands where we tied the boats together and drank cheap beer in cans and jumped off the rocks. We called them Asian Islands because of the artichoke leaf design of the two cottages built there by 19th century Chinese immigrants when they came to the area, or more accurately were brought to the area, to work in the mines and on the dam.

In the spring we moved from Rocky Bay to the Bear's Cave, the bar and restaurant on the main boulevard near the McDonald's and tourist lodges that Mom tried to open. She got a late 70s era red Cadillac El Dorado with personalized plates "MTNMAMA". She had big plans for her new image and for the Bear's Cave, but this wasn't the first time she tried opening a restaurant. For one reason or another, Mom's entrepreneurial ventures always failed. She didn't have a license and wanted to weasel around it or couldn't afford some fee and tried scheming to get away without paying. Something stalled the plans. Eventually they were halted altogether. I knew nothing good ever happened to us so it was OK, and even expected. Mom had her own way of seeing failure. The world conspired against our natural talents. We were good people—creative, beautiful, intelligent—but we were brow-beaten from the start. You could count on nothing, not even yourself. It was a conflicted self-fulfilling prophecy. You reject the world, which includes you, because it rejected you first, but the world rejects you because you yourself are doing the rejecting. You are the world or the world is in you or both.

Chapter 18
Saint Bertrand de Comminges

After the hike to the Cirque de Gavarnie, Henry and I tried to cross over the Col du Tourmalet in the rental car on the way to Luchon, but after the timberline, the road became ever more treacherous with rock slides and narrow passes, until eventually it was closed altogether and Henry had to turn around on the edge of a cliff. It reminded me of the many times my mom or brother drove us up and down the mountain when we were kids. The cliffs were so steep and precarious. Inevitably, a car or two would slip over in winter. My friend Dawn lost her mom that way in the fourth grade. She cried and cried at school the day we all learned the awful story. She moved to Australia where her aunt lived, and that was the last time we saw Dawn.

Henry and I drove all the way back to Lourdes and up to Tarbes where we got on the toll road for a short distance to drive back down to Luchon.

"Can we pull over for a little bit? I'm feeling nauseous."

"Sure, darlin." Henry pulled into a rest stop, and I lay on the warm grass letting my vibrating body get back in tune with being stopped. I was feeling sick: motion sickness, or baby sickness, or a combination of the two. I was torn between showing Henry the vulnerability and fragility I felt while precisely trying to hide it from him. I couldn't decide whether to take the safer or bolder path.

After we carried on driving, an hour and a half had passed when we finally stopped at the 11th century village of Saint Bertrand de Comminges, first visiting the Romanesque basilica of Saint-Just de Valcabrére a mile east at the foot of the fortified town's hill. Under the overhanging trees were more than several cars, and we saw a handful of well-dressed children playing on some grass with an equally well-dressed man looking after them. Many of the cars were adorned with white flowers and ribbons, and as we approached the church we could see a wedding was taking place. Henry walked right up to the door of the church and stepped inside to see the interior. I felt sheepish and begged him not to go, worried about the guests and privacy. Instead, I discretely walked around the crumbling gravestones in the yard and Henry caught up with me ten or fifteen minutes later. He didn't say anything about the wedding and I felt too uncomfortable to ask. I was conflicted with envy to have missed it.

We circled the grounds together admiring the *chevet* built from 1st century recuperated stones. Next to the church was a public herb garden where we read the leaflets and explanations of which herbs grew, how to care for them, when to grow them and how they could be used in food and medicine. Many of the signs had become illegible with rain and time and many of the herbs themselves were missing. To know what the garden should look like or what it had looked like when it was first created required imagining. I tried to do that. I tried to see what should have been there but wasn't, what once was thriving but was no longer cared for. I don't know if

Henry thought and did the same but he was also staring at the garden for as long as I was. We were silent and walked away together, instinctively taking one another's hand until we reached the car.

On the way up to the fortified village of Saint Bertrand de Comminges, we saw the Roman ruins of thermal baths and a theatre. We entered through a 14th century archway gate barely wide enough to fit our small rental car. I shifted around in my seat trying not to step on the bag of food that I'd set near my feet. I pulled out an apricot and passed it over to Henry who shook his head without looking at me.

"Could I have some water actually?"

I took a bite of the fruit and reached in the bag again with my other hand for the water bottle, glancing sideways out the window as I did. The wall of the ancient town was momentarily inches away from my door until the path opened up onto the narrow streets of the village. I took off the top of the bottle and handed it to Henry.

"Thank you." He turned right following the signs for the parking lot.

There were no more than 100 inhabitants, and Henry and I saw a handful of them in their gardens when we parked on the northern edge overlooking Saint-Just. We walked first up along the perimeter of the walled village and then down passing a café, restaurant and trinket shop before entering the cathedral where Henry deposited a handful of coins and a folded-up bill into a tin box. In exchange he took several cards with subtle yet remarkable ink renditions of the full Roman arches, Gothic nave and Renaissance stalls of the choir. We visited the cloister before being ushered out at closing time with the descending sun. It had already been a full day with the long detour to Luchon, and we still had nearly another hour to go. I tried not to show my fatigue in the ever-present effort to avoid being a burden on Henry, but my shoes felt strangely tight and my stomach was beginning to turn with the increasingly curvy roads. I took a drink of water and tried to fix my eyes on the horizon.

As we drove away and into the deep countryside ten miles or so later, I stared at the grain and hay fields around us and imagined the pilgrims passing through, making their way to the Catedral de Santiago de Compostela 600 miles away along the coast. Henry and I took slender, winding roads the rest of the way to Luchon, and their curves and trees and grassy knolls and low mountains made me feel I was living a life not my own—ancient and more beautiful. I felt weary but also serene, as though two conflicting sources of fatigue were upon me. The one came from our conflict; the other, a detachment from the world as a whole. I felt not myself in space and time but part of something more prehistoric and, at the same time, fleeting. The car humming gently through Pyrenean villages on a late afternoon brought both peace and anxiety. The arrival at our destination ended the moment and with it the suspension of fear and conflict, forcing me to enter back into the unknown of my every day.

Chapter 19
Going Hungry: 10 yrs

At the Bear's Cave, we played in the generous restaurant kitchen and in the bar and drank from the soda gun. It tasted funny and metallic, and I liked watching the clear, sugar water mix with the dark brown cola in forceful streams as it shot with the press of a button into tall drink glasses full of broken ice from the ice maker. That constantly humming machine was like the kind in motels where you opened the hatch to find a metal scooper, and you slid a handful of slender translucent ice cubes often connected to one another by the dozens into the bucket. In the fridge next to the ice machine stood bottles of beer and chilled wine and some juice, and rows of hard booze lined the shelves against the mirror behind the bar. The presence of all that liquor was somehow exciting even though we were kids and never touched it. We had a pool table as always, and Phil and Charlie set up billiard tricks involving chutes and angles using cue sticks lying on slants to make the balls roll a certain way. It reminded me of how the chicken hawk constructed an apparatus of precisely calculated lifts and pulleys, gadgets and gears, with the lighting of fire crackers, rolling of barrels, running of water, all so that a perfectly timed bowling ball would fall on Foghorn Leghorn's head knocking him unconscious, making him easy prey—though it never actually worked.

We lived upstairs in the apartment above the bar. It had one bedroom, which Mom and Fred shared with the usual bunkbeds. Emma and I shared one of two attic rooms above the apartment, accessed by a set of stairs that ran up the side of the building from the outside. Mom rented the other attic room to an old miner who went out to Honeycomb Valley each day to work his claim. He had a long black beard and was so quiet that we never knew if he was there or not.

The longer the Bear's Cave didn't open, the more time Mom spent at the bar in the American Legion. The three of us kids ate frozen tamales and potpies from the liquor store on the corner. We rode our bikes to the park or into the village to buy candy from money we found or earned selling hotdogs on the side of the road. Attached to a bright orange extension cord, the microwave sat on a vinyl chair that Fred and I dragged out from the bar.

On the way home from the village after a particularly good hotdog day, we had a contest to see who could coast the furthest down the last sloping hill, noting how far we could get without pedaling. Fred and I went first. As our bikes slowed, we shifted our handlebars back and forth in abrupt and rapid movements to keep from falling. Emma zoomed up from behind, and at the precise moment when she was about to overtake us, Fred jerked his handlebars to keep balance, unaware of her rapidly approaching from behind. They collided in the road. Everything crashed down, bikes toppled over, skinned knees, dirty tears, bruised elbows everywhere.

I got on my bike and road like a lit devil up to the American Legion just about one hundred yards away.

Tears were streaming down my face as I entered the bar. From my mouth came a high pitched fearful squeal.

"Mom! Freddy and Emma crashed on their bikes!" I could barely get the words out. "They're in the road! They can't get up!"

A stilled snapshot of them and the horrific scene of the crash burned in my eyes.

"Are they OK?" She was already angry.

"I don't know!" I sobbed. "They're lying in the road!" I imagined them still lying there, exactly how I'd left them, completely immobile, helpless, frozen in that space of the event of the accident as it was frozen in my mind. Another disaster for Mom to repair, like the time a bee landed on my shoulder just as Fred and I got off the bus. I was frozen immobile for over an hour until Mom finally came looking for us. She slapped the bee off without a second thought and shoved us in the car, angry we'd made her worry.

"Show me where they are," she demanded in a flat, serious tone taking my arm at the bicep fully with her grasp nearly pulling it out of the socket. We flew out of the bar like rats from a burning kitchen.

We hadn't but turned the corner of the building when we saw Fred and Emma, heads hung low, slowly, dejectedly walking their bikes up the street.

"You told me they were hurt! Look! They're fine!" She scowled. Her voice was raised.

Fred and Emma looked awful but alive. In fact, they seemed fine. A few scrapes, dirt streaks on their cheeks, worn out, even embarrassed, defeated, game over.

"You came and got me out for this?" Mom was upset with me.

I looked at her face and dropped my gaze to the ground with empty, confused eyes. I rethought my already thinking twice about when it was good to retrieve her from the bar.

During those times it was harder and harder to pull Mom away, and we had to look for food again on our own. I ate handfuls of chewable Flintstones vitamins, savoring their raspberry and orange flavors. Emma collected apples from someone's empty vacation house on the corner, and Fred used to go for breakfast on Saturdays at his friend Randy's down the block. He'd come back pockets loaded with hot rolls and half cut bananas snug in their browning peels. Sometimes we'd chop everything up and put it in a frying pan until the bananas turned into a kind of sauce and the apples were soft and warm and the bread both soggy and toasty. Sometimes we ate the contraband just as it was: cold and plain and good. If we were really lucky, there was fresh milk to wash it down.

In the spring, the gold miner moved out of the upstairs room, and a friend of Charlie's, Stan, moved in, sometimes going with us once in a while to the liquor store to get the 25¢ potpies and tamales. Mom turned up in the middle of the night, stumbled through the dark apartment and ran into my toys, crushing the My Little Pony stable and knocking over several items from the coffee table that produced a series of thick thuds as they landed on the carpet. When we woke up the next morning, she was nowhere to be found.

School finished for the summer at the end of June, and Emma made sugar cookies and Jell-O to celebrate. It was all we had left to eat but we pretended it was because we were celebrating the end of classes. It didn't take long for one after the other including Stan to come down with the stomach flu. Laid up for two days a piece like a series of falling dominos, I was the last one to go, thinking I would be able to hold out, but sure enough I got sick too. No one could eat those homemade cookies or Jell-O ever again. Commemorating the start of summer that weekend was shot, and Mom came back the following Monday with the icing on the cake: it was time to move again. The Bear's Den that had never opened was closing for good, and we were all 86'ed.

Chapter 20
Luchon

Bagnéres-de-Luchon was bigger than any other town in the region and there were many tourists and locals. In a large valley directly surrounded by jutting high mountains, Luchon itself was flat and symmetrical and almost felt like an American town the way the square blocks surrounded small parks and how houses had big front and side gardens with swing sets and dogs. What made it different from America was something about the creaminess, like an aged haze and invisible dust of the ages upon all things—a quiet wisdom in the material objects.

It was the beginning of spring. The hot springs weren't open, but the ski lifts still were. Henry and I stayed in a Victorian mansion converted into an inexpensive bed and breakfast owned by a kind French couple who had left Paris for the quiet of the mountains and woods. There were extensive hiking trails all through the mountains, and the first one we chose was a 12-kilometers drive south and a little east. We parked at *L'Hospice de France* and decided first to hike a more difficult trail and, after lunch, a milder one. We crossed the meadow in front of the Hospice, first reading the monument honoring the French exiles who fled there across the border into Spain during WWII. As city dwellers each originally from mountain hometowns, both Henry and I were eager to explore the nature France had to offer. It was meant to be a hiking trip but neither one of us had experienced such cultural history woven into the outdoors experience.

The trail was not hard at first. It followed a stream to the right and after crossing a small, wooden bridge a few hundred yards later, we encountered a dramatic incline. Thirty minutes of a steady ascent and we were looking down on a rugged valley with another glacial cirque surrounding us. We continued on the path until it was no longer visible under the rocks displaced by avalanches and the crumbling mountainside. Each progressive crevasse was more precarious than the previous one and we had to keep from sliding down the steep slope by treading on the still-visible brush, avoiding the patches of snow. The crevasses themselves were full of snow, and as we crossed, our legs sank deep into the center of the stiff powder where the smothered path lay underneath. Still we forged on and eventually it became uncertain if the crevasses had anything below them or if they were suspended above a hollow that shot down to the valley below. The old snow crunched under foot. Our breathing was steady and hard but not labored. It was a comfortable ascent with Henry comfortably in the lead.

We stood still and gazed outward into the vast gorge. Around us were the snow-peaked glaciers, shifting and trickling into green grass, trees and mountains as the eye fell. Sheep grazed on a great plateau directly opposite us. The only sounds were our breathing and the hollow rush of the air as it swirled through the immense basin before us, our bodies made minuscule by the far distance on the immeasurable summits. The stilled avalanches on the mountain faces captured the force of motion and power of nature and gave the appearance of enormous jagged, white teeth as the snow at once remained attached to the slopes while filling the chasms between.

This is one of those moments, I thought.

I looked at Henry peering into void, and felt the ever-growing uneasy sensation of radical joy that produced an immense sorrow.

Things could be so good. This is all we need. This is all we are.

That revelation immediately gave way to an overwhelming sadness. He was going to reject any path that might produce such an outcome, and so the greater joy I felt, the greater the weight of the grief that followed it, that was formed by it. I dove in each time for reassurance, for comfort, for affirmation of the present, of the perpetual present.

"This is so beautiful," I softly said.

He remained fixed into the horizon.

I tucked my body down into the side of his torso and under his shoulder. He put his arm around me and held me close.

"I love you, Hen."

"I love you too, darlin."

His language was no reassurance. It could not save my deepening despair.

"Shall we head back to eat?" I feigned composure, living toward myself in bad faith.

"Good idea, darlin."

We made our way back down the invisible path over the unstable passes, sometimes sitting and scooting to get across safely until we were on the green and flowering pasture at the bottom of the vale. We crossed back over the stream near the base and sat down together on a large tree stump at the edge of the bank. Henry found the water bottle in the backpack and took a long drink while I pulled out our sandwiches, apples, a package of cookies and a small bag of carrots. We silently began to eat and the creek did all those things we long for like singing and tripping. I felt reflective and trembled with life wishing the same for Henry.

When we arrived back at *L'Hospice de France,* we noted the patchwork of different building structures from a distance and learned inside about their constructions dating first from the 13th Century and again in the 17th Century. We entered through the modern doors, took off our muddy boots in the Medieval entry way and came into the generous and empty Renaissance dining room, spacious and encircled by a window. At one of the long, clean tables of fresh wood, we ordered two pots of infusion, a wild blackberry for me and the traditional *Deux marmottes* for Henry. While we waited, we opened an oversized history book with black-and-white pictures from the informal library behind us and read about the history of the hospice and how it was first used to collect taxes from travelers over the mountain pass and centuries later as a political Christian post and finally centuries after that as a bourgeois spa destination.

Warmed up, Henry and I headed out for our moderate hike that proved to be more difficult than the first. We found the trailhead at the corner of the hospice and it switchbacked steeply until it reached the height of the plateaus behind the sloping valley. The incline was severe and strenuous, and I hoped I wasn't overdoing it in my new body, although the challenge was always welcome in my old. At the top the path flatted out completely and stretched in various directions on the *Plateau de Campsaure.* Along the ridge we encountered many beautiful signs in rich wood with carvings of animals showing the ways to the *Chemin de fontaine rouge de l'Hospice de France*, which was the path we had taken, the *Campsaure par Roumingaou*, the path arriving from the opposite direction, the *Cabane du pesson*, a short-term refuge cabin for hiking, the *Etangs de la frêche*, a hidden set of ponds in a far-off dell, and the *Pas de la Montjoie*, one of the highest peaks of the range.

We walked long and hard and held hands and stepped through mud and broken fences until finally descending the dark and wide plateau two hours later along an unexpected and juxtaposed landscape of waterfalls and mossy rocks amid slender white trees and tender will-o-the-wisps. Finally, we crunched leaves underfoot and surprisingly found ourselves back on the end of the trail from earlier in the day that led back to *L'Hospice de France* near where we had lunched on the old tree trunk by the creek. When we arrived at our car we drank water long and cool.

"Can I have a hug?" I asked.

"Sure, darlin."

We stood there together in the parking lot with the sun finally setting in front of us until the last sliver disappeared behind the shadows of the trees and we climbed in their seats and breathed and sighed and drove down the hill back to our hotel for a full rest and another, longer embrace in the night.

Chapter 21
Garbage Bags of Doughnuts: 11 yrs

When the Bear's Cave scene went belly up, we moved in with Charlie and Phil and Phil's wife and baby, who had just gotten back from Chicago. We named it the Colusa House because it was on Colusa Street. It was a cheap, pea green stucco cabin with two bedrooms and stained carpets. Behind it sat a smaller cabin that looked just the same and came up to the edge of the road. Phil and his wife Jan and baby Phillip, Jr. re-located to the small one when Mom and the three of us moved in.

The Colusa House was built on afterthoughts. It had a massive red kitchen sink in the bathroom, an entryway that was a bedroom, a bedroom with two entrances like a hallway and a large, rear room that had probably been a garage. Emma and I shared the frozen garage room that was rather like a storeroom and had no insulation, Charlie had the entryway, and Mom and Fred had the bedroom, which was really just a passage between the bathroom and kitchen. Winter came, and we bundled up together in Mom's bed or in the living room on the couches. Several of the large glass panels in the full-window door were broken out, so we put pillows in the empty slots. The place stayed cold.

Events at the Colusa House:

1. Colusa had many different bugs. They were fabulously gigantic and even fought with the cat, hissing

and standing their ground. I started to think our street was named after the colossal size of the insects, but really all the streets of that neighborhood were named after the counties of California. We killed the endless bugs with any canister under the sink, usually lemon-scented furniture polish or WD-40. Those smells evoke strong involuntary memories.

2. Mom gave me a Susan B. Anthony dollar for squeezing her feet when usually it was only a quarter. Mom's poor feet—she birthed ten kids and worked upright in a kitchen since the first of them. Her feet were sore, swollen, black and blue, hard and calloused.

3. Mom regularly brought home full garbage bags of doughnuts retrieved from dumpsters behind the bakery next to the supermarket. We ate them for nearly every meal. Chocolate and maple bars, rainbow sprinkles on cake, glazed round, old-fashioneds, lemon curd, raspberry jelly-filled, powered holes, bear claws, apple fritters, chocolate glazed.

4. At the American Legion's annual Christmas party for the poor where each child got a free meal and gift, alone among the dejected mountain families, the Mexicans and the impoverished whites, the three of us watched the furious excitement of the underprivileged tearing open their age and conservatively gender-appropriate toys gifted by donors. At the finale raffle drawing, Fred won the grand prize: a full-sized, red ten-speed. We never won anything. We were there by ourselves and had no idea how to bring our unexpected ride home. Fred wasn't big enough to ride it—he was only eight—so we set out walking home across town, the three of us taking turns pushing it.

Mom got a new boyfriend early that spring, so we moved to the Alberta House right behind the 7-11. Never before had Mom's boyfriend been a penniless drunk who was still married. It was a sign. Her scheming had not only become careless but detrimental, and she had gone from hard player to sentimental alcoholic. She was near up to a bottle of vodka a day. None of us knew why Mom was with him. The guy wasn't a nice man. I quit playing trumpet that year after he told me it would ruin my lips. Things were spiraling out of a new, lost control, but Mom's descent wasn't evident until it was too late. It's as though none of us managed to see—or wanted to see—what was staring at us right in front.

They had a fight. Nothing new. But he'd shattered the windshield of our car with rocks as she pulled into the driveway to reconcile while we kids waited back at the American Legion a couple blocks down the street. She came back covered in pearl drop shards of glass. I watched her walk into the dark bar, glass-glittered arms halfway outstretched, curled back and up like she was holding out an animal hit by a car.

"Look! Look at what's he done to me. I'm covered in glass. Look!" She was staggering, pointing to her chest, pained, a sort of crying, wailing. Fearful, shocked, desperate. Seeing her vulnerable and trembling was unnerving.

Her friend Debbie gave Mom her car keys so she could go back, with still open arms, to the mindless perpetrator. Our house was just two blocks away, but it was unthinkable not to drive under the circumstances. The car itself had become her armor, a protection, a monument to the crucial and toxic distance between this tough, ruined woman and the old drunk in our house. Less than fifteen minutes later, Mom returned in an identical state. He had done the same thing to Debbie's car.

I don't know how their story would have ended. Maybe we would have moved out on our own eventually or maybe not, but we came home from school shortly thereafter, on a late spring day, to find the still-married drunk sitting on the porch with a wicked bruiser's grin on his face.

"Better pack yer things. Ain't gon' be seein' your mom fer a while."

We stood staring at him, frozen in slow motion before our own front door, paralyzed and thrown. Phil and Charlie showed up moments behind us in Phil's white pick-up truck that tore up the weeds and dirt as it flew into the driveway. Two big brothers bound out towards us.

"Mom's in jail." Charlie said. "She was caught and won't be coming back any time soon."

It was just the facts. Nothing to bargain with. Nothing to understand, just to digest and direct our immediate actions.

Several hundred years past in those next three minutes. Emma, Fred and I grew calcified roots into the dry earth, looking at each other, now with an underwater feeling. All things considered: the lumbering motion, the warble, the suffocation, the physical pressure of thousands of molecules on each inch of the body. We read each other's thoughts, swimming through middle school eyes standing as though in a kind of cult triangle on the dirt, each body equidistant from the next, supported by an invisible force that was thread through each of our chests toward one another. We didn't even know the police were looking for her in the first place.

"What did she do wrong?" My voice came out of Emma's mouth, and the gulping sob that followed came from Fred's.

"We'll talk about that later." Phil eyed the drunk still sitting still grinning on our porch.

Charlie began rummaging through drawers and boxes inside the house as though looking for some clue, some piece of evidence at a crime scene. Phil brought in more boxes taken from behind the convenience store next door, and both boys started throwing things in them seemingly haphazardly. They helped us pack everything worth anything which was nothing. In the space of an hour, our lives were loaded in the back of the pick-up. Charlie gave me a hammer so I could smash the screen of the non-working television that we left behind in the front driveway. The old drunk had finally wandered off on foot toward the American Legion. He hadn't spoken another word.

Chapter 22
California with Henry

The train back to Paris from the Pyrenees was long but uneventful. When we boarded, Henry reached his hand in his pocket and discovered he had forgotten to return the key at check out to that first hotel in the Pyrenees after Lourdes.

"I can't believe you unknowingly carried that enormous brass knob of a keychain with room key in your pocket the whole trip! And only found it there on the train back to Paris."

Henry nodded solemnly at the absurdity. "I'll mail it back to the hotel when we get to Paris."

I smiled in agreement.

We spent just one day in the round room before boarding a flight for California. The key would have to wait. It was early summer, and we planned to spend a couple weeks Stateside with our families before Henry's new consulting job had him popping around Europe for six weeks while they arranged his French working papers. We would first go to my family in California and then head directly to Idaho to see Henry's family before coming back to Paris.

Henry was awake with jetlag early that first morning in the California mountains, but I with my body clock woke at the normal time for morning and we found ourselves looking quietly at one another as I lay there.

Henry asked me for a walk and I agreed. The neighborhood was on the Eagleridge peninsula on the lake, and the houses all looked like Paul Bunyan cabins nestled quaintly among the pines. Henry had his arm around my shoulders, and we walked for several minutes in silence. We stopped at the corner, walked up the driveway of an empty cabin, and sat down on the stoop. We were side by side when he looked directly at me.

"We shouldn't be having a baby together." His voice was low. He continued to stare. It dawned on me that he must have been thinking of this all through the flight. My bowels and heart sank deep into the earth, and an invisible wave suffocated my breath. I was disappearing under its crushing force.

I extracted myself from his locked gaze and saw the still, electric blue sky above us. Ears filled with the familiar rushing sound of fresh wind knocking the treetops across the mountain valley up from the desert below. A roaring hush of a subtle, cascading waterfall. I could hear it so gently and sweetly surrounding me but also miles away, like an echo circling in on itself filling the vast expanse of space, and crawling up through the craggy hillsides around the dry brush until it soared and swirled among the heights of the tall softwoods—pine, spruce, fir. It made the entire valley feel like a small container but with wide-reaching edges, like the earthquake of 1992 when you could hear the deadly rumble coming from miles away underground, leaving jagged scars in the earth, and afterwards, after all the chimneys fell and the boy died, the community felt small, connected, sharing in the experience. Walking to the gas station felt like walking down the hallway of your own home. It was one big embrace. Everyone felt the same fear, the same menace and the same sense of care and repair.

"We don't get along. We should have split up long ago."

It was all an impossible echo. An insurmountable barrier. A repeated direct stab without any protection.

"What are you talking about?" I asked. My voice produced a renewed cheeriness, a lightness, a lilt that said, *Don't you remember? We've already gotten through this! Together!* "We've changed! It's all different now. Everything is wonderful." I stumbled over my words, quickly looking for the right thing to say and afraid of sounding too positive nullifying my entire attempt to lift his mood, change his mind, restore order, sail through the rough, not resort to hyperbole.

He dug in deeper. "Look. I'm telling you. This is how I feel. I've been telling. I've been trying to tell you. You don't treat me right. You don't respect me. It's not OK. I don't like it." His demeanor was stern and serious and angry, but still he remained calm, in turn agitating my need for exuberance and physical joy. "I don't like it, Aggie."

I was running out of resources. When he got this insistent, it was difficult to change his mind, or, as I saw it, help him through.

"I'm sorry. Yes, I totally know what you're talking about. I know... I know... I don't want to be like that." I needed him to feel I was on his side, that I understood, that we could work it out together. I would say anything. I was going to find a way through.

"You know, I learned from you, I learned, I've learned so much from you. And when we got here, I thought, wow, yeah, I don't want to be like that anymore. It's awful. It's so painful." I was self-deprecating by default. Was Henry really so much better that me? Why did I think so? I was trash. I was nothing. I was broken. I was from shit. My goal at that moment was to show him he lifted me up, I needed him, I needed to be like him, to learn from him, to show him he was better, and I was grateful. I hated that me and I also hated I had to do it. The fear ran 90% of the machine.

I sent my words out to him, to the world with full conviction knowing that they were tools to help someone and so knowing they may not be true, not true in the sense that I did not see the picture he saw, but I knew how to help him climb out of his depressive periods—sometimes. It was always an enormous battle, and I never quite felt like I was getting to the end of the tunnel, but at some point he would relent. I would be safe again for a while.

He looked at me, listening, waiting and hoping to hear something that really would change how he felt, but I could see it was futile. He could never undo things in himself once they had settled. He was stubborn to a fault. But, yes, he would hold on. He knew he had to. It was the right thing to do, but even now I knew his resentment was growing, was already becoming unwieldy. He dug in on his claim that he didn't choose this new path, and any crack, any fragment of a crack, it was enough for him to throw it all away. He was angry, and he wanted justice. For now though, for now he would do the right thing, he would remain a part of us, a part of the picture.

"Your family—they're great. They are sincere and… I don't know how to put it. There is stability. I never had that. And so much respect. Stability. Yes, that's it. I want to be like that. I am like that!" What was I talking about? Was I trying to flatter him? His family better than mine? Why? I had such a desperation to be liked, to regal any family not my own, to wish to join it, to be included.

I was overdoing it. I meant everything I said, but I was overdoing it. I wanted to beg to plead, to be loved, to make him accept me, accept everything, to be happy, to really be happy with it. Why couldn't he do it? What was wrong with me? I didn't understand, but I would pour and pour and pour. It was all I could do. I could do it.

"Haven't you noticed? I changed so much. I've changed so much since we've been together."

It was always hard for me to let anyone get close. I was afraid of loss, of abandonment, of being hurt, left behind. Once I did enter into the relationship, my fear increased from a newfound need for inclusion. It was irrational, as it created a divide between me and the other person whom I sought to be near. Henry was cognizant and, I thought, patient. I began to understand things better.

I started to become more self-deprecating, more apologetic and pathetic. Anything and everything to get out of the moment. It was all sincere, but it was in a panic. It was painful, terrifying. I needed to throw myself on the tracks. It was worth it. It was always worth it.

"Yes, that's true. You have." He absently looked towards the lake, though it was barely visible through the thick blanket of trees and cabins. A tension released in him.

"I've changed so much!" I started jumping up and down against him, my chest hitting against the zipper on his sweater, as it flicked up and down. "I love you. We can do this. We need to. We are huge. We are amazing."

I came up close to his face and stared in his eyes. I needed it to work. "We can do this." I paused, my voice lowering. "We can be bigger. It's our chance."

He looked at me without responding. He looked sad. He didn't really feel anything. He didn't really feel the thing for me. He was trying to find the right thing to feel. He loved me or called it love, but something had cracked or was left behind or destroyed. He didn't feel whatever I was feeling, perhaps it was missing from him altogether and so all he could do would be to go along with it. It was not the first time he had to force himself to choose the path that the usual feelings follow. He felt detached inside. At a young age, he had learned how to choose right even if it felt wrong.

I became excited once more. I would be his cheerleader. Creating positive tension, tackling the challenge. "Hen! We have to be bigger than that! Don't you see? The world… everything… listen. It's all so beautiful. I just want us to be huge. To be new and extraordinary. Remember? We can do this!"

He stared through me. Time froze and passed. He stared at me. Time was suspended. It was missing. He found me again. Time came back like a soft wave on the sand. He found the peace within him.

"Yes, OK." He said softly.

He looked away and paused then looked back at me. "But, look, I don't want to be reproached and criticized all the time. It's not OK."

"I understand. I've learned so much from you."

I would compliment him. It was a gesture. I would prove to him. I would subjugate everything, anything. I would save it. I would always save it at all costs.

The birds in the trees were singing. They were screaming. A cacophony coming from every corner above their heads. They were listening. Beautiful and fearful. They were full of sorrow and of knowing. The rockets in my head were calming down. I felt a sickness in my stomach. I felt an electric coil turning tighter and tighter. A glow from within me was enshrouded in something dirty, black and sickening. I forced the glow through to the front, to the center, to fill me with hope and joy and resilience and perseverance.

We walked back to the house arm in arm. It was saved. I felt almost whole again. I wanted to run and scream and laugh or hold him close and bury my head in his chest under the warmth of blankets. Yes, I felt almost whole again, but there was a crack in me now. Something was seeping out or seeping in.

Chapter 23
Mom's Sentencing: 11.5 yrs

Shackled like a mountaineer with twelve other prisoners including a smooth Mr. Leon Johnson, Mom was taken to the county jail still in California, then extradited to Chicago three days later. All thirteen prisoners, caught while on the run, were secured in a federal police van that drove across the country from California to Chicago traveling 30 hours straight.

"We were both wearing silver jewelry when we met!" She told us about her new boyfriend, Leon—a joke she loved repeating afterwards, although I still wonder if it was actually meant to be funny.

With Mom gone, Emma, Fred and I went back to the Colusa House with Charlie. Phil, his wife Jan and their baby, Junior, were still next door. The first night Phil and Charlie took us to the video store where we rented a movie and a VCR to watch it on. This became a new pastime. On regular rotation was *The Sound of Music*. In between weekend screenings we sang all the songs, recited scenes, every line by heart matching family to family: they, seven children and a governess-turned-mom, and we, seven children plus three more from the drunken brother-in-law. Poor, dirty, motherless, at sea without a rudder, we were nothing like the Von Trapps. Still, we aligned ourselves with them and let our imaginary selves take over.

We were waiting to find out what was going to happen to Mom, and then we learned she was going to the big women's prison out near Peoria, almost 200 miles south of Chicago. We didn't know yet for how long. At the last minute, the public defender told our older siblings it might be a good idea if we little ones were at the sentencing—to maybe soften the judge—so at the last minute, John drove out with his buddy Paul from Chicago to take us three back in record time. When John drove, Paul slept. When Paul drove, John slept. The three of us kids rode and slept in back, one on the floor and two on the seats. Fred tried sleeping by lying across the base of the rear window, but he rolled out the first time he dozed off.

After creeping over the long, windy, mountainous road late at night, we stopped at the 7-11 in the desert to fill up and get our first meal: Slurpees, Cokes, hot dogs and candy. An hour later with the hot desert night air all around us, Emma opened the window to dump out her warm, flat soda. It came right back in, vacuum sealing itself to my hair. We crossed the country without stopping except for gas and gas station food and got to Chicago after 30 hours straight—just like Mom herself had done.

Hot off the road, we got to Mom's sentencing just in time, walking into the federal building still dazed and dusted from the whirlwind trip. Her courtroom was in the George N. Leighton Criminal Courthouse on the lower westside. As we each one waited for the others to pass through the security checkpoint on the ground floor, we peeled the road off our skin with dozens of packets of moist toilettes that we had lifted from the condiment counter at the Loaf'n'Jug outside St. Louis. Emma brushed my sticky stiff hair while the elevator ascended, the number for each floor softly illuminated and extinguished behind an engraved brass plate. Fred used the grubby, wet tissues accumulating in his hands to wipe down the tips of each of our road trip bedraggled shoes. Emma and I solemnly nodded to him in approval. Everything counted.

We entered the room in silence, bleary-eyed, wood-splintered bodies, hearts racing. John ushered us down the aisle, and we sat down in the fourth row on the left behind a sign marked "Defendants". There were just a handful of people around us. I could make out the two lawyers because of their suits and perhaps an assistant or two, the stenographer, several serious and proud-looking police officers and two or three other people on a bench opposite us. Ten airless minutes later a door in the rear of the room opened, and Mom entered. She was wearing an orange jumpsuit, her hands shackled together, and was led by two female and equally serious and proud officers. The joy I felt in looking at her again was impossible to contain. We hadn't seen her in months.

"Mom!" Bodies restrained, we all mouthed the word without its accompanying sound, slight squeaks and half breaths falling out instead.

She tried to blow us kisses, her eyes misting over, mouth frowning. The officers turned her body and sat her down. She was forced to look away.

The courtroom wasn't a room anymore. It was a taut balloon with hard, unmoving air. Each figure was static like toys on our bedroom floor: only those in our hands lived and moved. We put them down and new ones took their place. None of these toys were in any hands.

Unmoving toys. Suspended. The air pulled tighter around our arms and cheeks and nostrils until we couldn't breathe.

The tension was broken with a blood-red sound crashing down from the unknown height in the center of the ceiling.

"All rise." The booming voice of a figure I hadn't seen before announced the arrival of the judge. In her familiar flowing black robe, she was imperial and grave. When she sat, we all sat. The inevitable hush fell across the room, and we waited.

"Would the Defendant please stand for sentencing."

The judge laid the case out before Mom and the rest of us.

"To the Defendant: This is not the first time I have seen you in my courtroom. I am disappointed. Can you tell me why you're here again? I saw you on similar charges over a decade ago. You spent that intervening time fleeing to California and having more children, but you managed to commit crimes in my State and City again."

Mom was small and submissive. "I'm sorry, your Honor."

"You seem have a made a living of cheating people of their hard-earned living. Is this a lesson you want to pass on to your ten children?"

"No, your Honor, I do not." Still small and submissive.

"You actually have ten children now, don't you?"

"Yes, your Honor."

"Are they here in the courtroom today?"

"Yes, your Honor. Some of them are, your Honor."

My stomach dropped. I felt like I was going to be sick. Emma grabbed my hand keeping her head facing forward.

"They will learn a lesson here today then. Do you understand the crimes you committed that bring you here before me today?"

"Yes, your Honor, I do." Mom stood there in the middle of the room in her orange jumpsuit.

"I'm not sure I agree with you. Today's sentencing is a result of a guilty verdict in which you attempted to involve several of your children in an auto-theft scheme."

So there it was. We finally learned what Mom had done to go back to prison. The judge said it was similar to previous crimes—crimes she had committed before Emma, Fred and I were born. Crimes she had committed that caused me to be born in prison. Crimes, I knew, related to fraud and 'bad checks'.

Mom stared, her chin falling against her chest.

"If you understand the crimes you've committed, as you say you do, have you learned from your detention to this point and from your previous detentions?"

"Yes, your Honor, I have," Mom's head remained bowed.

The judge, like a glowing white light sucking in the life around it, growing fuller, rounder, all consuming, the judge, unaffected and unmoved by our presence, unconvinced by Mom's words, unconvinced as though she had heard nothing, staring at the same mark on the wall on my mother's face, unblinking, unfazed, austere, bored, familiar with the production.

I suddenly had the feeling her last question was rhetorical.

"I don't think you have. Two years." She brought her gavel down.

"All rise!"

In that instant the formalities of the judge's departure became a blur. I didn't watch the flowing robe. I didn't see the stenographer or watch the movements of the attorneys and assistances. The judge's words rushed back toward us in the wooden seats on the left behind the short gate like a wind that enters a room and slams the door closed. They whipped through us and sucked out our breath instantly. They exited our tired bodies and socked us right in the gut, Fred especially. His body bent in two next to me as he doubled over in a nine-year-old's sobs.

We watched them quickly take her away, and we watched her leave the courtroom through the back as she had come. A new, clammy silence entered into the space where she had been. It was thick and heavy and full of mildew and sweat and air-conditioned nightmares. It shrank down around us curling our hair and giving us waterlogged fingers. Our shorts were soggy, shirts sagging like the insides of a wrinkled balloon. We stood with difficulty, our bodies fastened to the benched.

John slowly walked us out of the courtroom in the opposite direction from Mom. We stood calcified in the grand elevator lobby in a blank, slow stillness that opened and swallowed us up as we stared out of the massive windows looking over the city from the lower westside of Chicago, Illinois. Our bodies moved against our will, held in place by tentacles that reached up from underground. We had to push against them, tearing open wounds on the backs of our legs and on the palms of our hands. *There aren't enough Band-Aids in the car*, I thought.

Chapter 24
Henry's Idaho

The plane arrived at 11:57PM on the tarmac in Boise, Idaho, landing strangely quietly but for the steady, insect-like hum of the propellers. The passengers disembarked, and Henry's parents and sister were waiting at the security exit point.

"Hi, you two!" His mom yelled. "How's your family, Aggie? How was the flight?"

"Someone died on our flight," I blurted out, wishing I could pull the words back in. Henry looked at me with disapproval.

"Oh no!" Expressions changed to pained emotion. "Really?"

"That's the only reason we made it. The flight out of California was delayed so that by the time we got to Seattle, we were literally running for the gate. They hadn't closed the door yet even though it was way past take off time because, it seems, someone had died on the plane right before leaving the gate and so they had just taken the body off, and everyone was still sitting there waiting to go. That made it so that we were still allowed to get on, but normally it would have been way too late. We didn't know what had happened though when we got on, and everybody looked so somber and were staring at us. We thought it was because they were mad. There were two empty seats behind us, which we thought was really strange especially because they had turned away two non-revs at the counter for being too overbooked." I couldn't stop talking. I didn't know what I was doing. I could feel Henry's displeasure but it was too late to stop the story.

"What's a non-rev?" Henry's teenage sister asked.

"Non-revenue. Someone who usually works for the airline. People who fly for free, like pilots and attendants and their families and stuff," I explained.

"Anyway, it's nice to finally be here," Henry said.

I unclenched my fists. I was sweating and nervous and glad to get out of the spotlight.

"Yeah!" His sister replied for the group.

"Are you excited to graduate high school?" He asked.

She turned red, eyes darting around, "I don't know. I guess so."

"Congratulations! And way to go on being valedictorian. That's amazing." I was recovering my social skills.

"Thanks," she mumbled, still smiling still red still endless curls hanging in her face. "I'm so glad you two could make it."

"We're glad to be here." I rubbed her on the shoulder and she shyly leaned toward me. I liked Henry's family. I wanted to be part of it—a replacement or new start, more stable than what I had known. I was projecting.

"Let's get your bags and get you home to bed." Henry's mom was always all smiles.

Papa drove the SUV out of the airport parking lot, and the sky was inundated with stars and mountain silhouettes on the edges. We headed north across town, passing the state university after a couple miles. Just beyond, we crossed the river, dark and rich, and headed into the quiet downtown. On the right the blackened Greek dome of the Capitol Building came into view, recalling just a little Sacre Coeur. Papa took a left on West Front and a right on North 15th, the SUV automatically shifting into low to ascend North Harrison Boulevard where we pulled up to their home. The air was brisk and refreshing as we stepped out into the night. I was comforted to be in the company of Henry's family, and we all bundled into the house, everyone helping carry the odds and ends.

Henry's parents lived in a generous and handsome home tucked in a wooded valley on the edge of town. Balconies wrapped around each of the main home's three levels, the bottom one connecting to a pond, a vegetable garden and a private wood. The backside of the home hung over a pronounced ridge overlooking the city and valley below, with a view ricocheting off the Boise River and the Sawtooth National Forest in the distance. The front side of their home led onto rich landscaping complemented by numerous spring, summer and fall perennials while the interior was ornamented by an eclectic and valuable variety of local artistry, mostly bright pottery and reclaimed wood, giving homage to the wild, Western landscape and Native American heritage.

"Anyone need a cup of tea or a snack?" Henry's mom always on the ready.

"I'm going to hit the hay, Mom, but thanks." He put his hand on her shoulder giving it a gentle caress.

We said our good nights and slowly carried our things upstairs, falling asleep together without words.

The sun burst in the next morning through the east-facing window. Henry and I were sleeping in a guest room decorated with an authentic, blue Matisse figure hanging uncertain behind glass in a frame against floral wallpaper.

"I don't want to have a baby with you." Henry lay next to me staring straight at the ceiling with his eyes open. They were like ice and they saw ice and they gave ice. It was hard to continue the fight. My anxiety was causing me real physical ailments. My breathing was quick and shallow.

"I'm not afraid of you anymore," I found myself saying, trying to pull the bold words back into my mouth as they fell out and away.

"What do you mean by that?"

"I mean—" Oh god, I was scared. Why had I said that? "I mean that you can't force me to do anything." I didn't know what I was saying. I didn't know how that had come out of my mouth. It was too defiant. I meant it. It was bad to say. It wouldn't work. It would drive him away. I was scared. I was glad I'd said it. I needed a new tactic and that was it. I needed to say the truth, what I felt, what I meant. I needed to stop walking on eggshells. Everything was at stake. The baby was at stake. My self was at stake. The future of the world was at stake.

"But you are the one forcing me, darlin," Henry replied calmly and coldly, eyes still facing upward, body rigid. His self-control was a horrifyingly brilliant performance.

"What I mean is," I struggled to figure out what I meant and how to say it. "What I mean is—" I didn't know what I meant. I tried to nuzzle up against him, hiding myself, half of my face, my right ear and cheek and eye, all of my hair and the edge of my chin into his shoulder, into the warm depths of the blankets and the beautiful sun rays pouring in, that constantly reminded me of a world bigger than this somehow petty, futile dispute.

"We need to split up," he declared.

I lifted myself off the pillow and stared at him, the sunlight dividing our two bodies.

"We have to split up," he repeated. "We can't be together anymore. I don't want this. I'm angry. I won't be forced."

Each sentence was a dagger, was more than a dagger. Each sentence was a death sentence. The violent roar of an approaching diesel-fueled garbage truck outside became noticeable and grew louder. Though I couldn't see the truck from the bed, I could see it with my imagination and join the jolting sounds with each stage of the process. I imagined the bins being mounted to the pulley and lurched high before they slammed against the top of the open container and their contents fell inside. The next sound told me all of that material was being crushed and pressed, churched up and made faceless. I saw inside the body of the truck full of viscous black oozing decay. I tried to tune it out and focused on the wallpaper. The juxtaposition between them gave me vertigo and the floral print began to grow larger and unsteady. I was Alice soon shrinking and expanding, shrinking again. Lost inside the room without an escape. Lost inside my own body.

"It's more than that! It's… we're…" I was running out of ideas. I was running out of repair methods. I was running out of fear. Out of a desire to keep it together. I had to find a new tactic.

"We have to figure out to make it work. Separately," he insisted with frost with no human heart with 80,000 miles between our two bodies.

"OK, fine." I was nearly hyperventilating. "But, you know, I really thought—"

"What? You thought what? Are you going to insult me now?" He angrily cut me off.

"No. I just wanted to say..." I took a deep breath. "You know, I just know you're more than this. You have it in you, I know you do. I just thought we could be bigger than that. Bigger than this kind of smallness..." It wasn't exactly making sense, and I was sick of the one-sided effort, so instead I chose the beginning of defiance.

"I don't need this," I finally said. "I don't need to be treated like this. So, fine. If that's how it has to be, fine. But I just thought we could be amazing, and, you know, explore the universe in a way that was unconventional. I mean, you know, have this baby and travel, explore, do something special, something different, something..." What was I saying? "Unconventional"? How? Maybe just different from where I had come? What I had gone through? How was that unconventional? What was I trying to sell here? "You know, go through this together and be part of a new connection and do it our own way. It could be so interesting, so rewarding. We are intelligent, you know? We are loving, and we are so good together. I just think that it's a great opportunity for us even just to see ourselves. And to move away from that, it's really a shame. It would really be a shame." Is that what I really thought? Is that what I really wanted? It didn't matter. The fear powered everything, every word.

"Let's get breakfast." He didn't know how to handle conflict, and he didn't know how to speak back to defiance. Not that he was afraid, but he knew he would just crush me again. We didn't want the same things. He knew I was passionate. It didn't matter, and he also didn't care if I was sincere. He wasn't convinced, maybe only perhaps softened or simply hushed. As usual, he felt sorry for me because I desperately needed to believe what I said—to protect myself to protect my body to protect my future—and we both knew I would lose.

The rest of the trip was a blur. I was waiting for the crisis to erupt again and again and it did.

We took walks in the woods and he stabbed me. We took walks in the town and he stabbed me. We had tea with his parents and he stabbed me again while they were watching and they watched. His family knew what was happening. They were frightened for the outcome because they loved Henry and knew it wasn't going well for us. I wanted to scream out for their help, but they were Henry's family, not mine. Was there someone who could help me? There wasn't. It was like a nightmare where you try to scream or run but the sound doesn't come out even though your mouth is open, and your feet don't move even though you're trying as hard as you can to escape. The difference was that this was real life.

Sleep was safety, and in the morning again was the terror. We watched the soccer games of Henry's niece and nephew, and he stabbed me when no one was looking and when they were looking and when the children were playing and when he was carrying the children and when he was giving them candy.

At the lake house his family went swimming and I watched on the shore. We took boat rides and I sat dead next to them in the front seat, my flesh feeling fused with the leather seat as we cruised across the top of the water and I was looking at them with a violent scream in my absent voice and they were not looking at me.

When we returned to town from the lake house ten days later, I had been buried ten times and then I knew I would not be buried one more. I ran away to the summit behind their house, and when I decided to come down, I was ready for full battle. The clean air was strong in my lungs, and I inhabited my body and myself. I was ready to bear the consequences. I returned to the hilltop next to their house and as I approached the cliff, I saw Henry approaching from the other direction. The terror took my breath away, but I was ready.

"I have something to tell you," I said.

He looked small. He was half his usual size.

"I also would like to speak, but please. Go ahead."

"I don't have to live with this." I had to hurry or I would be unable. I would be nothing. I would be shattered. I could barely catch my breath. It had to come out all at once or I would splinter into 40,000 pieces and scatter to the wind. "I do not have to feel bad like this for bringing a life into the world. I should be supported. I should feel wonderful about this. I should be around only love and support. And so I don't need this. And I'm not afraid." I am air. My voice was air and the wind was caught in my mouth and opened it wider and gave it both depth and lightness. "I'm not afraid of you anymore. And that's fine. If you don't want me, if you don't want this, if you don't want our family, that's fine. I'm not scared. I am not afraid of the future." I was floating on the surface of the precipice, my body fanned out lifted suspended ready to fly. "I'm not afraid to be without you. So, you choose whatever you want, but what I choose is not this. I do not want to be near someone who treats me poorly. I don't have to put up with that. I will be fine without it. This baby will be fine too. We only want love. It's what we deserve."

There was a hum to the tension in the still air like the world was holding its breath. I had finally said what was needed. I looked across at Henry. Henry looked up at me. The world looked up at both of us from the valley below. I waited for his response and I was still afraid and expected to be obliterated on the rocks.

"I want to try," he began.

The air exploded with a violent rush, and a cold wind was released and consumed me on all sides with a physical surge and a stark throbbing in my head and ears and hands and heart.

"I don't feel it now, but I want to try because I know that I have to give it a chance." He was stiff and pained and forced. His eyes bulged and his mouth twitched and his body was not his own. "I know that you deserve more than being treated like this, and I am not sure I am the one to provide that to you." He paused. "But I want to try. And I want to be a father in the baby's life."

I wanted to fall down dead with relief.

Interlude III
The Last History of Mom

"She's not going to last must longer." Emma's voice climbed through the old rotary phone in my dumpy, cockroach-infested living room that early Thursday morning. It was the year before I moved to Paris and met Henry.

"I told myself if she were still alive this morning, I would go." I restated my plan to Emma. "I would be there. The flight is only about an hour, and the hospice center is ten minutes from the airport. I can be by her side in three hours from now, tops." I paused. Thought about the distance from Seattle to Boise. I looked out the window. It was sunny, quiet, peaceful. The breeze was blowing the uncut grass in the front yard. The birds were chirping.

"I told myself I would be there." I repeated, detached, trying not to panic.

We were silent for about twelve years.

"I have to find tickets. I gotta go," I said into the silence.

"OK, good luck. Love you."

We had never had such a brief conversation.

I pressed one of the plastic cylinder switch hooks on the base of the ancient telephone, cradling the receiver between my collarbone and chin. I still didn't have a cellphone. I dialed a colleague to cover my class, then my downstairs neighbor, a grad student in the English Department on the ready. I had finished my Ph.D. the year before and was working as an instructor at the same university.

The line picked up. My neighbor was home. "Of course I'll take you. Let me know when you're ready." We hung up, and I quickly booked a last-minute flight.

We drove in silence. He dropped me on the curb for Departures. I had no bags and went straight to the security checkpoint with my preprinted boarding pass. I was sweating uncomfortably, my eyes darting around loose and vacant. Working hard to concentrate, unable to focus on the world in front of me, trying to hold my papers together, to not drop anything, not fall, not tumble, not crawl into a ball under the conveyor belt pushing along with everyone's personal items in gray plastic trays.

As soon as I passed through, I put on my headphones and walked quickly toward my gate, though there were still fifteen minutes until my plane boarded.

I'll be there in an hour and half. I'll be there. I'm almost there. I was anxious, nervous and felt like my body was weighted down with wet cement while simultaneously floating above the floor, disconnected, amorphous. I went to the toilet and stared at my feet while I peed, remembering I wanted to tell Diane to tell Mom to wait for me.

I'll be there in two hours tops, Mom. She needs to wait for me. I'm coming.

I rushed out to look for a payphone. Taking out my headphones, I exchanged a dollar bill for four quarters from the Mexican food stand next to the row of phones. At first they wanted me to buy something.

"My mom is dying. I have to call my sister."

Without another word they made the transaction. I turned down the neighboring corridor and dialed Diane with two of the quarters.

"Hi, it's me."

Diane's response was delayed. "She's gone." Her voice was trembling. "Didn't they page you?"

12,000 years passed.

I felt weightless. The air compressed around me. All

sounds vanished. The phone in my hand and my hand itself became unknowable objects. I looked for my body. I looked for my voice and found it.

"I was wearing headphones," I managed.

"She's gone." The sound of a deeply heaving, warbly breath.

The silence of twelve years compressed.

I could find nothing to say. It was like an unopened, blank Sunday afternoon. Nothing to say. Nothing to feel.

"Oh," I let out. My humanness fading away.

"She's gone, Aggie. She's gone."

"Oh."

"She's here next to me." Diane started crying. "She's gone!"

She said it as though it weren't supposed to be true, as though she, Diane, hadn't been sitting there for the last three days waiting for it to happen.

"What do I do?"

"She's gone." Diane repeated it again as though she hadn't heard my question, as though to confirm the death was real or maybe to undo its realness by announcing it so absurdly.

"What do I do?" I asked again. "Come anyway?"

Diane was sobbing now. She finally heard me, her baby sister. "Yes, come anyway," said with force, conviction, determination.

"I don't know. Why? What do I do?"

"Come, yes, just come! Yes, Aggie. Come! Come anyway!" Her voice was unstable, quivering, wavering, moving over waves, uncertain and suddenly certain and excited with new clarity as though she were going to pull me through the telephone, as though her life depended now on my being there.

"I don't know. I don't know. Let me let me... I don't know."

"OK, call me back."

I wandered around. The air expanded and contracted. I felt the bodies around me were massive, roaming everywhere, filling the space everywhere, moving in all directions in patterned and un-patterned formations, silent, roaming, directed, undirected, still, cacophonic, fast, slow, angular, smooth, suitcases, babies, legs, sweaters, long hair, short hair, lights, announcements, walkways, wheels, carts, colors, no colors, sounds, sounds, shapes, bodies, and I in the center of it not knowing what to do where to turn how to turn how to be my body.

So many faces, people, voices, and yet none of them were for me. A crowd that did not know me, could not help me, had nothing to do with me. Human bodies surrounding me not for me, none to know me, to help me, to lean toward me.

I walked a few steps, stopped. Walked again, slowly then quickly then again slowly, aimlessly and soon found myself in front of my gate. I was standing before two agents who were sympathetically frowning at me. How did they know?

"My mom just died," I blurted out.

"We know, sweetie," said the one who was already coming out from behind the counter delicately, affectionately as she touched my arm above the elbow. "We have a message for you to call your brother."

"I don't have a phone." Then mumbling, "I didn't have a phone. I didn't know. I had music on. I got quarters. I wanted her to wait for me." She wasn't listening. I was speaking to no one, recounting. "I wanted her to wait for me." If I said it again, I thought, more loudly, more forcefully, it would change what happened. I had that lingering feeling of figuring something out too quickly where the desire to tackle the problem still remains, and you become distracted, still focused on accomplishing the task when in fact it has already been settled.

"Here, take mine." The agent offered me her cell phone. "In fact, come this way." She looked back over her shoulder to the agent on the other side of the gate desk. "Jen?" The agent gestured across the terminal. "I'm going to take her to the lounge for a second." Jen nodded her consent.

The gate agent ushered me into one of those mysterious side doors at the airport that everyone always wants to know what's behind, sat me down on a sofa in a regular, cramped employee lounge, told me to take my time, to use the phone to call my family.

I called Emma this time.

"No, don't go. You don't need to go." Emma was calm, direct and confident.

"How do you know? Why?" I was feeling weak, panicked, uncertain. Emma gave me perspective and grounding.

"Because," Emma answered without hesitation, smooth and steady, "you don't need to. It's over. What would you do there? There's no reason to go now."

Diane was with Mom. No one else had gone. I wanted to go. It was too late.

"Oh, Oh. OK." The employee lounge didn't live up to its imagined reputation. There were several old vending machines including one for coffee. A very old-looking table, like the ones I remembered from elementary school, with matching chairs, one half broken leaning against the wall in the corner, and two beige telephones with about 50 unidentified buttons a piece. I also spied a ratty teddy bear lying haphazardly on a tattered doctor's-waiting-room-style sofa, and I wondered what that was doing there. "OK, you're right. Yeah, OK."

"Just go home for now," Emma instructed me.

"OK, I'll just go home then," I repeated mechanically.

"And call me when you get there. Love you."

"And I'll call you when I get there. Love you."

We hung up. I didn't take the flight. The agent began explaining that she would process a refund even though I didn't ask and didn't know how or why to ask. The agent escorted me gently by the elbow for some reason back to the gate just across the terminal, and the refund was settled before I walked away, again aimlessly, again toward the payphones. I used the second two quarters to call my old Ph.D. director at the university, the greatest and kindest man I could ever imagine knowing, who always invited me into his home as a child of his own. He arranged for another of his graduates to pick me up.

On the curb, a man in his 50s greeted a younger identical looking man, a student at the university, his son, and they began loading the elder's suitcase into the trunk, who, at the last moment, looked over to me before getting in the car and said with a wink and a smile, eyes locked on me though directed to his son and/or everyone and no one in particular, "I'd like to go where she's going!"

Then I got elevator eyes from the two of them, and the son and father shared a brief laugh uniting them in their

American manhood before they drove away.

My own ride pulled up two timeless minutes later. Inside was an extraordinary young woman, a Chinese immigrant and professor of comparative literature. She handed me a bottle of water, a packet of crackers and a box of cookies.

"Where do you need to go?"

"To the university." I didn't know where else to go.

"I'll take you to the university."

"I need to teach my class." I had no idea what else to do.

The drive was comforting next to this person whom I didn't know but who was there for me at this dark moment. We retraced the route I had just taken with my neighbor and I computed on that journey back home with her that it was ten minutes into the twenty-minute drive, as I was passing downtown with my neighbor going toward the airport, with the view of Mt. Rainier and the Olympics, that Mom died.

When I got out of her car, she gave me an envelope. Inside was a $100 bill.

"Please, I can't accept this," I said as she handed me the envelope.

"You're going to need it." She squeezed my hand.

I realized, in all my stubbornness and frugality, I had to accept it. Who was she? In the chaos and grief of the moment, I knew this kindest of gestures from such a stranger would never be forgotten.

I didn't teach my class that day. I walked down the dark corridor on the fourth floor of Thomson Hall and found Adam there at the head of my classroom. Adam whom I had called right after talking to Emma and before my ride that morning, telling him I wouldn't be able to make it. Could he cover for me? When he saw me, he briefly left the classroom, and with him were eyes and lips and teeth that showed me his empathy. My name came from his mouth holding in it a gentle kind of laughter that supported my body, my physical body, there, in his arms, as he held me, withdrew and smiled, then turned me away by the shoulders, and I walked back out of the building, this time across campus to my office where I sat for many hours with no clear task, before it was a reasonable hour to go home and sleep.

That was Mom's death. Four years after Mona's death, there was Mom: dying in an equal manner, on a hospital bed full of morphine struggling for breath gurgling the death rattle. All her children were not with her though. Mona's story was different. Mom was nearly alone, toothless, a flask of vodka and a dozen skeins of cheap bright yarn in her hospice bedside table. And there I was: in the Seattle airport ready to board the less than one-hour flight, on the toilet on my way to the gate remembering only then to call Diane to tell Mom to wait for me.

Not long after her death, I learned my precarious position at the university as an adjunct professor was not going to continue more than another year, and I needed to move on. Move where? Academic jobs are hard to come by in the best of times. New teaching positions were fewer and fewer in the struggling market. On a whim, I took the advice of a fellow doctoral student I saw one day in passing while on campus.

"Why don't you move to Paris?" Ismene casually asked.

I stared at her. I was sitting in the department lounge having a chat with the department administrator, Kumiko.

Ismene walked in and began making a cup of tea. She was Egyptian. Bold, bright, radiant, no-nonsense personality.

"I'm serious." She slid the bag out of its wrapper and dropped it in the mug. The electric water cooker was beginning to steam.

I half-grimaced half-smiled. Kumiko did the same.

"Why not? What else is there? You can easily get an adjunct teaching job there, and you won't have to worry about health insurance and all those things here that make it totally impossible and unlivable."

The water began boiling and the switch on the cooker clicked off. "That's an interesting idea." I paused. "I like it."

Kumiko laughed. She was confidante to all of us grad students and young professors in the department. The stories she knew were limitless, whereas we knew nothing about her but that her parents were Japanese immigrants. "Sounds like an adventure! Great advice, Ismene."

That's how the decision was made. Less than a year after Mom died, I packed everything I owned into the cheapest priced storage unit and took a one-way flight to Paris.

But in the airport that day, Mom's death was on replay: I walk down the narrow and dim passageway to the payphones, take out my earbuds, plunk two quarters in the machine. I was a cell phone hold-out.

"She's gone," Diane's tiny voice coming out of the depths of hollow, reverberating into a wide-open emptiness. "Didn't they page you?" And that's when I hear my name over the speakers with instructions. "Please see the nearest gate agent."

"No." I'm holding the heavy, blue receiver of the payphone in the dark corridor to the toilets near the food court at the Seattle airport. The tentacle bodies of the swarming traffic of travelers loom and gurgle around me, raucous and silent as though in a soap bubble, buzzing, moving, standing rigidly still, caught in a burned image in my mind like a celluloid strip. I stand there for an eternity.

Mom's final decline was only three days. She was up and about to the end, calling the nurses idiots for thinking she was dying, calling the other patients "old geezers" and refusing to interact with them. Mom was 72. By the time I had arrived for a fated last visit a month prior to her death, her eyes had begun to look through things with an emptiness that made me uncomfortable. I felt sheepish, visiting my dying mother who was denying her mortal decline, who was someone I never really knew but loved as a mother is always loved. It was as though Mom saw far off with those gray-green eyes, but somehow the gaze was turned inward or was absent even from herself. Empty and vacant, lost and frightened in an effort to grab hold of something that had permanently slipped away and was still slipping. She showed me a basket of torn checkered fabric she was using to make a bathmat for Diane. It seemed absurd—to have that as her last project. She never finished it of course, but while I was there we pulled it out and played with it like children and scrappy kittens, holding up the crisscrossing long strips to our chins and shoulders, hiding our faces, tousling our hair, smiling, giggling and taking pictures.

If love doesn't come back to you, you empty your own well giving away all that you have. Perhaps not the wisest or safest move, but as one love gets taken away, you find a way to replace it with your own.

Mom died there in Idaho, spending her last days ditching hospice in a borrowed wheelchair and crossing the street to a boxy black and smoky casino with free, stale plastic-wrapped brownies and greasy chips on small paper plates. One or two other patrons also sat at slot machines in a timeless blur, slipping in the coins, pulling the lever or just pressing the button instead. Over and over the three wheels rolled side-by-side, offering up mismatching images, the flashing lights, the dark seats, carpet, machines, no windows, the smell of liquor and old soda from a gun. *Ching! Ching! Ching!* The deception, no money dispensed but occasionally a handful of coins by the nickel here and there. I saw her there in October on my last visit, exactly one month before her death that came days after my birthday—just like when she disappeared days after my fourteenth birthday, or even at my birth itself.

There in the casino, I leaned my head on her shoulder as we watched the lights dance. I thought about the squirt guns and the cackle of the electronic clowns as their balloons inflated at Circus Circus when we left Chicago for California 30 years ago. I was four years old. Ten years after that, Mom was gone. Ten years after that, she was back. Ten years after that, she was dying. My breath on her neck, hers undirected toward the machine. My pulse against her arm. Bodies together, hair blended together, same color, same eyes, nose, lips, same flesh.

Chapter 25
Return to California: 11.5 yrs

After Mom's sentencing Emma, Fred and I spent the summer at John's in Chicago making weekly trips to the women's penitentiary in the countryside beyond Lincoln, Illinois, an hour south of Peoria. Each time, we went through a series of security checkpoints and sat with Mom and talked at normal tables like at school, long and smooth, colored a dusty, light blue. We paid to have our picture taken together on the prison Polaroid camera.

I had imagined it would be different. It wasn't at all like visiting our father in prison in California a few years before where we met in booths with thick glass in between and talked with those phones. We were allowed to touch and hug Mom, and she wasn't wearing the orange jumpsuit but regular clothes and had some make-up and pins in her hair.

John was nineteen that summer, and he paid us $2.00 a piece to clean his apartment each week. We also cleaned his buddy Paul's apartment across the hall for the same price. We were like John's mini roommates, and he and Paul were fantastic and treated us like pals. We spent time together and cooked for ourselves making fried egg sandwiches for lunch. We played catch in the alley, watched movies and bought ice cream at Dairy Queen. Sometimes we ordered take-out from a family-style restaurant down the street that smelled like industrial refrigerators and re-purposed grease. We had nothing in our small town to compare. Counting out exact change, picking up the order in the dark lobby with the hostess in a crisp white shirt and long black apron, smiling boredly behind a faux cherrywood lectern, leather-bound menus hanging off the side. We sat at the outdoor-looking park bench by the door, staring at the crazy patterns in the busy, thick carpet that reminded me of the casinos in Vegas. A waiter came out from the kitchen, wearing the same black and white outfit as the hostess, carrying a mid-sized paperbag with the edge folded down twice and a receipt stapled to the top. Big city living.

John took us to O'Malley's where we had sundaes with a combination of ice creams of East Coast flavors like cherry cordial, chocolate malted fudge, maple nut, raspberry cheesecake swirl, bubblegum and pink lemonade. The toppings offered for our three shared scoops were just as exotic: cotton candy sprinkles, crushed jellybeans, candied ginger, toffee chips, lemon flakes and even stranger were the sauces like *créme brulée*, chunky pineapple, white chocolate fudge and butterscotch. We sat at a small booth on the indoor carrousel just like the one at our casino in Vegas, constantly turning at a slow pace. Everything was pink with little white and green flowers, pink wallpaper and a faux green brick pathway to the toilets, and the windows with pink curtains and lacy trim. We didn't always wonder what was happening to Mom or how long we were going to be in Chicago.

At the end of the summer, we visited Mom for the last time and got ready to head back to California for school. Phil drove out to get us. When we went from east to west, it was much more leisurely than going west to east with John and his friend Paul. With Phil, we took about a week to cross the country. When he arrived in Chicago, he stayed with us at John's place, sleeping on the sofa, and we spent two days with both brothers doing a last bit of exploring in the city of our birth: the Lincoln Park on the waterfront, the woods of the Forest Preserve and Cranberry Slough and, finally, in getting our things sorted and packed. We said goodbye to John and pulled out at 10AM in Phil's old, white pick-up truck.

That first day, we drove all morning through Illinois and into the early afternoon until we reached somewhere between Davenport and Cedar Rapids, Iowa. Before entering the town, we cleaned up from the heat and grime by swimming in a stream off the side of the road. Refreshed, we rolled down the main street and found a joint where we could eat cheap fast food.

Slurping on milkshakes, we walked over to the playground and eventually went bowling, killing time, finally stopping by the grocery store on the way out to get day old donuts for the morning. When dark night fell, we slowly, quietly crept into the campgrounds unnoticed. Phil told us to be extra quiet, and we slept on the ground with the stars all around in mildewy sleeping bags that smelled like mossy grass. We left early in the morning to avoid paying the fee.

The second day Phil drove to the corner of Colorado where it juts out into Nebraska. There's a little lake there called McCanaughy Lake, and this time we paid the fee so that we could swim, have a picnic for dinner and eggs for breakfast over a campfire and under the high rising sun. McCanaughy Lake reminded us a little of our own lake. We were all homesick, and once you're homesick you're mom-sick and so all the feelings flooded back and sometimes it was hard to choke down each bite of the meal. Luckily there was the four of us, and so at least someone else was in a good mood and that one helped to change the mood of the ones who weren't.

On the third day, we left the lake late, and Phil took us through Colorado where we surrounded ourselves with the Rocky Mountains. They were what I had hoped, and I envisioned a future life in Denver as an artist, driving a convertible forest green Mustang through the city with my *attaché* case in the backseat and into the rugged peaks beyond. We camped that night on the west side of the range near the Utah border, and my imagination helped me reconcile what I could not change of the things happening in my family.

Phil's ancient pick-up broke down not too far after crossing into Utah on the fourth day, so we got a motel for two nights in Thompson Springs while he fixed it. Just the three of us went for a hike that afternoon while Phil looked for parts, and we swam in the motel pool and drank Slushees from 7-11. When it rained the second day there, we ate frozen burritos cooked in the lobby microwave and watched old westerns, sitting side by side on the slick motel bedspread. That's when Phil taught us how to whistle through our cupped hands to recreate the menacing, wind-whipping sound in *The Good, the Bad and the Ugly*. We drank hot chocolate with mini marshmallows late into the night and played card games like 31, Rummy and Crazy Eights.

We arrived in Vegas on day six and stopped for lunch at an all-you-can-eat buffet. Phil parked the pick-up in the lot of Circus Circus and gave us each 50¢ to go in and play one game a piece—the same ones we remembered from back when we moved to California with Mom. It was strange to be there and stranger not to be with the rest of our family like the twins, Sarah and John, and two of our big sisters, Amber and Lynn, and of course our other big brother Charlie and especially Mom, but there was nothing to be done. We didn't stay very long and somehow the magnetic sheen I remembered from before was no longer there and may never have been there in the first place.

Phil pushed through on the driving so that we arrived back home four hours after setting out from The Strip and ten hours from Thompson Springs that morning. The three of us were mostly asleep as we rolled into California and awoke as the truck started the lengthy, slow ascent into the somewhat impressive range where our own evergreen town sat. As we climbed higher up the winding mountain roads, the air became dramatically cooler and the sky seemed to grow darker and the stars brighter.

Chapter 26
Off to New York

When Henry and I got back to Paris from Idaho, he had two days before leaving for New York for almost a week, followed by a week each in Zürich, Frankfurt, Berlin and Milan. Then he'd be in London for just about two weeks before coming back to Paris.

"I'll be in London at this hotel for a couple days before New York." He handed me a business card. We were standing in the round room apartment among boxes, crates, suitcases, bags, cords, computer equipment, coats, and thousands of books. I had moved in all my stuff.

"I'm going to miss you." I pulled him close.

"And I'll miss you too, darlin. But it's not too long 'til I'm back in Paris, and you'll come every weekend to each city, right?"

What would be the state of things when the time was up? What would be the state of me? Of my body? Of—

"That's the plan. It'll be fun to visit all these different cities."

As the sun rose, and the sky was thick with morning dew, Henry and I turned together in clouds of sleep trying to shrug off the painful need to get up very early. Twenty minutes later I was bidding him farewell, watching the door close to the round room. From the window I saw his slow and hulking silhouette leave the building and make its way under the bridge to meet the taxi near the stairs toward the metro station. My heart ached and was drawn as though physically toward the moving body as it is separated from me. Under a composed sky the colors stretched themselves thin across the horizon, spread as if by limited means with only barely enough substance to cover the entire expanse. The red of the east was as pale as its white and blue counterpart in the west. Everything was still and somewhat forlorn in anticipation of another dawn, though it seemed as if there was no strength in the coloring and that it might as well have been pre-dawn.

I watched him as he set his bags in the taxi's trunk and rode off to the Gare du Nord. I cried for the sentiment of the moment—a departure, a fond farewell. A still strange uncertainty of what was happening.

Henry called me that night when he got to London and then several days later from New York. "Hey, darlin." His voice was deep and rich.

"Hi, my love! How's New York?"

"Everything is moving pretty fast. I haven't had the time to slow down yet, but it's been interesting. I'm going to get a chance to walk around tonight with some friends from college. How are you, darlin?"

I wanted to wrap my arms around him through the telephone. I wanted to make sure I transmitted enough love over the lines, transferred enough constant love so that he would never leave me. He would never have a reason to leave me. I made sure only to do or say things that he would find appealing. Kept my voice positive and was always using my upbeat tone whenever he discussed confusion or hardship or uncertainty. I had to be his cheerleader just like that first morning in the Matisse room. I had chosen to be his cheerleader. I needed to address things in ways that would not set him off. Make sure he didn't feel threatened or tread upon, but this was not easy. Even harder now. The pregnancy occupied my every moment. The way my body was changing, the way I physically felt, the way I was organizing my entire life, from now until it would be born. I was terrified to talk about any of it.

Henry was loving and giving, but he had a hidden interior. Dark and brooding, often restless and disappointed. He carried himself as a gentleman, always a professional, but he internalized his pain, his anger, and now with me, his ever-growing resentment.

"I'm fine. The apartment is all fixed up. Wait until you see."

"I can't wait, darlin. I'll be back soon. How's the cat?"

"He's great as always. Keeping me company without you. How long are you staying there before the next city?"

"I'll be back in Paris for just three days, and after that I won't be back until the month and change are up, and the working papers are all in order."

"OK. I can't wait to see you. I love you."

"Love you too, darlin. Let's talk tomorrow. I should get going."

I hated the end of calls. I felt my heart break a little each time, unwilling for it to end, unwilling to give up that moment and let it fall into the past, to be disconnected once again until next time.

I didn't see Henry that coming weekend or the next.

Chapter 27
A 1967 Mercury Montego: 12 yrs

When we got back to the mountains after the summer in Chicago visiting Mom in prison, Charlie had arranged with Mona, our father's longtime girlfriend, to split the rent at the new Madera House on Madera Street. I don't know which one of us decided to start calling the houses by their street name, but that was the tradition and it stuck. When the older siblings were growing up in Chicago a decade before, they had lived in as many as houses as we had, and they had done the same thing. I think they realized it was the only way to remember them all. We moved to the Madera House from the Colusa House, exactly two blocks away. We didn't have a car for transporting our stuff so each of us took a box: across the street, up the hill to Center Street where the neighbor girl sunbathing on her deck lay covered in baby oil frying like a cake and glistening like a greasy spoon, across Center Street and right down into our new backyard on Madera.

It was a cheap, boxy, duplex house but it was different than any other place because there was something dependable about it. Mom wasn't there, and Charlie took care of us on his salary as a junior electrician. He even saved money to take us to Dodger and Laker games and football and hockey too. Sometimes one game per season. He sold his motorcycle to buy a family car: a slick, tan

1967 Mercury Montego with sage green vinyl interior, bought from the original owner who had barely driven it. All three of us young kids learned to drive in that car and it was a shame when a couple of years later, some gal careened off the boulevard and rear-ended it while it was parked at the office where Charlie worked. He didn't find it smashed up until after he got back from a job rewiring the botched electrical in one of the new condos across the lake where the marshes used to be. The lady didn't have insurance, and Charlie didn't make her pay. Phil tried to fix the Mercury up, but its glorious washing and waxing days were over.

We decorated the Madera House with second hand furniture and appliances. Added to these were some of Mom's things like a cheap brass display shelf for knickknacks and a mirror above the fireplace with "Jersey Lil" engraved on it in a sensual, cursive font. Sometimes our father came over from his place at Mona's across town with a bag of oranges and Little Debbie's cakes and cookies. Mona sent over casseroles and Christmas presents and threw us family birthday parties with specially ordered cakes with stiff and extra sugary frosting from the supermarket. We didn't compare Mona with Mom, because Mom was Mom, and the love and care we got from Mona was reciprocated and never taken for granted, except in the forgivable ways of pre-teens.

Charlie was 23 when he took us on. It was the fall of the year of mom's arrest that spring and our long summer trip to Chicago. Emma was turning thirteen. She did the laundry. I was turning twelve. I was the cook. We ate a lot of TV dinners, pizza, hamburgers, donuts and canned

Chinese food. It wasn't until college that I learned a bulb of garlic does not resemble an onion on the inside.

Every two weeks, we cashed Charlie's paycheck at the bank before going grocery shopping.

"We need fifty… two dollars and…" He told the teller, glancing back at us, giggling. "…and… thirty…" looking at us again, "…and… thirty-four cents."

We were all smiling like giddy monkeys.

"Is that right?" He asked us.

"That's right."

"OK, $52.34 for groceries."

The grinning teller obliged, counting out the money. Charlie made sure each bill resonated in its significance as the teller put them one by one in his hand. Next coin by coin. We looked on in approval. The weight of Charlie's hard work was evident in each crisp bill and in each shining coin.

"Yes. Great. Thank you. That's exactly what we need. Perfect. Have a glorious day." You could never tell if Charlie was serious or ironic. It was the same with all my brothers. Usually it didn't even matter.

We walked across the parking lot to the Safeway, and after the grocery shopping, we drove backwards as fast as possible behind the supermarket and through the shopping center parking lot in the middle of a rainstorm at full speed charging the boat of a car through the gigantic puddle that always formed in the same spot where the concrete was sorely cracked.

"PUDDLE!" The four of us simultaneously yelled and the thousand drops that the skidding wheels threw into the air thudded against the Montego in a disparate, tidal splash.

Charlie took care of us from start to finish. Sometimes the mood was solemn, and we joined in that too. After school, we explored his tapes and listened to Black Flag, Lizzy Borden, Led Zepplin. On dark nights, we sat around listening to Neil Young, James Taylor, Pink Floyd, Peter, Paul and Mary. We watched regular television shows together on certain nights of the week and put ourselves to bed at 9PM sharp. We played video games after school, and on weekends went to the arcade for ski ball, air hockey and pinball. On the way home from the arcade, we stopped off at the market for lunch, and Charlie would buy a box of ice cream sandwiches and split them up four ways. We sat on the lawn of the elementary school lying around in the dry grass proudly eating our 'sandwiches' for lunch.

Charlie took us skiing, hiking, to games, to the movies, to the park for the playground, for tennis, softball, football and kickball, throw the ball, roll the ball, tackle the sister with the ball, pizza, soda, invite your friends, tell jokes, make the teenagers laugh, make people stare, act strange, act wild, walk backwards, walk it off, walk home, walk hand-in-hand.

Before the start of every school year we got new clothes and shoes at Target down in the city an hour away by windy mountain roads. We each had $25 to spend, and Charlie made sure we got our money's worth. In high school Charlie worked nights at the ski resort, and Emma and I had parties at home. He trusted us, and we had the safe house for kids. We did what he asked, earned the highest grades and went to college. We were the first in the family to do it, and he made us believe we could do it and we did and it was easy.

Chapter 28
Before Switzerland

I was in the shower when I heard Henry enter the room, his tall, broad body shift sideways, the door unable to fully open, blocked by the ad hoc shower.

"Hey, darlin," his booming voice called out, and I saw his shape move into the center of the room.

"I'll just be a second." I turned off the water and grabbed the towel from the top of the clumsy, sliding plastic door and stepped out onto the mat.

"Hi! You're here!" I scurried towards him with wet limbs and hair.

"Hey, darlin." His voice rose with a short laugh as he embraced me, pulling me on his lap. "How are ya? You smell good."

"I missed you. How was New York? I've been writing a lot since you left."

"That's great. Tell me about it. Are you writing about your mom? You should tell her story. Tell me her story."

"No. Tell me about New York. Tell me about you. You're wonderful, and I love you, and everything is amazing."

I kissed his neck, and we fell into bed together and remained there until dusk.

"I got your card. So beautiful. I love the MoMA. Thank you."

We were lying on the old foldout bed in the round room with the sun fading to the west. The card had an old scene on the front of the Brooklyn Bridge and the Hudson. We lay in each other's arms for hours until we were staring long and quietly at the searchlight of the tower across the river.

"So, tell me finally: how is your writing going?" He asked. He always asked. Whether or not he cared, he always asked.

"I'm nearly finished."

"I love you," he said holding me against his warm body, and I thought about how I would never forget that moment, remembering that feeling of seeing him for the first time again after barely a week, of his eyes drawing me into him when I opened the door. His eyes were bright and wide, below eyebrows that were soft and broad and curly. Heavy cheekbones framed full, flush lips that smiled easily and often.

"I love you," I said back into the cool, open space from the cocoon between the two of us on the bed, knowing that I had chosen his love myself this time, chosen it deliberately so that I could be comfortable living with it and not expecting it to live for me.

In the morning before leaving, Henry asked me to take a walk before he was to catch his flight for Zürich. We were standing in the center of the round apartment, and I kissed him between his shoulder blades standing on my tiptoes, tasting the must of his old T-shirt and filling the space with my cheeks, jaw and chin. I lingered against his neck a while longer to savor the taste and touch, knowing everything was about to change—again.

"Come on, let's go." He gently pushed up against me, and I stood.

In the elevator I asked him questions about his trip. His answers were short and distant. It made me anxious, but I affected my usual behavioral change, upping enthusiasm, making up for the diminishment, his ever-increasing lack.

Out on the pavement, the sun shone down coolly and directly, hidden from above by the elevated metro track line that created a bridge across the river and into the station in front of us. We walked along it underneath, turning left before the stairs to the top of the hill, toward the nearby park one block to the south. We passed over the short cobblestone road with gates at either end to keep nonresidents out. We waved to the concierge of our building who was out walking her dog. When we reached the park, Henry held the gate open for me, and we silently strolled once around the perimeter, observing the seated couples talking, laughing, kissing, the families picnicking, the children playing, the teens joking, listening to music. After we looped around, we hiked up the grassy plot into the center where we sat near the shade of a tree. Henry lay down, and I put my head on his chest. We were staring at the clouds. I felt a frightening second of peace that was paradoxically full of tension.

He began speaking as though in mid-conversation. "You can still have an abortion, you know." His voice kind, detached and unmoved.

The words formed into a sentence in my head far slower than I could comprehend. I felt my body rise off him on its own in one instant, turn around to face him and scream, "What?!"

He stared back at me as calmly and gently as always.

My desire to shriek and thrash and invoke the absurdity, atrocity, incongruity of his statement was deflated, was crushed was robbed of all viability in the way he stared at me, in the way his eyes spoke of his self-assurance, rationality and carefully thought-out conviction. He did not let me take the control from him. He would not engage in any emotional drama. He would not give outbursts an ounce of recognition. This case, of course, was different, and I knew it. Not only had I learned to obey him and not behave that way anymore, I knew my response now was warranted, and I knew he knew. But Henry was never one to care what anyone knew to expect or wanted to expect or should expect from him. And he never bent his rules for anyone but himself. Now he was standing by this feeling if ever he stood by anything in his life or even in death. He knew he was choosing to feel something to believe something that would become the detriment of all things beautiful.

"Aggie," he began. His voice was a smooth river of persuasion and well-placed intention. "Aggie, you yourself said you weren't sure you wanted a baby."

"That was before I was even pregnant! That was last year. We hadn't been dating very long. I had no idea what I even wanted back then. You or otherwise!" It was unkind to bring that up here, and Henry knew it. I had never thought he would bring that up now. In fact, I had expected the opposite. He was the one who had told me he wanted children and said he would change my mind.

I was confused, wanted to turn back, to retract, to start over, to see him walk in again, I'm in the shower, I love him, I'm happy to see him, I kiss him, his neck, we are lying together, start over, walk in the door, in the shower, kisses, love, future, you're back from your trip, I love you, walk in again, shower, please, no, ok, walk in again, there you are! I love you! So happy, walk in again. Walk in again. Walk in again. And a discussion of logic, of who said what and when, holding me to something as though it means something, as though it must make me do something, change my mind, lock me into a deal, weaken my position, force me to have a position, make a decision, put in a position where a decision needs to be made, put in a position now weeks later where a decision needs to be made, put me in a position ever in this situation where a decision needs to be made.

The sun was so bright. The sun was too bright. The trees were so far apart. The trees were suffocating. The trees were ancient. The trees were buried like dead bodies the trees were planted by the groundskeepers in green suits. Sickly trees small and urban and sad. Full of life and smells and the history of the universe. Flat like paper. Explosive and knowing. There were so many people in the park. There were no more people in the park. The sounds were unbearable. The sounds were all so far away. The sky was so bright. The clouds felt cold. The ground was dirty. The ground was wet. It was dry. There were ants. I flicked an ant off my elbow. The sky was painful. The texture of his shirt made a sound when he turned his body. I heard my zipper like the fierce roar of a waterfall or the banging noises of the freeway. It wasn't moving. Nothing was moving. It was frozen. It was cracking and sparkling and flying in all directions. My eyelashes were blinding me. My eyelashes were burning they were full of noise. The ground made sounds. The clouds were sounding. The people all around made sounds. The children played and were loud and sounding.

"Look, it's all we can do," he said. His voice, speaking calmly. "I can't be forced into this. I didn't want this. I didn't choose this. And you weren't even certain yourself."

He would repeat what he'd said. He would repeat it over and over. He didn't care that it had been dispelled, logically negated, rejected. He was a record with a skip, and you couldn't get past it. Over and over was that repeating line where the record was scratched, not really playable, though I had hung on to that one wonderful song and always ignored the scratch. It came again and again.

"I only ever expressed doubt because of your fears! It made me so scared. I wanted you to want it so bad. Back in California, that talk we had… I tried to say what you want to hear. Please, no—I…"

I trailed off. I was stuck. I didn't know what to say. He would always lead me to the same repeating spot. There was no getting past it. He pursued it. Gently. Steadily. No way out. The skip came again and again. The record over and over.

I looked away. I looked anywhere. There was nothing to look at. I could only see inside. I could only see a blur of images that had already happened and were passing again in front of me.

There was a heavy hollowness in my gut that was now in my bowels and was now in my throat and was now coming out of my eyes and pressing on every orifice in my body and was pressing the hardest on my heart in that physical, dying sense of grief.

I was holding back a torrent.

"Let's go home," Henry said. He looked around. "Let's

not talk about this here anymore." Henry was eager to get me out of the public eye.

"What is happening?" I pleaded. I could have been an insect falling out of the sky.

He took my hand, and we stood up together. He put his arm around me, and we walked back, now unsteadily, toward the gate to the park.

As we crossed the alley, I stopped. I was small and broken and no longer full of rage. I couldn't move. I'd lost reality.

"Come here," Henry said. He pulled me close to his open chest, burying me against him. "Don't worry. Everything is going to be alright."

It gave me relief. Ah, he understands now. Yes, of course. Everything is going to be alright. Just like that.

We went back up to the apartment, and he left thirty minutes later to the RER train across the bridge for Charles de Gaulle to catch his Zürich flight. I stood frozen in the center of the room for an indefinable period then left the building and walked back to the park, to the spot we had just left. I saw us lying there having a different conversation.

A panic seized me. Like a searing shard of metal into my chest and all through my body. I tried to hide from myself, but it wasn't working. Walking quickly nearly staggering suddenly, walking two steps ahead of myself to get away, I went in a nearby shop where I bought three boxes of cheap cookies and with heart racing and eyes darting and ate them as though they would save me distract me change me. Then scurried through the nearby park of the Champs de Mars as a strange man in a top hat and coattails rode up to me on an ancient bicycle asking if I were '*littéraire*'. I didn't know what he meant. Was I dreaming? I disappeared into a public toilet and vomited every cell of my body into the putrid toilet and sweat into it and begged to be released into it and searched the walls for a way in and then a way out. When I pressed the button to exit, a man was waiting, and he entered before my remains disappeared into the sewers. *He will see what I did. He will know my shame and find my lacerated body parts in the toilet and on the walls the blood and vomit and shit.* I ran again in fear and hid behind myself and the trees, and I heard the trees and the man and my remains laughing at me.

Under the bridge of the Metro Line 6 into the tower to the room at the top of the tower finding a card from Henry with a Manet print on it postmarked in New York had just been slipped by the concierge under our door. I climbed into bed though the light of day shone through the glass. I shut it out with my eyelids and groaned as I slid into the space between the pillows and the comforter and the mattress and I was a small ball of an object compacted as tightly as possible, and somehow it wasn't tight enough so I crawled under the bed and lay there and sobbed and made noises that are heard in the fear of the dark of the night.

Chapter 29
With and without Mom: 13 yrs

Mom got out of jail just shy of the two-year sentence when I was in the eighth grade. Emma moved into my room, and Mom moved into Emma's. She hung up art that she had made in prison all over the place. She had made a lot of things in prison. She used to send us homemade dolls with crocheted dresses and silver gum wrapper earrings. She was creative, kind of an outsider artist. Her style had no connection to anything learned. She just put things together the way she knew how. Fred, who was ten, and Charlie shared the third room. You couldn't see the floor in their room.

Maybe it was expected or maybe it was not, but it didn't work well with Mom living there. We had already found a new rhythm with Charlie, and Mom made herself feel out of place. Life with Charlie was something we never could have expected, and it was too bad Mom didn't like the arrangement he had made. She felt we didn't need her anymore, she said, or at least she didn't know how to operate in her way while living in the house the way we had it set up with Charlie. She knew it wasn't her house, and she couldn't be the woman she was used to being in that house, she said. There were no seedy but promising boyfriends, no new self-sabotaging plans to hatch and no new schemes hidden away in the cabinets. We were still poor, but we were clean and straight and clear-headed, and Charlie made sure we were fed and warm and working hard but having a good time.

Maybe it was all an excuse to leave again. Just a month after moving in, Mom left town altogether to the city at the foot of the mountains down the windy roads just over an hour away. We visited her some weekends. She found a job as the cook in a fancy country club, and soon enough she had moved from a rented room to her own apartment. Suddenly though, when we arrived one weekend, she was driving a Mercedes and claimed to have bought an incredible house. She began buying us gifts using swindled money from new widowers that she discovered through connections at her job. We would show up and find her bed covered in strange, expensive clothes we didn't need or like. One weekend there were ten or fifteen old-fashioned ballroom dresses. Where had they come from? And why? During that comfortable monied time, Mom regularly took us to the mall, perusing various clothing shops for which she suddenly had personal credit cards. She claimed to be their rightful owner, though the name never matched her own.

"I always wanted to be called Marley O'Donnell, so I changed my name last month."

We believed her. Even still, I was thirteen and didn't want clothes from Lane Bryant, Macy's or Sears. I wanted tapes by The Cure and The Smiths, and I had been paying for my own clothes from the thrift store working as the ice cream clerk at the local drugstore. Mom didn't know this teenage me and didn't care. Marley O'Donnell had been dead who-knows-how-long. Her credit was there for Mom's using, and Mom used it. The widower husband was kept as long as possible in the dark.

With sufficient funds at her fingertips, Mom was bent on getting us things she could never afford. Those things marketed to a desperate middle class at shopping malls: sneaky sales of overpriced, low quality clothing and shoes, department store housewares, bundled cosmetics packages, silver jewelry and white gold, knock-off diamonds, plastic, brightly colored hair accessories, fizzing bath soaps packaged with facial creams, rejuvenating lotions, restorative shampoos, fake nails.

One of her plans I could get behind was to get us a full, adult version Encyclopedia Britannica set. The salesman came to our house, explained the buying process on the installment plan and reassured us about the importance and value of having such a set in our home. He was right. I found my escape and my future in those books and used them every day. They told me to keep asking questions, to get away, to find a large, extraordinary world to explore. I packed all 32 of them up for college when the time came, and after many years gave them back to Charlie, whose own children used them 15 years later.

With Charlie unexpectedly set up with the payments, Mom just as suddenly corralled Emma, Fred and me for a cruise to Mexico, the preparations for which required another trip to the mall for the outfits and shoes, the jewelry, makeup and all the trimmings. Things were getting more and more fishy that year so I wasn't too surprised that days before my 14th birthday Mom left California without a word. We heard it through the sibling grapevine from Diane that Mom was back in Chicago. She had run away from the O'Donnell affair and probably a few others. She stayed in Chicago for a couple months and got into trouble with another widower's money, Diane said. Then her father died in Michigan in the early spring, so she drove up there for the funeral. Her sisters arranged to meet for lunch afterwards. Mom never showed up. We didn't see or hear from her again for ten years.

I wondered if there was something missing from me, in Mom, from Mom, that I never knew that I should have known. I knew things about her but it didn't really matter and there was nothing to know that would have changed my life, so I allowed myself not to care. I tried to believe that Mom's life wasn't any more meaningful or interesting or mysterious because she kept it from us—that she never described her growing up, or that there was never a chance or a time to hear the stories, that I had to piece her history together. To believe that something elusive was there, some important thing that shaped her and might have me would have been a harmful way of allowing myself to feel hollowed by what I would never know.

Whatever Mom was, it didn't really seem to have a whole lot to do with me, and that was fine or it would have to be fine. It wasn't wise to go searching for something or to feel the need to find something that was removed from you, that didn't affect you anymore, that was unknown to you. That would just be a grail quest and those thoughts would only lead to dark places because they remained unfilled. There was no mystery. She was a lady who happened to be my mother who was born with circumstances and lived and died with circumstances. I could only speak about what I knew. Charlie took care of me from when I was eleven until I was sixteen when I left for college and those were the best years of my childhood.

Chapter 30
Dying across Europe

Henry left for Zürich. I arrived on Thursday night four days later and died there.

Henry worked on Friday and I ran along the river until my lungs froze. On Saturday the two of us walked to the top of *Zürichberg* through the grounds of the university and hospital. When we first crossed the river, before the ascent he bought me a book on Wittgenstein that I had with me, and we talked about philosophy and literary salons as we walked. We trekked first through neighborhoods of very fine houses and narrow streets onto the mountain itself and into the deep woods in the cold sun. Leaves crunched under my feet, and I felt some peace and thought about the fresh air and I loved him and was glad I made him happy, though I tried with great fear and delicate steps to talk about a future that would have children yet. I felt fragile and was fragile and knew he felt my fragility and I felt him aim his heart towards me in care and guilt and the two of us looked out over Lake Zürich and the surrounding valleys from the top of the Germanic and pristine tower of stairs that were built of clean wood. On the way back, he bought me an expensive bottle of geranium oil.

On Sunday I returned to Paris. I flew to Frankfurt on Thursday and died there.

The Christmas market in its curved, flickering lights and temporary cottages with the smell of sausages and

Glühwein covered the central square, and he forgot to tell me he had changed hotels so I waited in the quiet snow becoming numb and unsettled until he found me in the hard, cold alley and comforted me with his heavy breath and full embrace. We had Thanksgiving dinner that night at *Zum Schwarzen Stern* and ordered everything that seemed like home. The waiter nearly refused to serve me sauerkraut alongside a cherry tart, mushroom gravy and applesauce.

On Friday, Henry worked as usual, and I made myself sick on strudel with raspberry jam and soft pretzels without salt and bad coffee. On Saturday the two of us walked along the river and visited the museums. I didn't see anything on the canvases and in the cases, or I saw through them or didn't see anything at all, and I tried to get rid of the day as quickly as possible.

I flew back to Paris on Sunday and on Thursday I flew to Berlin and died there.

In the morning it was bright and beautiful. The sun was pouring in through the curtains, and for a brief time I exited the sickness of childless fear, and I could walk and eat, and he held me, and the light hurt my eyes, but he held me. It was possible to view the river and think about blinking and he opened some pages of a book as I stared blankly at the wall and into the space outside the window until I could rest again. When it was time for dinner, I was able to eat something without thinking. I spread a softness across my face for him and aimed the love out of my body somewhere there across the table and into the sky as it needed to go, and I had lots of sweets and tea. In the late night I went to exercise at the top of the hotel.

The gym overlooked the roofs of Berlin and the *Fernsehturm*, and as I ran on the treadmill, I watched a program about a girl from Mexico raised in Germany who went to find her birth mother, and the woman cried and the girl did not cry. I watched while Henry forgot to find me up there after an hour as he said, and he left me. I searched all around for as long as another hour up to the room and down again to the lobby and up again to the gym and back to the room and down to the lobby again and I finally found him naked coming out of the sauna, not remembering I had said I wanted to go in there myself and not remembering to bring me when he had decided to go.

That was Henry, and I had wished and hoped for something different especially now. For both of us, I wanted a new way of being. These were things I said only to myself though. Lost, confused, fear too great. I saw how Henry had a security and confidence or entitlement that I did not, and those were linked tightly to family. I expected things from him I shouldn't have. I could not expect Henry to make up for what I lacked and had always lacked since my prison birth.

On Saturday we walked into my old neighborhood back from when I was a graduate student. I made my escape out of my hometown as soon as I could and chose to study in southern Germany for a year once I was in college. I knew I needed to return, that travel was part of me, the discovery, the creation of a new life, the release from a pained history. I lived and traveled around Europe in graduate school, living in Berlin and elsewhere, eventually choosing Paris to settle. In Berlin that weekend, Henry and I visited the cafes and parks and talked about how wonderful it would be to move there, though it wasn't an honest conversation. Dinner was at the bohemian soup restaurant near all my old favorite haunts, and at the end of the night we walked through *Alexanderplatz* and saw the teenagers dancing to their music in the dark behind the church. I thought maybe it will be OK or maybe I was learning to disappear into certain moments and avoid the death that followed me around, waiting for me to wake or sleep or open my eyes.

I went back to Paris on Sunday, and I flew to Milan on Thursday and died there too.

I have nothing to remember about Milan. Maybe I wasn't in that city.

My head was slumped on his shoulder as we rattled along in the train to Malpensa Airport where I would fly back to Paris and he, on to London.

"Darlin," he quietly said.

I didn't look up at him. My eyes were open now staring at the empty seats all around, watching the windows violently move up and down as the train moved forcefully and unevenly along the track.

"You can still get an abortion."

I melted into the seat and let the roar of the metal wheels fill my ears and eyes and nostrils and mouth and all my pores and hair follicles. My limbs and torso were a hard, dead shell and no longer belonged to me. I was wasted. Empty. Defeated. I had nothing left. His voice was solemn, granulated but soft and deep, stern but gentle, spoken like an "I love you, and I'll be OK" to a mother on her deathbed. And me, I didn't even make it to my mother's deathbed.

Then came the transformation. All in a swift instant my whole body stiffened and rose up on its own. Before I even knew where it was coming from, an unearthly cry came from my lips. I was surprised by the excitement of my own voice and jumped up. "It'll be too late!" I blurted out. "It won't even be legal anymore." I looked at him directly. I felt safe. Rescued. I found a way out.

With his usual composure, as though reciting a grocery list, conducting a business meeting, talking softly in his sleep: "It'll actually still be legal in England—where I'll be."

I felt like puking. "You looked it up?"

I sat back down. I stared ahead. My voice was tiny, wavering, thin and watery, lost in the string left to slacken between two tin cans. He'd looked it up. He'd been thinking about it. He'd spent time on it.

Can you lift your arms, I wondered, and fly off into the air? Can that happen? If you just lift them and point your body towards the sun? The would be cool and warm at the same time, and you would be lifted weightless but with your body dense and strong and full of air guided by the waves of wind streaming through you and around you, supporting you, more and more into the sun and the trees and away! And away! Just away. Like that. Peaceful and away.

"It's still legal in England." He repeated. "I'll be living there for a couple weeks starting tonight. You'll be there as soon as this weekend, this Thursday even. If you did it on Friday, we would still have Saturday together before you had to leave for Paris on Sunday."

There is nothing more to remember about Milan. I think I wasn't in that city.

Chapter 31
Mom's Idaho: 24 yrs

During the first years when Mom was gone, Charlie kept things going as smoothly as he knew how which meant that he had to give up his own opportunities to take care of us. Emma and I graduated together five years later, and that was the end of the Madera House. We had never lived anywhere so long in our lives—five years. Five great years. Charlie was aimless for a while afterwards and drifted around until moving back to Chicago and again back to California where he settled down. Fred was forced to go to Arizona for his freshman year of high school where Phil was working construction and had a good home with his wife and two little ones. Fred got homesick, and after that one year he came back to California mountains and stayed with Mona and our father for the rest of high school.

After we three were all grown and gone and out of college ten years later, Mom came back. I was 24 years old. I hadn't seen her since I was 14. It was a reality everyone wanted, and no one expected. It came and went, and our three oldest sisters got her set up in Idaho, where they had moved sometime after Mom left, trading the fair California mountains for the bigger Idahoans. All ten of us plus families went up there once a year to visit. We camped out, sleeping in Diane or Amber's backyard, and the evenings digressed into a variety of events involving sibling arguments, make-ups, laughing, crying, bickering, hugging and harmonizing. Childhood stories were told by the truckloads, always involving some kind of disappointment, a peculiar family event, domestic abuse, alcohol abuse, Mom working her knuckles to the bone as some underpaid cook in a dive bar, kids crawling all over the dirty, industrial kitchen floor, Mom drunk as a fish but always going at it. But the stories were always told in good humor, as if they were funny, as if they were episodes on a sit-com with funny and favorable outcomes or unavoidable natural disasters that we overcame and could smile and laugh and be grateful about. It began with someone asking the lyrics to some old 1940s tune that the old folks used to sing.

"Oh, yeah! How does that go?" Phil asked eyes lit. Lynn worried he was on something. Smiling, leaning in with his guitar, one leg up on the broken lawn furniture, he was anxious for the answer so he could start singing and strumming.

"Oh! Oh! Oh!" Diane got even more excited, arms slowing rising in unison as if on their own, her glass of wine steady, not a drop spilling on her lap. She stood up partway, also as if by séance, knees bent, unaware of her body anxiously moving itself into position, leaning in too now, eager and ready with the words on the tip of her tongue.

"I got it!" Sarah said. All eyes enlivened fixed on her. "Let—me—call—you—sweetheart..."

Diane tearing up joined in: "...sweetheart... I'm—in—love—with—you!"

Lynn joined in harmony and suddenly four or five were singing along in other octaves and harmonies while

Fred, who didn't actually know the song but was a musical genius, picked it up on guitar and improvised a lead, Phil on melody.

"Keep—the—love-light—glowing—in—your..."

"No! No! That's not it. Wait, wait..." Amber corrected everyone during the mayhem and a brief, confused pause while each person hummed a bit, took another drink, thought of the next song or suddenly began telling someone nearby a new story. Coming in from other parts of the yard were bits of children's loud conversations, laughs and spats. The older ones singing looked around and gradually one or two caught on and they were all back again.

"Let—me—hear—you—whisper—that—you—love—me—too."

Smiles all around and voices rising.

"Keep—the—love-light—glowing—in—your—eyes—so—true..."

Everyone was smiling now, carrying on, a glow emerging.

"Let—me—call—you—sweetheart,—I'm—in—love—with—you!"

Everyone scanned the scene beaming corny and earnest grins, mouths hung open, teeth gleaming, tears caught in corners. Guitars strummed other chords other songs already moving away from the moment that captured some other moment that no one really lived but knew about its being lived and here living it new but a new that was old, so old, as old as everyone's lurid, painful childhoods full of booze, music and dirty restaurant kitchens.

In the morning, there were children running around,

playing this or that game, looking for something to do, teenage girls flipping through old photo albums or trying to get a ride to town to meet with a friend. Younger kids played with random toys or made toys out of paper, cardboard, glue guns, potato guns, BB guns, whatever was lying around. Someone else was looking for a ride to the auto parts store to get a distributor cap for an always-faulty car or two in the yard. Someone else was asking "what's there to eat?" popping a few-days-old perogies in the microwave. Someone else was off somewhere, no one knew where, but "he said he'd be back by lunch." Someone else was "working until the afternoon". Someone else was trying to round up a few bucks to buy cheap, tractor-sized inter-tubes to go floating down the Boise River.

Mornings, if Phil was around and not down in town doing some odd job, he'd make off to the country market and show up with a couple packs of bacon, two dozen eggs and a loaf or two of white bread, plop it on a bench and disappear under the hood of his car or behind his guitar, knowing that one of his sisters would pick up the fixings and make an egg and toast meal cooked in the bacon grease. Diane was already brewing coffee. Sarah having just rolled out of bed was making jokes about tequila shots and wearing a sombrero found in an old thrift store on the main street in town the day before.

In the afternoon, we rode up to Baybrook Bridge and took turns jumping off. The boys showed off, doing flips, frightening us all by landing head-first in the shallow river. The younger kids hid their fear and leapt like the rest in some rite of passage. Three or four cousins held hands and went all at once. Another group readied themselves counting down from three, no one jumping but Sarah. She rose to the surface cursing the group through wet laughter.

We piled back into beat-up cars with shoes clothes soda cans littering the floors, heading off to Amber or Diane's or Lynn's place to eat leftovers again.

When Mom was there, things weren't so much different. There was just a lot of home-cooked food and that tangible sense of security only a mom can bring even if that mom was the same one who took away that very security during your entire childhood. There was never any talk of why she did what she did. She couldn't answer and it didn't matter because hardly anyone could ask. No one had the heart. It was unexpectedly awkward. No one could or wanted to come out with it: *Mom, where were you all those years? Mom, why did you leave us?*

I didn't know anything about having a mom or even being a girl or a woman. Raised by my brother, I learned about myself along the way. Charlie took me to the store when I first got my period. I had told Emma, and she told him.

"You know what you need, right?" He said when we got to the supermarket avoiding eye contact.

"Oh, yeah, totally." I didn't have a clue and went down the aisle by myself while Charlie went to the back to pick up a gallon of milk.

"I'll meet you at the check-out." I nodded in agreement. I tried to remember which thing, what kind, what size, what purpose, what purple perfumy box with flowers was under the sink at my friend's house who had already gotten her period a couple months earlier.

During those ten years with Mom gone, I had my brothers and my sisters and it was lucky for us too when Mona helped us out when she left. We were pretty young when she came into our father's life, started throwing us birthday parties and getting us Christmas presents. When Mona died we were all there in the room. A vicious, ugly and fast death from pancreatic cancer. One minute she was complaining of an aching foot and the next she was flown by helicopter out of her mountain town to an advanced cancer center in Los Angeles. She died six weeks later gasping for breath, gurgling phlegm, eyes watery blue, cracked lips pulled back tight, ice crystals on her parched tongue.

We gathered around, as she lay back and we watched her slip away—slip away? Stop. We watched her stop. We watched her struggle to indicate pain in her neck in her spine, and the doctor said it was because she was "shutting down." Her body was sending a final surge through the spinal cord and the brain to "turn off." We watched her eyes turn to gray, her pupils dilate enormously, violently, obscenely, her lips purse back, her neck stiffen, her body lose itself, finally, into that cold, eternal emptiness—and she left us like that.

In the first ten minutes my father had drunk an entire flask of vodka. Like it was water. He pulled it out of the bag and lifted it to his parched lips and poured it in, gurgling and slurping and trying to get it in as fast as possible. He was wide-eyed, panting, teeth-bearing. Sitting next her body, on the edge of the bed. Having moments of delirium when he was sure she had moved, that she wasn't really dead.

"Did you see that?!" The anxiety and terror of joy shone in my father's bulging blue eyes.

What if he's right? Realizing only much later that it didn't matter. She was dead, as much as dead ever is. And if she wasn't dead, she was dead in ten seconds or was bound to be dead shortly, even if there were a breath still there which there wasn't.

The lot of us had been sleeping in her room or motorhome in the hospital parking lot since our town was too remote to drive home each day. We dragged him out there that night and lay him down, but he kept getting up. We couldn't sleep. He was moaning and wailing and carrying on in frightening ways. He overpowered Fred and me at one point and managed to get to the front of the motorhome, attempting to leave through the driver's door and run on to the hospital, forgetting perhaps that Mona's sons had already sent her down to the morgue for cremation. When he got to the steering wheel he fell forward, with us trying hopelessly to restrain him, and crushed his face against the panel, breaking his glasses and bloodying his nose. We pulled him back. We put him down. That defeated him. Buried him. We were exhausted. Not just from lack of sleep but the desperation, the emptiness. The bewilderment.

The next day we awoke, newly exhausted, and the weight was still there. We got up in silence, my father with that look that he gives that begs for some help like a child, some understanding, a mother of his own to say it's OK. But it wasn't. And we couldn't. And I wasn't. That desperation to try to hold on to a lost reality only caused it to shrink and fade, distort and become deformed. My father had never been able to take care of himself and now his caretaker was gone. He suffered from her death more for the absence she caused him than the loss of her life to herself and loved ones.

When I was little, I saw a lot of fighting between my folks—if that's what you can call it. If that's what you call watching a man chase the mother of his children with a baseball bat or pin her to the floor with arms crushing the life out through her throat. My childhood was violent or rather my father was violent in my childhood. The two split up when we moved to the mountains, but even then they still fought and it was still violent. Later he fought with Mona. We never saw that because we were gone. Her grown sons never forgave him whatever they knew about it.

Back then as a kid, you saw a purity to the fighting that meant it was white and bright and horrifying and penetrated into you so that you didn't just fear the violence, but you felt it rattle you inside and it made you want to be sick. Something bad was happening. It wasn't about pain or death or cruelty. It was more primitive. It was a reaction towards loud noises, darkness, and that bright white flash behind my eyes, and those eyes that weren't mine that were my father's and that weren't seeing straight anymore and rage that was going to crack my bones without them even being touched. Cracking into my head shattering the implicit stability in the world that is born in you when you're born. That exists and you feel it and even if you don't get your mom's embrace and warmth, there is something there already inside of you, even if you sleep in a dresser drawer when you're a baby or on the floor or on a piece of wood outside or in a chair or in some old lady's bed because she's dead or in a trailer or in a tent or in a room with no beds or a room with a shared bed in the houses of many different random men. It's in you because you know what it is when you're born and you know what it is when someone is shattering that stable solid place that you are that is you in your head and the white violence cracks it.

Chapter 32
London: maybe 3 months

Henry was in London for the end of his period abroad. Sitting on the Eurostar for my last trip before his return to Paris, I thought about the previous weekend I visited him in London, when we went to Monk's House. I examined my reflection in the darkened glass of the window as we entered the nearly-hours long subterranean tunnel. I thought I could detect a shape and was finally over the nausea. I was maybe three months, but our meetings had not gotten any easier. The pressure was constant. The conversation always followed the same sequence. I was afraid to lose him, and when the train entered the tunnel, I felt the continual sickness all over again of confronting him of not confronting him of making it through the weekend of finding a hardened, solid peace from the weekend. But no, nothing was safe. Nothing was determined. Time was passing, still passing. Each week increased my anxiety and fear. I felt radically stupid to have thought everything could be all right. I was winning and losing at the same time. And time. Time still passing. Time passes. Time detrimentally and defiantly victorious.

The speed of the train, its rolling north toward London away from my own assurance and solitude in Paris and toward Henry's piercing severity, staunch rejection, pressure pressure pressure, made me ill with panic with an acute awareness of the inevitable doom that lie ahead no matter what happened.

The train pulled into the station, and after passing through the unmanned border patrol and customs booth, I made my way to his hotel on foot. It took about an hour, and I traversed London on an unfamiliar route. I arrived before he got off work, showered and relaxed, anxious to be alone with him. We would go to the pub for dinner.

That night we walked down Fleet Street down passed Ye Olde Cheshire Cheese to The Tipperary. We passed St. Paul's Cathedral, and I thought of Mrs. Dalloway and the airplane carving out a message in the sky with its vapor trail. To be in public was pleasing and somehow reassuring as though I was being protected by the smiling strangers around me. Nothing could happen to me as long as I was among them. I was terrified of the walk back to the apartment, the opening of the door, stepping powerless into that exposed, menacing den, not knowing how to fend for myself and for my body. Enacting bedtime routines quickly to avoid the looming conference weighing upon every cubic inch of space in which we existed.

I woke up the next morning to Henry staring at me as I lay next to him in bed. There was a renewed coldness and vacuity in his eyes. "It's your decision to make, but this isn't what I want."

My hollow knot grew larger, tighter, consumed all of me, in my belly, my bowels, my throat, my heart, the tips of my fingers.

The fear in me was enormous. The weight was crushing.

I sank and sank, I swam away into a dark tunnel that called me into its depths the recesses of nothing, not-ending, no going back but no going forward, just darkness and swimming suspended in the thickness of empty nothing of water all around not breathing not hearing but flowing with the gloss and weight my hair like seaweed or like cotton in a breeze, carefree and flowing and my body unknown to me swimming swimming moving and gone.

We struggled in words. It is unrecordable.

I stood up. "OK, I'm going running."

I quickly put on my sneakers and left. The air was fresh, clear, painful to my eyes. I ran towards London Bridge, I crossed the river and ran along its banks. I breathed in, lifted my knees, moved faster, let the nausea climb from my belly into my throat, trying to un-imagine the very real weight in my abdomen. I ran back into myself and found it safe there. The time passed, and my face and body were covered in a layer of salt. I tried to outrun first Henry, then the decision he gave me to make through force, then myself and back around again, time eating away at everything, the run never ending, never needing to end. I looked up and looked away. I looked out of my body and reclaimed my body and told my body this is my body and I will be OK to reclaim it to ignore it to reimagine it to forget it and reinvent it as only mine. And I needed to cry because I had chosen and it was done, but I could not cry while running and so I had to keep running and not cry.

And finally my body said, it is OK. I looked up and out and aimed myself into the sky that was just a sky but I was enveloped perhaps by myself and by my body and not by the sky at all, and my heart yearned and ached and climbed out and fell back inside and cooled and hardened and said things that might not always be easy, like "don't look back, you can do this now for today," and "don't look back or you will never make it out again," and then I was done running.

He was in the bedroom. Time was still. I entered and crossed the room and showered and pushed and pushed and pushed away everything that wasn't on the path that was now that was the only choice the only way to save anything. I pushed it away, forgetting that it is impossible always to push away or even to keep away what has been pushed when the pushing will need to stop.

He was in the bedroom. I sat at the desk in the other room. I took the telephone, and I called the clinic.

"Yes, tomorrow. Maybe three months. Yes. No. OK. What does that mean? Oh, I see. OK. OK. Yes. Yes. I… yes, I have. OK. I understand. Yes. Thank you."

I wasn't breathing. I was still breathing.

"I have an appointment." I said.

"OK." He didn't look at me. He didn't cease looking at me.

I stared at him with nothing in me. He stared back in his calm, painfully serene way.

The ground fell away. I fell great distances.

I struggled into bed and felt the warm skin of his body next to mine and the cage inside of me was cast open and out climbed enormous beasts that tore and clawed my flesh as they poured out through my body not just my mouth and eyes but every inch so that I was flayed and raw and a burning totem of rotten decay eaten away by monstrous figures that climbed back into me with every breath.

I climbed out of bed and went near the door and lay on the floor like a child like a fetus, in the position of the fetus, in the position of what is the most primal, the position when there is pain and hurt and a desire to move back towards something that is safe and primal and maternal and whole and blood and warm and love.

My body convulsed as it froze to death. My mind, my body, every last minute understanding of my own existence, it was wiped away, ripped away, torn away, burned away, forced away, disappearing into an invisible fire of burning flesh, shattering like brittle glass, all the fragments flying back upon me with an inescapable weight. What I was returned and destroyed what remained.

There was nothing on me or near me, just the cold tile floor, and he came out too when he found me absent, and we lay together on the floor near the door. He held me in his arms, wrapped around in that gesture of love and protection but which now was the emblem of death, of holding my body out towards death, of a last embrace to give me over, knowing and willing and wanting, and lying there in the last embrace of death.

Book II

Chapter 1
A Drink With Friends

A cool Friday evening as I waited for Francine to arrive so we could head out to Randy's birthday gathering at the pub. Francine and Randy worked together at the English bookstore where I spent a fair amount of free time. They had both become good friends. We were all on very different paths, but we connected once in a while. I didn't get out that often and was excited for the invitation. I turned the record player on low, Chopin nocturnes. From my window the traffic passed by silently behind the *double-vitrage*. The hair salon across the street had just turned its lights off, and I watched the girl walk downstairs to the main floor of the shop and then leave the building through the wide, central passageway. When she came through the gated, blue, double doors, she turned right toward rue de Rivoli, pulling her coat stiff and tight around her neck moving briskly.

Just after she passed came a group of slow-moving, well-dressed young men that collectively gathered around the public toilet next to the coiffeur. They seemed to be arguing if the receptacle was unavailable or just not working at all. Two or three dismissed the rest and wandered each in their own directions: one toward a car bumper on the boulevard, the other toward an invisible corner against the building and between the same double doors the girl had just exited. The third simply aimed his stream against the exterior of the public bathroom itself.

Next to the hair salon was a travel agency, its yellow, sun-shaped sign left illuminated all night long, and next to it was the dark exterior of the *Duc des Lombards* jazz club with its neon red sign and accents made to resemble wild, cursive script. The sidewalk and road were wet. The sodden scattered leaves were highlighted like an irregular polka-dot pattern in the temporary blackness. The doorbell rang. I turned off the record player and put on my coat before answering.

Francine stood on the landing holding her limp umbrella upside-down. She kissed me on each cheek. "It's cold out there!" Her face was rosy and bright.

I turned up my collar, put on a scarf, taking my umbrella from the box by the door, and shouted a quick goodbye to my flatmate. Francine and I walked down the stairs rapidly. The sound of our shoes against the wood and then marble deafened and reverberated through the six-story stairwell. When we got to the bottom, I glanced through the slot of my mailbox in habit and pressed the button to unlock the door to the street with my left hand.

Francine exited first and immediately opened her umbrella. I also opened mine after inspecting the quality of the rain. We proceeded east toward the Marais.

"Who's going to be there?" I asked.

"I don't really know. Randy rang me up this afternoon to say he'd forgotten to invite me. I told him I'd be round yours and we'd be there by 9PM."

"I wonder if Debra's coming."

"I hope so."

"That would be funny. I just spoke with her the other day, and she said she had plans. Perhaps these were the plans." Debra also worked at the same bookshop, but she was more elusive and didn't always join in. It wasn't easy to know if she just wasn't interested in the event or in our collective dynamic, or if she really did often have other plans.

"Yes, that would be funny. I do think she may be there. I hope so."

The bar wasn't far away, and Debra was not there. It turned out to be the same bar where Henry and I had one of our first dates. He had been sitting reading a book in the corner by the front window when I arrived those years ago and was wearing the same paddy cap and sweater that he had always worn. When I entered, we had both smiled. He put his book back in his pocket. We had ordered Guinness and gone straight downstairs for the bluegrass.

Randy was in that same seat now and was alone. "Ladies!" He waved us over.

"Hiya, Randy! Happy birthday!" Francine gave him a wallop on the back. Randy grinned.

"Happy birthday, Randy! What are you drinking?" I asked.

"Whiskey."

"The next one's on me. And you, Francine?"

"I'll have a white wine."

"Be right back." I took off my coat and scarf, setting my wet umbrella in the rack by the door, and walked up to the bar.

"Thank you, dear!" Randy shouted at my back.

Le Quiet Man was small with a short bar, sparse stools and a room in the cellar with tables. Amateur bluegrass was on the menu during happy hour—all welcome to join—with the real-deal later in the evening. The unpaid musicians had finished, and the professionals hadn't yet begun, but the place was filling up. I had to wait before giving my order. The barman drew my Guinness first and set it aside nine-tenths full while he poured the other drinks. The waiting seemed to take forever.

"Where you from?"

I looked over to see the guy on the neighboring stool staring at me.

"A few blocks from here,"

He laughed so hard, it was a lucky thing he hadn't just taken a drink.

"That's a good one. What I meant was, what country."

It was impossible to escape the American-in-Paris conversation. Annoying as hell and endless, everywhere in the city, no matter what circumstances, year after year. Always the same. It's like you choose to live and breathe the 'about' being in Paris and that's why you move abroad. To live a meta-life about around the possibility of the life where you now are.

"Oh, well. I grew up in the States."

"Which one?"

"Oh, well, hmm. Yeah, so I grew up in California, but I studied in Washington. I have family in California, the Midwest, Oregon and Idaho."

"California! Yeah! I've been there. L.A.! I loved it! Road trip, you know. Saw the Grand Canyon too. It was about five years ago. Well, I was there once when I was really little, you know, with my parents. But I don't really remember it so much. The Grand Canyon! So nice!" He laughed. He liked telling this story. They all liked telling this story. There is nothing wrong with the story, the only problem is that I've heard it about 4,000 times. They all had the same story. I wondered if it was a "camping car" road trip. Of course it was. The story was scripted.

"Yeah, California. Er, the Grand Canyon. That's great." I tried to muster some enthusiasm. I didn't want to be rude, but I was tired of the old script.

"What are you doing in Paris?" He picked up his half-gone beer and took a drink. I could barely register him. He was average looking, clean cut, wearing post-work clothes: button-up shirt, slick office shoes, suit jacket and briefcase hanging on his chair.

"Oh, you know, paying taxes and so forth." Tempted to add the question reciprocally, but I knew better than to give him another window.

"Oh, that's funny! Paying taxes!" This time he was ready for it. No fear of beer out the nose. He looked around to engage with another audience member for my increasingly humorous stand-up routine. He drew himself wholly back toward me, "I mean, what I mean is—" He was apparently worried it was his English that was making me not quite understand his questions. "*Qu'est-ce que tu fais à Paris?*"

"Ah, yes. Right. Well, anyway, excuse me a sec here." I directed my whole attention to the barman, as though he had just spoken to me although he hadn't, but he was about to, and I was more than ready for it. I could feel the fellow's gaze still on me, but I didn't relent and focused on the bottles of whiskey against the wall.

Once the Guinness had settled, the barman finished the quick pour, and I took my time bringing my wallet out with elaboration, demonstrating to my neighbor how busy I was. The barman shook his head and said, "*C'est toujours ouvert.* Your friend's tab is still open."

"Well, I would like to pay this round, however." I should have known Randy had an open account.

"OK, that's 15,80€."

I gave him a twenty and slid the change in my pocket without looking sideways. It took two trips to get Francine and Randy's drinks over to them first, followed by my Guinness. I gave a quick nod to my old neighbor to indicate things were officially coming to an end.

"*Santé!*" Francine, Randy and I touched glasses and made obligatory eye contact. The beer was cold and thick and went down easily. I drank half in the first lift and set it down on the ledge watching the chocolate foam slowly slide down the side of the glass. Three girls left the bench seat in the window, and Francine, Randy and I quickly took it over. I was just finishing my pint when four scruffy friends of Randy showed up bearing gifts. Pete handed Randy an old jar filled with some kind of hot soup.

"This, my friend, is a Polish specialty."

"What is it, Pete?"

"It's chicken barley soup made from scratch. No bouillon in this baby. I boiled the bones myself."

"We ate that chicken two weeks ago!"

This comment came from Ricky with his greasy long hair and a shit-eating grin. Speechless, Pete stared at him. I felt compelled to help.

"Oh, but that's what makes it so good. There's nothing wrong with that," I said as if I had read all about it in some Julia Child cookbook.

Randy looked skeptical.

"I would eat it." I added. "My grandfather was Polish." All eyes on me. "Uh, you know. That's how they do it in the old country. That's the best way to do it. That makes the best, heartiest soup. There's nothing unhealthy about it." I had some unspoken capitulations. Pete was saved for the time being. Randy had slid the jar to the corner behind his right elbow where it was forgotten for the night. I'm not sure how many folks present knew I was vegetarian.

Charlotte ordered a Perrier and became new fodder for teasing. She told any late arrivals it was a vodka soda. Pete was also drinking water, said he had an itch in this throat. Only Alexandre and Maxence ordered pints. Randy was also taunted for having drunk so few drinks before the others arrived. I began to feel like I was in high school. Francine followed her wine with a *demi*, dropped out of the conversation and left by 10:30PM. I was having a good time and headed downstairs on my own to hear some of the bluegrass.

As I crossed the bar, I heard someone suggest that Randy perform his "Lord of the Dance" moves downstairs. This was followed by a gaggle of laughter.

"Where are you going?" Someone asked.

"I want to hear the music." I spoke into the air behind me without turning my head.

I had to squeeze through a group of redheaded, bearded English men playing darts who offered me several sets of elevator eyes along with one or two *bonsoirs*. I didn't reply.

The bluegrass was loud and vigorous and clean, and it felt good to get away from the chat scene into the music. I leaned against the wall in the back and watched the violinist's elbow jerk violently up and down as the bow slid across and back but mostly jerked up and down too. The banjo player looked like he was holding the most delicate of objects the way his hands seemed barely to touch the surface of the instrument. The sounds came out vibrant and strong and blended in nicely with the others though they also stood up distinctly on their own like piercing flashes of solid sound. There was a guitarist playing mostly rhythm though he did some nice finger-picking during his solo and a mandolin player who brought that enchanted night air feel with the fast strumming across the sets of string pairs. No one was on the piano tonight, at least not yet.

I went back upstairs and ordered another Guinness. By this time four or five others had arrived for Randy's gathering and were throwing snarky comments around. I felt alive and buzzed and had a conversation with Zack, Randy's old flat-mate, about literature and then writing and if a writer would feel better to write what sells or never sell what was written.

"My answer will differ week by week," I told him.

I don't know what kind of answer he wanted. Zack was suspiciously younger than he looked, currently had a twenty-something Russian girlfriend, was finishing a Ph.D. at the Sorbonne, directed various political clubs and even campaigns on the side, lived in the exquisite historic flat of a college buddy's parents, and had all and sundry wondering how he managed to pull it off. He was a New England boarding school natural on the piano and somehow had the right smile and comment for any situation you could throw at him.

I stepped outside to call my own flat-mate who had one ear out for the baby sleeping in the room right next to hers. When I went back in, I realized the fresh night air had quickly transformed my sense of the evening, and I should have already left while I'd had the chance. I gave a quick round of farewells and zipped off before anyone tried to stop me. The walk home was short and cold, and I got to thinking about Henry as I always did, especially when it was night and now I'd had beer too. I wondered what he was doing and remembered what it was like before he left. As usual, I did myself a disservice by leaving out the bad parts.

I thought about how we kissed that first time under the gazebo in the Jardin de Luxembourg listening to jazz, each with one earphone and how we walked along the river and talked about making plans for a future that involved casual parties and books and ideas but nothing fancy or intellectual though still full of ideas and reflection. I thought the whole way home about what it might have been like and then what it used to be like and what it's like now.

At home it was quiet and still. The baby was sleeping soundly. Her arms were raised above her head, and she was lying sideways in the bed. I went to the bathroom to brush my teeth then chatted briefly with my flat-mate who sat in her neighboring room working all night. She said that she didn't hear a sound while I was away. I went back to my room and traded my skirt and stockings for pajamas and sat next to the baby's little, warm body. Her soft blonde hair was billowing up on the pillow, and I looked at her large and fragile, paper-thin eyelids closed over her glassy, green eyes and her full, puffy lips open partway as she breathed.

I wanted to cry at the holiness of it, the beatitude, at how angelic she was or just how precious the moment felt but it was also mixed with the feeling from the beer and how sad I felt to see the beauty alone by myself and also just to be alone. On the table was a bottle of mineral water. I took a long drink and set it down next to the bed. I was remembering watching Henry leave in the earliest hour of the morning while the sky was still dark. I had gotten up and run out onto the balcony to see him pack the taxi's trunk with his suitcases. It was cold as I stood there still in the dark with the orange glow rising and I waited and watched him and wasn't sad to see my enemy leave and was so sad and distraught to see my lover and beloved leave. He knew I was there, but he didn't look at me.

"The keys!" I yelled down, but he didn't hear or had pretended not to hear. He had forgotten to give me his house keys, and leaning over the balcony, I remembered that day in the Pyrenees where he had forgotten the hotel key on the giant keychain, and it had sat in his pocket all week without him knowing. He got in the taxi, and it unceremoniously drove away.

I turned off the electric heater under my desk and pulled off my socks and got into bed. It was hard to get Henry out of my mind. Even if I had a good night, it still made me feel like crying once I got home. I thought of him walking out of the apartment and down onto the street and stepping into that taxi, as I had last seen him, and of course it killed me every time I let those images pass through my head even if I knew it had to be. It's a lot easier to get perspective in the daytime and without drink. Night is always something else. Night brings the demons. That's why I don't drink alone or when I'm sad, though tonight I didn't know I was either of those things, and I guess I got tricked.

Chapter 2
The Greeting Card

All that ache of the nighttime was transformed into the daytime ache, which is more manageable. It was Saturday. The sun had come out, and I felt pretty fine. The baby and I awoke about nine o'clock, got dressed and I brushed my teeth while she played on the floor with the ukulele like it was an unwieldy log. The whole time she sang *Bateau sur l'eau! La rivière! La rivière!* It reminded me of the songs we would sing growing up. I had sung so much as a child, with Mom, with our siblings. All the tunes from *The Sound of Music.* So many old war songs that Mom had taught us, so many from school, so many between Emma, Fred and me.

We had yogurt with oats for breakfast, and I made myself a cup of black tea with milk. We read books about Babar the elephant and played for a while. We listened to records by theme, Cat Stevens, Cat Power, Stray Cats. Two hours passed that way, and we left the house before the morning was out. At the market we picked up some items for the apartment like toilet paper and a box of matches for the stove. I wanted to get the errands taken care of before I went running. I had to strategize our schedule so that the baby didn't fall asleep in the stroller while I was running. I needed her to sleep at home afterwards to be able to get some work done while she napped. Everything had to be perfectly timed. Everything counted.

We got back from the shops, and I hoisted the stroller up the first thick step into the Haussmannian building with my right hand while strategically typing in the code on the keypad with my left hand. The grocery bags swayed on the handles of the stroller and were slightly crushed on either side of the building's massive wooden door frame. The fresh bread fell out of the stroller's canopy, when I shifted my weight to pull everything through the doorway rocking the wheels to and fro twisting and turning the stroller until it finally gave way and smacked down inside the entry. I picked up the bread, luckily still in its open-ended paper bag, and pulled open the mailbox at the same time without using the key. The lock was recently busted and now the door was coming off too. Inside was a cream-colored envelope addressed in Henry's hand. I shimmied the crooked mailbox door back into place.

Memories of each time he had sent me one of his carefully selected cards in our handful of years together fell upon one another in the trap of my mind. I had kept the full set of them in a ceramic box he once got me for no reason at all, unable to part with them after he had left. The last card I had received from him was unkind, three weeks past my birthday after he left for San Francisco and returned his house keys by mail. No gift, no mention of the missed date. It was painful to read, the lack of love in that card both in its selection and in its writing, especially in knowing how much care he used to give those gestures—or perhaps still does give, just not to me. It was The Cat in the Hat. "Oh, the places you'll go!" And inside "*Bon voyage!*" It had absolutely no context. I wondered if it was an old card he was simply re-using to return the keys or if he had just grabbed whatever was at the counter when he was paying for the package.

Henry had such an eye for delicate things, I had always thought, in contrast to what I saw as my own bumbling and awkwardly deliberate approach to understanding or appreciating aesthetics. His family collected art earnestly and lavishly, mostly ceramics from local artists. I was often impatient when he was choosing his cards, leaving a museum or on a trip or idly passing a shop on a walk or on the way home, a desire provoked in him to share a tender thought with someone. Still, I had admired him for it and detected in his gesture something sincere that gave me pause and served as a source for reconciliation whenever we fought, or when I'd find myself judging him for bad behavior toward me. I counted these caring things. He and I both counted but in different ways.

I stared at the script, the narrow, vertical letters. My name, my Paris address and the return address in San Francisco. I imagined him writing it, the second he pulled the pen from his back pocket where he always carried a notepad, a book and a pen, and I visualized him in the motion, tried to understand the feelings he may have had in doing it, to want to commit something for me in ink inside the card.

I slipped the envelop next to the bread on the canopy of the stroller so I could hoist the stroller again to get through the second security door, this time one-two-three-four-five plunking stairs, the grocery sacks sashaying, the wheels hitting down on the stone in rhythmic fashion, the baby bobbing up and down up and down. I maneuvered again with the right hand on one of the handles, the left on the keypad. I let the front wheels hit and then rolled the stroller backward ten feet to the elevator and pushed the button. The air was still. The elevator smelled like heavy perfume and body odor. I waited until the doors closed before I tore into the envelope.

Twenty minutes later, I was on a video call with my sister looking at the early afternoon sun through the balcony window.

"So… we're going to go see him," I blurted out.

"You are?" Emma's eyes bulged. She looked shocked.

"Well, you know, we just have to do it."

"What happened?"

"He sent me a card."

"What did he say?"

"Emma, there's no other way through this. It's going to be good."

"That's what he said?"

"No, I'm just saying that because it's true." I was exhausted.

"Aggie, are you sure? It's not him you need."

"It's not about that. The baby will always need him."

"Aggie, listen. I get that. I think it's great. I mean, I understand it's hard. I'm sure it's very hard. But I don't think…"

"Emma, really, it's not what you think."

There was a silence.

"Really," I insisted.

"OK." That was Emma's way of saying she accepted the statement but either didn't agree or didn't understand but knew it wasn't her place to share that.

"I feel like I've had so much loss in my life. I won't let that happen anymore."

"I know you miss him, but…"

"But what? It's not about that. It's the right way forward."

"I get it," she said, "but, I mean, this is all like a broken record. You need to get out of the cycle of this conversation with yourself. Please—just remember that. Don't repeat the hurt."

"I'm not. This isn't that. Really."

"Well, that's great. You're doing great and I'm happy for the baby. I mean, only you can decide, but keep us in mind—your support, just in case you… I mean, just in case you go… in case you go for the wrong reasons or something. Only you know, I guess. I don't want to say anything to discourage you. I hope you know what you're doing."

"Thanks."

"Just be careful."

I could tell Emma anything. She was diplomatic and clear-headed. No nonsense and supportive. I always called her when things were rough. She listened.

"I've got to go. The kids are waiting."

"Thanks, Emma."

"OK, love you. Bye."

As soon as we hung up, I jumped out of my seat and took off my sweater and shirt and pants. I pulled a pair of running pants off the old bookshelf where they were stacked with the rest of my clothes and put them on along with a black, long johns-type shirt and a bright green Paris Marathon running t-shirt. I took a pair of compression stockings from the small dresser by the bed and started going through the baby's things on the other side of the room to get her ready to go back outside.

After both of us were laced up, I opened the door to the elevator and strategically shoved the running stroller inside not without difficulty. With its extra wide size and large inflated wheels, it barely fit and required a certain simultaneous lift and turn to get in place, but we were down on the road in less than a minute. Afternoon light was creeping in. I slipped in my earbuds and took off for the Tuileries garden.

Looking up at the sky while running, as Murakami says, is a futile gesture toward unity with something that is quite cold and neutral. We must look into ourselves, he says. Well, anyway, he must look into himself, he advises, and I think that's a good idea. Yes, we do gaze at the clouds and the sky and find their indifference, but it's a beautiful, striking indifference. In fact, it's an indifference that pulls us ever more toward it, in our own gesture to simultaneously look inward and to find something inward that first started out there in the pink sky. So in a way it works, and the sky is after all not cold and ungiving but helps us find a way back.

Do I see kindness in myself? Yes, I think I do, I am not Murakami with his harsh self-assessment, but I wonder what either one of us is trying to say when we say or show our answers to that question. If the audience is not looking, does Murakami still not see kindness and do I still see kindness? This question might be more about the role of writing in the world and what it does or creates between a writer and a reader. I can still say that I do see a kindness, and it's more like Ben Lerner writes about Whitman, and I too want to populate my writing with Whitman in the way that he calls us back not just to the joy in the sight of the *seagulls above and the web-tide below* and *knowing how it is for you, men and women of a generation hence*—but right in the writing of those things and right in the gesture of how it connects, even though it's connecting nothing but writer to letter.

There are twenty references to Walt Whitman in Lerner's *10:04*, the last one on the last page, almost like a joke, a reference to the seemingly peculiar 21st century experiences of a young man in the center of New York on a bus with his pregnant friend, not girlfriend but friend he impregnated at her request, and indeed in the old-fashioned coital manner, with the similitudes of the past, and those of the future, corresponding.

I am with you and know how it is.

Chapter 3
American Expat Writers in Paris

Monday morning, the baby and I walked up to Arts et Métiers for an appointment with the pediatrician. The trees lining the Boulevard de Sébastopol, which runs directly and only north, had been bare for several months and were just starting to look alive again. The clinic was down a small, cobblestone side street off rue Beaubourg a few blocks past the Centre Pompidou in a neighborhood with many cheap goods' import shops selling handbags, lighters, sunglasses, scarves, bridal gowns and knock-off designer clothing only *en gros*, that is to say only in commercial quantities. On the little rue au Maire off to the right, that is to say the east, stern-looking men with cigarettes dangling from their stubbled lips and wearing blood- and dirt-splattered, full-length white aprons pushed massive carts filled beyond capacity with boxes containing imported vegetables, fresh fish and large plastic bags of soft, fatty meat. The street dead-ended with the pediatric clinic and my own health clinic directly next door. When Henry and I were planning on moving out of the round room at Passy, we nearly rented the apartment on the second floor of the building at the direct center of the dead-end road. Each time I walked to the pediatrician or my own clinic, I faced it head on which is to say I thought of it and saw it and stared at it and spent the eternity of time moving from the corner of rue Beaubourg to the green gate entryway of either clinic. All along I pictured our soft silhouettes living moving breathing behind the gauzy white curtains.

Yet we never lived in that place. At the last minute we backed out. Something didn't seem right. We had a bad feeling and we stopped pursuing it. The owner was a round and comfortable man in his 60s who owned the jewelry shop below (*vente en gros*) and was extremely keen on us making the deal. That was the first thing that put us off. I had visited the apartment on my own and was pressured immediately into deciding then and there if we wanted it.

"I need to talk to Henry first."

"Here, please, use my phone."

I hadn't expected that offer, but it was the hard sell. I took his phone and called Henry. I explained the layout. Henry wanted to know my opinion. I liked it. He trusted me.

We were naïve. The owner kept trying to insist that the decision to rent wasn't up to us. That we had to go through the process of being chosen. He agreed to hold the place for us in order to give Henry time to see it two days later. Henry liked it too, and afterwards we were invited into the back room of his jewelry shop where everything was in boxes under decades of dust. The windows were boarded up, and a giant desk in the back was covered in a collection of other business deals. He offered us espressos from his machine that we drank out of thimble-sized, brown plastic cups in the front room of the shop while the owner took care of some other pressing business with one or two other well-dressed older men who were waiting just inside the door when we first came downstairs to the street.

"I like you, Henry. Where are you from?" He began speaking to us in English.

"Idaho."

"Ahhhh, Idaho..." He spoke in a lingering, wispy voice as though he was retrieving old cowboy memories of his own. "Isn't that where Hemingway lived when he shot himself?" His character was predictable. "I love Hemingway. A real American. A real man," he continued. Henry was not charmed but as always remained professional.

We headed around the corner as instructed, to leave our dossier with the real estate agency that did the actual renting and managed legal affairs. It wasn't until the next day we were informed that the security deposit would be 10,000€. The owner tried to corner us, humiliate us, shift things around to make it seem as though that figure was evident from the start, that we had forgotten, misunderstood and needed to cooperate and follow through with the "prearranged agreement." Henry knew the guy was trying to take us for a ride not only for being foreigners but also gullible Americans. We broke the deal off and looked elsewhere. He tried to bully us for another few days but we didn't take the bait, and that's how it ended with the apartment at the dead-end of rue au Maire.

After the baby's check-up, she and I went back across rue Beaubourg to a nice café for a piece of their homemade carrot cake. It was a cool and bright afternoon with one bold cloud crossing out the sun. There was that electric afternoon feeling that could easily turn to anxiety if nothing was done about it. I chatted with the owner of the café and caught up on some news about folks I didn't know. Someone was leaving town, moving to Germany on a post-doc or transferred back to Canada or America, or their papers expired, or someone's neighbor was having a baby or got a new job at the library or the embassy or they were opening an artisanal coffee shop with organic coffee, even decaf. I enjoyed being in the warmth of the café and was reluctant to leave it.

A group of loud young boys on their way home from school walked by with their backpacks and laughter and pranks. A young woman with a computer and an open notebook sat at the front of the café. Her long Celtic-red hair kept tumbling forward from behind her ear, and she would tuck it back again without looking away from her work. The café was on a side street next to the rue Beaubourg. Busy traffic was passing south just at the east corner of the street, as all the cars and trucks and bikes headed toward the Seine. The baby and I heard a *camion-poubelle* roar by, but we couldn't see it, and the baby was excited. You know it's a big green *camion-poubelle* because of the way the diesel engine starts and stops every few moments for the workers to step down, unlatch the old garbage bag from the ring stand and replace it and then step up again onto the green ledge on the open back of the truck. The only person in the café who could confirm this was the young woman with the orange locks, but she could neither be consulted nor presumed to have seen it herself.

We left without eating all the cake because I wanted to have a little something to look forward to when I got to work that afternoon and also because the baby never eats all of anything but mostly nothing of everything. I set its remains gently in my bag and tried not to cause the old-fashioned bell overhead to ring too loudly when we walked out. I did not like leaving the kind, warm café, but it's more important to have a place to go back to than to wear it out all at once.

It was a straight shot down rue Beaubourg which becomes rue du Renard to get to the Hotel de Ville from the Arts et Métiers area. I took that road to get the baby to daycare that afternoon so I could get to work. I left her as usual with mutual reluctance or perhaps a reluctance that was greater on my part. In great haste I headed back up Boulevard de Sébastopol on a city bike to the university study abroad center that I called my employer near Chateau d'eau. I arrived with seven minutes to spare before my class started—minutes I used to make a decaf coffee using the office's trendy espresso machine in the small kitchen.

The center occupied the third floor of a Haussmannian building with an open central room with four computer desks butted up against one another, a lounge, two offices and two classrooms off-shooting. Patricia's desk was right in the entryway making it feel like entering a dentist's office to make an appointment. She was the only administrator and Lawrence's assistant—Lawrence, the program director whose office was stationed in the corner, the other office occupied by the visiting professor from the States.

"Aggie, can I get your month's timesheet before next week?"

Patricia should have been paid better. She took care of everything. We all should have been paid better. I was teaching university courses per hour for chris-sakes.

"No problem. I'll give it to you during our break today."

"Sounds good." She didn't look up from her work. She was 25 and had been a Fulbright scholar in Chicago during her undergraduate days, moved back in with her dad in the Paris suburbs when she returned, shared a room with her teenage brother, and commuted to central Paris for this administrative slog.

I walked into my classroom, and half of my ten students were still missing, lingering in the lounge or checking email on the central computers. I didn't mind. I had been there over three years and had learned the particular way of the center and the home university in America. My students needed support but personal space: a hand on their hand for guidance coupled with encouragement of independence and accomplishment.

I started class by making a few pop culture jokes followed by projecting a quiz overhead. It drew groans, and I told them to grade their own quizzes and keep both the quiz and answers. Yay! Keeping my job involved a particular combination of good grades and even better evaluations. Next came a student presentation on the Beat Hotel and my spontaneous inspirational mini-lecture on the joys of being in Paris.

"You are just like Burroughs! Barnes! Hemingway! Stein! Fitzgerald and the rest of the gang!" I paused, took a deep breath and drew up my energy. "And what is the significance of 'place' for these writers?" I looked around the room and tried to make eye contact with each young face. "Use your own experiences to identify with these writers and to identify the forces at work! Take full advantage of your own placement here."

A student raised her hand. "Do you mean because we're, like, in Paris we can understand better what they were, like, writing about?"

"Exactly. But it goes both ways. How did they write about America from afar? How do you see America from afar, living here as you do? And turn it around: how did Paris see them? How do you feel about your presence here? How is Paris seeing you?" I had this kind of ridiculous passion. I loved living the cliché. I meant everything I said, and I enjoyed how rudimentary it was. I was adjunct, and given the meager pay, tried to give only what was required though I was fanatical and excited and a damned specialist in the subject.

"I don't get it. So, like, for example, like why is this book called *The Autobiography of Alice B. Toklas* if Alice didn't, you know, like, write it herself?" An undercurrent of half-breathed complicit laughter across the room. "I totally don't get that. It's like, not true. I mean, where do they even put this book in the bookstores?" She gained confidence as she spoke, excited and proud of her criticism. The class joined in.

"Is it, like, because Gertrude Stein was from America and so when she came to Paris she could, like, kind of pretend to be someone else? Or what?"

"Right, OK. Yes! Sort of. Well, anyway. Good thoughts. Something like that. Stein is disrupting expectations of genre, form, truth and fiction. We'll be getting to Stein next week actually. For now: Hemingway!"

The students were great. The study abroad idea was great. But the job was scandalous. It was Paris though, so I let myself delight in the students' youth and naivety and the wealth that allowed them to have these experiences. I didn't have much of a choice. What else could I do? It was impossible to get a job, a teaching job, a real teaching job. I was lucky. Before the baby it wasn't much different, but at least I had been able to travel some with Henry and places on my own too, like Mongolia, Iceland, shelters in New York and Washington to volunteer, to do what I could, to flesh out my past, to give care to replace the care I never got. Now I had this. It was absurd and reductive, and it was still beautiful and rewarding, and it worked simply because I lived in Paris where I had automatic healthcare and childcare, government-subsided support.

"Just like you, you see, these writers used their expatriation in Paris as subject matter precisely by exploring the significance of that geographical change. It influenced their writing sometimes through Paris itself serving as a focus or simply through the mood and atmosphere within the writing regardless of its setting, or oftentimes both." I looked around; they were listening. "After World War I, they were dealing with alienation, crises of identity, PTSD, although the term hadn't been invented or understood yet, the war in general, but also language—experimental prose and poetics, like Stein!—and bohemian living, alternative lifestyles, transgression, subversion, all of that stuff."

They were taking notes. That was good. Only one guy appeared to be texting.

"We want to talk about perceptions of the self, their-selves, your-selves. How did they—do we, do you—

construct a sense of France, of Paris, through the lens of expatriation?" I was sweating a little, my voice getting higher, a bit carried away. "How they impacted literary studies today as we know it!"

"But, I mean, are we—I mean, what is an expatriate? Are we really expats? I mean, we're just here for a semester..." He looked around with a grin, and the room again gave back a hushed, collective knowing laugh. I wasn't deterred.

"Yes! You're expats! Why not? Don't you want to be? It's how you feel. It's that you're here. It's the very fact that you live here. In French you're considered a Parisian full and true and legitimate if you live here. That's all it takes. Nothing to do with origin. Nothing to do with timeframe." What the hell was I talking about at this point? I didn't really know anymore but I was on a roll. They were nodding, scribbling notes.

We dove into *The Sun Also Rises* and spent the next hour dividing the characters between war veterans and non-veterans, favoring the veterans and excusing them their excesses and shapeless, dramatic and harmful existences. We took a break, and I went to get a glass of water and use the toilet. I came back to my classroom and filled out my timesheet while the students mulled about the computers and the lounge.

A student entered the room. "Professor, can I write my first paper about how the bullfights are a metaphor for the sex lives of the characters?"

"That sounds like a great idea. And be sure to consider the steers from multiple angles. For instance, is Jake Barnes a steer because he's impotent (possibly castrated like the steers)? Or is Robert Cohn a steer because he's not a war veteran and is part of a herd mentality? Are all the men who desire Lady Brett Ashley the bulls or are they mindless steers? Is Brett the bull herself? Destroying whoever is in her path, like Mike, Cohn, Romero and so on? And don't forget Hemingway himself: he is the puppet master after all."

The student nodded slowly, mouth hanging slightly open and eyes looking vacant. I left it at that. I had faith. These kids weren't just smart, they had guidance, which made all the difference.

At the end of the lesson, 5PM sharp, I rushed off to get to the baby in time. It was routine, it was tight and it had to work. The daycare gates were locked shut at precisely 5:30PM. I had to get in, pick her up, get her coat, shoes and other items and get out before the guard arrived with keys at the ready.

I quickly walked to the nearest city bike station, wiped off the rain wet seat with the cuff of my coat, cycled down Beaubourg to Renard in the drizzle, turned left near the BHV department store, went down the one-way street facing thick head-on traffic all in a blur and parked the bike in front of the gates of the Hotel de Ville. I had just a handful of minutes to spare before they locked the doors. I always wondered what would happen if I didn't make it.

Once I picked her up, we performed our usual evening routine of hysterical tired and hungry fits on the way home to burst through the apartment door twenty minutes later with bags, shoes, coats, hats, scarves, *pain au chocolat*, picture books, stuffed animals flying. I peeled the layers off both of us as quickly as possible and plopped down in my office chair with the baby in my lap to nurse. Fifteen minutes later calm was restored. I turned on the record player, Debussy piano, and we headed to the bath.

After I put her to bed, I sat for what seemed a long time by the full-length, glass balcony doors and watched the salmon and indigo sky turn a charcoal color. The periodic streak of light became more visible as it passed over the buildings opposite as though from a lighthouse but was the far-reaching spotlight of the Eiffel Tower in the 7th arrondissement. It crossed over the horizon in front of us every few minutes moving from right to left down toward the Seine, both ominous and luminous and reminiscent always of those first days at Passy. The moon was hanging strangely low over the horizon, and this very same day the baby had suddenly said, "*La lune! La lune!*" I couldn't show it to her in her sleep though I wanted to. The moon, *la lune*, was enclosed in a glowing ring-like lunar halo or force field, protecting it from what my imagination was capable of conjuring at 8PM on an empty Friday evening. I was tired but knew I needed to stay awake to get the work done that I wouldn't be able to do over the weekend when the baby didn't have daycare. No great complaints but some pain, unresolved heartache I couldn't keep myself from finding again and nursing again.

I tried to work hard so that I could sleep well and not be afraid of my dreams.

Chapter 4
Jim and Susi

I continued to try not to think about Henry's card. That next Friday I was invited to dinner with an old friend. Jim is that old man and old friend and he lived near the Parc de Montsouris. Jim and I were both invited to dinner at an old friend of his and then of mine: Susi, Swiss courtesan extraordinaire and rock'n'roll sex icon of the 70s. She invited Jim as always and then she invited me herself to come with Jim, and I liked that. Even though my weakness is sentimentality, these two were my imagined bohemian parents, but I often had to remind myself not to take my care too far. The two of them were live wire libertarians and didn't give a damn for the sludge of the heart. Nevertheless, they were old, and they were human and through them I felt like the world was something for me to discover and to learn from and to learn from them and to show them that I learned from them. I wanted to show them that they meant something to me and I wanted to show them that they meant something, just meant something. I always want to show this, but it is almost impossible to express those feelings in a way where they are really conveyed to the depth of what they are and to do it without being a sap.

I have this problem with everything. I want to show everyone they mean something to me. I want to show the world that it can mean something to itself, to me, to everyone, even if I risk my own protection. My silent wish, I know, is also to have it done for me. I imagine how I project myself into the world and think constantly of how and what I can continue to do.

I decided to bring banana bread to dinner. It is important that my gifts are homemade, not only because I can't afford anything else but because I feel the effort to create something personal is the best I can do for someone. I turned on the record player—not Chet Baker, but The Doors *Greatest Hits*—and began setting out the ingredients. I was thinking about the first time I met Susi at Jim's place, four years ago. That day on the way to see Jim, and meet Susi, my new bohemian libertarian parents, I had taken a considerable and frenetic bike ride through the city, letting the rushing energy surge and climb out of me like electric beasts, like an electric current whose end I could not yet feel in my body. I thought about the long ride I took that day long ago, plowing through joy and spirit and strength rolling through me on its way out and how I would do it again tonight.

While in the cycling reverie, I was greeted by my tuxedo cat rubbing against my calf as I pulled the items out to prepare the banana bread for the dinner. Flour, sugar, ripe bananas, sharing a piece with the baby, sometimes an egg in the mix sometimes not, sometimes walnuts, baking powder, a dash of salt and that was it. Throw it all together in a loaf pan cook for an hour. Henry loved banana bread. I had made it for him all the time. I still make it all the time. I wanted to think about those sensations that I felt before everything that happened with Henry, and how it felt now visiting Susi and Jim again tonight. Strange to think I met Henry six months after Susi and Jim those four years ago.

I had ridden a good two hours across the river and back, up and down boulevards and small alleyways, around train stations and cemeteries until finally flying up the Champs Elysées while the sun was setting. Music was pounding in my ears, and I reached the top of the boulevard on my tottery bike and joined the throngs of cars in the massive roundabout of the Arc de Triompe. I felt wild. I was in it. In something. In the world. In life. In a moment. Of all the world's moments. In my own death eating at me from the inside, in the pulse of the blood in my veins and the sweat cooling on my forehead and the wind in my hair and the sun, and the sun on my face, the sun setting across the sky of Paris in so many shades of pink and glorious gray and orange. I could never tire of the colors of Paris even when I tired of Paris. The cotton candy glow of the sun on a winter afternoon, the soft dumpling white of the clouds, the ashen almost blue of the rooftops, the shades of brown and beige on the centuries of old stone in every building, the contrast of the rich green of high trees against slick black streets.

I circled around the Arc de Triompe and flew back down towards the Place de la Concorde. This is not a short road. This road is roughly two miles long, but you can see end to end because it is the Champs Elysées. It is straight and wide and menacing and vast, full of cars and lights, and it connects all the roads of the world. Every hair on my body was standing on end. There was nothing else in existence but me and that sun and that road and my bike. Nothing. I reached the end and passed around the Place de la Concorde, not ready yet to let go of the majesty of the place, of the experience. I crossed the Seine again and finally headed down to Susi and Jim's arrondissement at the southern border of Paris.

I stirred in the last of the wet ingredients and washed the thick brown sludge from my hands, letting the mixing bowl fill with warm water. I poured the batter in the loaf pan and slipped it into the oven, setting the timer to 60 minutes. I cleaned off the baby's face and got her dressed and ready for daycare. When the oven bell sounded, I slid the warm cake out onto the stovetop to cool. The bike ride moved a little beyond reach and was replaced by the warm scent of the cooked fruit, nuts and grains. When the bread was cool, I covered it with foil, put on my jacket and shoes and headed out of the apartment with the baby in the stroller and down to the street.

It was just after 1PM. Most days I could leave the baby at daycare at 1:30PM and no earlier, with the usual 5:30PM cut-off pick-up time. Most days I taught from 2PM to 5PM. It was a tight fit on both ends. We cut through rue des Lombards that became the rue de la Verrerie as it passed L'Eglise Saint Merri where my friend Jacques curated the music events. We turned right onto rue du Renard and down towards the fat artery of rue de Rivoli and crossed over it toward the backside of the Hôtel de Ville. When we came to its second entry gate, edged against the Seine, we rolled up to the police guards, and I held out my flimsy laminated paper pass, frayed and faded from so many hours spent in my running shoe on rainy days. They smiled and let us pass into the grand 19th century inner courtyard of the extravagant and ancient city hall—the inside defying its stunning Renaissance exterior. From there we entered the wing on the left, unloaded the stroller and walked up the low, child-friendly stairs, entering a small foyer where I pulled two paper shoe covers out of a bag hanging against the wall and placed them over my boots. From the hall we passed the kitchen with a large chalkboard on the door indicating any special news of the day (*Aujourd'hui: l'anniversaire de Salim!*). On the neighboring wall was a grease-board calendar outlining the lunch and snack schedule for the month, accompanied by colored magnets and playful drawings in multi-colored inks. The rest of the walls were covered with stickers, pictures, notices, cut-outs and artistic creations including an orange and pink scribbled dinosaur holding a guitar. I was sure I knew who had worked on that one. Through a gate and into a large room with miniature tables and chairs, down another corridor with toys, play mats, balls, a small trampoline and enormous windows onto other various rooms with changing tables, beds, swings, bouncy chairs and groups of children. Finally descending another set of stairs to a series of rooms occupied by two other assemblages of children, one to contain my own.

Once in the last corridor, I removed the baby's shoes and coat and placed them in her cubby. We entered the main room, and when she saw her group, she clung more tightly to my body and began to whimper. I slowly attempted to set her among the other babies and toddlers, but her despair increased. The caretakers intervened, spoke to her, offered her toys and explanations, and in her distraction, she gave in. I quickly gave her a kiss and said *au revoir,* retracing my steps back to the main entrance of the Hotel de Ville.

I grabbed a city bike once outside and sped off to teach. The return process was repeated once again just after 5PM. Finally after getting home, the two of us played and read and ate dinner and washed and passed the quick evening hours until the day ended, and then I readied to meet with Jim and Susi. The time vanished in the way it knew how, and when it was almost time to go, I put the baby to bed slowly and carefully and we lay there together until she fell asleep. I was exhausted.

I slowly got up, spying Henry's card on my desk, and returned to the kitchen, gently placing the banana bread in my bag so that it did not turn on its side. I went back in our room and lay down again with the baby and waited for my flat-mate to get home. When she arrived, I kissed the baby softly in her sleep and met the flat-mate in the entryway giving her the details of the evening. I put on my coat and shoes, petting the cat who pushed his head, neck, and spine against my palm as I chatted. I locked the apartment behind me and took the stairs four flights down to the courtyard, walking up one block to unlock a city bike. I used to have my own bike, but it was stolen on one of the first nights I spent at Henry's place years ago. I preferred the city bikes anyway, especially now with the baby, where I could do things like ride one from work to pick her up, return it in the station at the Hotel de Ville and walk home with her without also having a bike to push.

After twenty minutes of riding in the cool night air down a few straight miles to the south of Paris, I arrived at the gate of Jim's *atelier* apartment. It was 8:30PM. I put the bike back in a nearby stand, crossed the small cobblestone street, then dialing the code to get into Jim's courtyard. Up the broken stone path, crunching leaves underfoot and looking up at the long windows along the line of artist workshops on the right side and the wild trees on the left. In the days before my own bike was stolen, I stored it between the shed and the overhanging trees but now that space was empty, and I turned around to ascend the four steps into the building. When I reached Jim's door, just inside the corridor on the left, I knocked once loudly and entered without waiting for a response.

"Who's there?" He shouted down from his bedroom loft.

"It's me!"

"Are you ready?" His voice was loud and gruff as though he were irritated, as though it came from 200 meters away.

"Ready when you are!" I called back in the way that I do, with palpable cheer, to deflect any possible low spirits, knowing too, however, that Jim was not low, he was just Jim. My good pal, 80 plus years old.

Five minutes later, the two of us were out the door heading across Allée Samuel Beckett for dinner with Susi, the old dame on the 14th floor of the only Modern building on the block, wedged in between a handful of classical Haussmannians.

The road on both sides of the walking path is called Avenue René Coty, whereas the path itself, which runs down the center, is called Allée Samuel Beckett. Jim walked along very, very slowly now, and with a bit of a limp. He had been to the doctor that morning and was on new medication for high blood pressure and for swelling in his ankles. He was in pain and quite unhappy, speaking morbidly. This was balanced by his otherwise sarcastic charm.

"Ah, I remember," Jim began, "I remember walking here with old Sam."

I listened.

"It's funny, you know," he continued, "It's funny, because he was old then."

I watched him. His straight, gray mustache, his hair combed for dinner, perfectly to the side, slightly greasy, his neutral-colored trench coat hanging open loosely.

"He was old. At the end of his life, old Sam."

I imagined Jim, this retired professor and publisher, walking there forty years ago with Samuel Beckett.

"He was old, and I was young."

This old man walking on Allée Samuel Beckett before it was called Allée Samuel Beckett with Samuel Beckett, "Sam."

"And now I'm old," he said.

I heard him. My thoughts moving as slowly as his old, strained legs. *And I am young, and we are walking*, I thought but did not say.

Instead I spoke quietly, softly, gently, "And now we're walking here."

"And now we're walking here. And you're the young one. Yes."

"And we're walking down Allée Samuel Beckett together. I'm glad." I paused. I was being too moved and earnest.

Silence, and then, as though he didn't hear all of me, "Yes, and we're walking down Allée Samuel Beckett together." He paused. "It's funny, you know, and here I am at the end of my life." He was silent for a while and then concluded, "No. No, I guess it's not so funny. It's not so funny."

I knew there was nothing to be said after that. Nothing to be done, but my silly love was pouring out for him. And he certainly wasn't at the end of his life. I loved his oldness, I loved his life, his kindness, his openness, his gentleness, his presence. I loved Susi the dame too, and I was welling up inside. I wanted to care for them. I wanted to do something. To be alive. To show them they were alive. That they'd lived and were living still. And they were loved, and are loved still. That they mattered, and matter still. I went home that night and wrote about them in my notebook, but even there I contained my feelings and remained mostly silent, trying to investigate why they were so powerful. Later I realized it was because I wanted someone to feel those things about me.

My own mom was gone before I was born, to return only in silhouettes on a barstool through the window through my childhood, and again across the cafeteria tables of a prison visiting room in my adolescence, and again, during her ten-year absence, in underwater dreams. My own father, the last time I saw him, the white violence roared up like it does when you don't expect it but you know it's coming. It was when he told me to get the fuck out of his house and so I did, with trembling limbs and baby.

Just before arriving at Susi's, Jim and I stopped off at the *épicerie* to buy her an excellent bottle of wine, one which Jim always brought her, which always made her angry.

She lived in a small penthouse at the top of that solitary Modern building bought for her many years ago by Jean Paul Getty. When Susi answered the bell, she saw the wine first in Jim's hand, because she knew it was coming.

"You know I hate when you buy me this fancy shit!" She exclaimed.

Jim shrugged with sagging shoulders and looked at me with a happy sheepishness across his face.

She pulled it from his hand and pushed the door open, silently inviting us in. "I love this wine! I don't want this kind of money spent on me by you. You know that!" She looked at me, "Don't let him do this again!" She demanded with a frightening, unapologetic seriousness. She meant business. I was startled though not surprised. I solemnly vowed to make sure it never happened again. I was earnest and timid and bursting with love.

We entered her suite. It was a museum of curiosities in homage to her reputation as a great sexual beauty and brass, free-spirited personality of her era. Her door was open to thousands, where extensive dinner parties were a regular event. The entire place was covered in faux leopard patterns—including her own skin-tight pants that she still wore now although she was approaching her 80th year. She made all her clothes herself. She had four small, dirty, white dogs, clumped curly hair, brown wet mouths, licorice tongues, marble eyes, bouncing off the massive leather sofas, extensive paintings, pictures, portraits of her and celebrities covering every centimeter on the walls. Trinkets, knick-knacks, the coffee table covered in phalluses, ceramic, glass, rubber, wax. I spotted her portrait by Salvador Dalí against the wall of the dining room. Elaborate mirrors designed for her as gifts hung in all corners, reflecting her portrait by Helmut Newton from every angle, period and genre. On the terrace was a private spiral staircase leading up to the roof, with an inflatable hot tub and panoramic view of all of Paris.

"I masturbate up there in the summer with the jets on," Susi explained.

"Oh." I had no adequate response. I smiled.

Jim had heard it all before and wasn't paying attention. He had his share of the same memories. The same free flowing fun and games of an era of so-called sexual liberation.

The dame Susi made an amazing dinner, and I told her so. She was gentle and kind and giving with me, this old woman who was full of a long history of controversy and known to have an incredibly hard exterior. She was funny and very abrasive.

"You have great tits," she told me.

I blushed. "Thank you."

"No need to thank me. It's just the facts."

"OK."

"I like you, Aggie."

"I like you too, Susi. Thank you for inviting me." I tried not to let my sentimentality spill out and embarrass me. I was already embarrassed.

She had a reputation of volatility and exclusivity. I was even more nervous now that she said she liked me. I knew I would have to work hard to preserve it.

"I will give you fish next time you come. I make great fish." The dame Susi was not modest.

"I would love that," I complimented her as she desired.

I did not explain that I don't eat fish. "The pastries are wonderful."

"Of course they are. I made them myself. I make everything myself. They are German." Though Susi is Swiss, she'd lived in Paris since she was eighteen. She was a sought-after starlet who married an heir, had a son, divorced and became a courtesan to princes, politicians and rock stars. Legend goes that she "retired" from the business when a sheik offered her $40,000 USD for one night. She made him lay the money out on the bed and they cavorted on top of it from dusk til dawn.

I excused myself for a quick trip to the toilet, and when I turned on the light, I found it covered in Polaroid photographs of her with a French baron, her with a Spanish prince, her with an Italian count, her with an English minister, her with Mick Jagger, her with Robert Plant, her with Iggy Pop, her with David Bowie, her with Germaine Greer, her with Salvador Dalí, her with Helmut Newton, her with Pablo Picasso, her with Gerard Depardieu, her with Monica Bellucci, her with Carla Bruni and her with many others.

I wondered about her son. Jim had told me Susi didn't see him often, and he'd gotten mixed up with the wrong crowd. And I also wondered if her son had a papa. If he was there. If he had been there. If he was good.

At the end of dinner, I thought about what I could give her as a thank you. At some point she mentioned she liked when her friends made her mixed tapes. I made a mental note to make her a mixed tape, however complicated that would be, but instead the baby and I picked wild flowers from all the nearby city flowerbeds and left her a bouquet the next time we were in her neighborhood.

I have a homemade Christmas card she sent me with a photograph glued on the front of her posing nude for Salvador Dalí.

Chapter 5
Running

Saturday. We had a lunch of pecans, dried brown apricots, green apple slices and flaxseed-pressed crackers with cherry tomatoes and a large avocado. Most everything was local except for the pecans, which strangely enough came from a Dutch chain store like a pint-sized cross between IKEA and Walmart spread across Europe. The baby gathered many numbers of the small food items and put them first in a bag then a basket then into another container and after some tantrums and book-reading ate some yogurt, applesauce and a few bites of strawberries. Afterwards I took her to the daycare, and since I didn't have to teach that afternoon, I headed off on a run before getting some work done.

I ran. Not because it keeps off death but because it opens up life. Murakami says too it has nothing to do with the idea of keeping off death or extending life or living in health but, and I say, in the delivery of joy. Every day if never otherwise, I come to love myself and the world and my mother and Henry in a new way and imagine ferociously kind engagements with my pains and sorrows.

Now I ran because Henry had sent me a card. Had I imagined it? It was a new kind of torment. It was similar to the way I imagined Mom coming back, during those ten years she was missing, and then her finally coming back—and then nothing. Then ten subsequent years with this person "mom" but still without answers and still without giving back or bringing back my childhood. I ran through the hurt, though sometimes the hurt would well up and it'd be hard to breathe and to run but if you run right through it (and you can) you get somewhere else and the story changes and you smile while you're running and you might start leaping as well. I was trying to run through Henry's card.

Wearing cheap white robes draped over donated graduation dresses, my sister and I held hands nervously waiting to enter the gymnasium to cross the stage and receive our high school diplomas. More than twenty years ago.

"What if Mom is in there?" Emma asked me.

"She isn't."

"But what if she comes for this? For us? What if she comes back? What if she surprises us? That would be amazing. What if she's in there?"

I looked at her unable to contain my frown. Mom had disappeared two years before.

We entered the gym and saw hundreds of parents, family members and friends on the basketball bleachers to the right. There were 123 unfolded black metal chairs on the left with no one yet in them and next to them, a stage with the school principal and teachers. A line of teenagers in similar white and blue gowns (white for girls, blue for boys—the gendering of colors made me cringe) filed slowly into the room, two by two, toward the stage and then the black chairs. We saw Charlie and our father and Fred and Phil and almost everybody, even John who had quickly returned to Chicago to finish high school and hadn't come back out to California since, until our graduation.

—Suddenly, standing there in the corner was Mom, tall and proud and making an entrance. We gasped and nearly fell down. We wept and ran up to her, embraced her, were embraced by her. We were shaking, filled with overwhelming love and surprise and relief and—

No, that didn't happen. That never happened.

The record scratches to a halt.

The others were there, yes. Mom was not there.

Emma and I graduated high school together because I went to summer school and took night classes at the community college as a sophomore and junior so that I could get the hell out of that town as fast as possible. I graduated a year early. I went to the San Francisco Bay for university, and Emma went to Orange County with her boyfriend. We had planned on being "vagabonds in Europe together" straight out of high school, but with the majority of our seven older siblings having dropped out of high school altogether, I decided it was best to head to college right away after all. Emma was pretty mad for a while when I told her, but we made up for it later when she moved to Belgium for a few years and we saw each other once in a while, and even did the whole train thing together through Eastern Europe. She got a master's in Music Teaching. Her high school sweetheart got a Ph.D. in Biochemistry. They got married a week after their simultaneous graduations, and the next year Mom turned up. That did happen.

So then there was Henry's card. Running wasn't getting rid of it. It still felt imaginary. Maybe it was. I eyed the stoplight as I approached Châtelet and crossed either south or west based on which direction would still be green but nearest to becoming red when I arrived in two point five seconds so that I could run out in front of the string of idling taxis without either plowing down any pedestrians waiting to cross too or getting hit by the four lanes of one-way traffic piled on my left. I leapt across the concrete barrier of the bus lane and dodged several strollers and even a wheelchair before jumping up on the curb and continuing faster now down the quay towards the Louvre.

We would go see him. I would find a flight. And then, that morning, we would wake up early and take the RER to the airport and get on a flight that had a layover somewhere like D.C. or New Jersey or Chicago and we would be tired and might even be delayed and miss the connection and have to spend the night and have a difficult time getting a refund on the hotel. We would finally get to San Francisco and we would stay the first night with Fred in Berkeley because it would be strange to see Henry like that all of a sudden at the airport. It would be much too dramatic for an already dramatic situation.

The sidewalk against the Seine was crowded with tourists along the bookstalls and I ran on the edge of the bus lane until I reached the Tuileries where I cut right into the park but then quickly left and stayed up on the raised edge away from the fountains that ended at the Orangerie where I took the stairs down and traversed La Place de la Concorde. Along the stretch before reaching the Orangerie, I thought about the 500-year-old stone barrier facing the river across the boulevard, where

Henry and I stood and watched the Tour de France in the spring before he left. The cyclists whizzed five or six or eight times down the *Champs Elysées* and passed under the Carrousel du Louvre right next to us, preceded and followed by a huge caravan of politicians, celebrities and sponsors in sleek black Mercedes with tinted windows and glamorous sports cars with the windows down and camera-folk poised strategically on motorcycles. Each time after the complete entourage passed, the police watching guard along the edges of the park threw the discarded water bottles at us among the cheering and pleading fans hoping for an authentic souvenir. The Eiffel Tower was in the distance. As I ran toward Concorde, I could see Sacre Coeur to the north, in fleeting glimpses between the buildings.

I had imagined going even before the card arrived, though of course I never knew if I actually would. I was unhappy with myself for entertaining the thought in the way I was entertaining it. It was an inappropriate fantasy. It was inappropriate. But it didn't stop me from having it or from having it a lot. I had imagined turning up in San Francisco like a despondent Romeo at the foot of Henry's apartment building that I found on Google Maps. I stood there hopeless and hopeful and pleading under the glowing, grey night sky of the East Bay. It wasn't raining in my fantasy, although it felt like it should be raining or could be raining. Actual rain would be much too dramatic for an already dramatic situation.

The city block stretches that are parallel with the Champs Elysées before the river turns south are covered with a full canopy of trees with green grass underfoot, and I sprinted part of each of them until I reached La Place de l'Alma. I caught the end of the red light and went before it turned green even though the cars were coming down from Avenue du Président Wilson and back up across the Place onto the Pont de l'Alma. Everyone always expected the cars would cross the complex intersection before I made it all the way across because of the impractical and very French way the lights changed. The people on the sidewalk were visibly worried, but I knew this intersection if I knew anything. The light turned red before the cars reached me, and they waited halfway through the intersection there in the middle of the open road like stranded driftwood on a desert isle.

Henry would take me in his arms in a big bear embrace and bury his face in my hair and whisper sorry and I love you and I would say—no wait. Too dramatic.

The needle skips.

When I got to Trocedero, I dodged groups of tourists snapping photos with selfie sticks and the Eiffel Tower behind them. I plunged down rue Benjamin Franklin until I reached Place du Costa Rica and suddenly realized I was aiming myself toward Passy and our old apartment all along and to continue the route there at the roundabout I turned left on rue de l'Alboni and went down the long flight of steps past the outdoor metro station and saw our place there at the bottom up on the right at the top of the tower. I began to lose my breath, as I imagined the conversation in the park around the corner and all the other moments both good and bad. I shifted my attention back to what was in front of me: the foot bridge over the Avenue du Président Kennedy. I landed down on the Pont de Bir-Hakeim with its riveted metal colonnades and hanging, raindrop *Art Nouveau* lamps and covered cycling and walking path below the metro line 6 that rattled by our single-pane, watery window every five or fifteen minutes until one in the morning, two on weekends.

Now I tried to visualize seeing Henry there on that bridge in the early days when I knew him in his big Rocky Mountain coat and tweed cap and blue scarf before he lost it and I made him a new one. It turned out that image was also no help, so I sprinted from the halfway point, where the Île aux Cygnes shoots out into the river from the bridge. I was trying to get away from him. From him and me. From myself. My lungs were bursting. Hair plastered against my forehead, sweat dripping into my eyes. I came soon to the end of the Pont de Bir-Hakeim and quickly turned left onto the sandy Promenade d'Australie and visualized being there at my running halfway point so that I could project myself to the end and breathe in the end as it began moving towards me. After I passed the Eiffel Tower now on my right, the path became the Promenade Quai Branly until I reached the Musée des Egouts and shortly thereafter I was at Les Invalides, and I followed the Seine like that toward home four miles back to the center of the city.

It isn't possible to chase him down. It wasn't possible to chase Mom down. It isn't possible to chase anyone down. You can chase after them, but you will not catch them and if you catch them they will still never come to you and be what you want or need or deserve. It isn't possible to give or offer something or yourself to someone if they think of it as being forced upon them. It isn't possible to force yourself or a thing on someone and have them like you or it, even if that thing is love or being alive.

I wonder how I managed to be born.

I sprinted across Rivoli and one block up Sébastopol where I stopped abruptly on the sidewalk and cut the music from my ears. The run had ended and now I was in the world again and the tension that I thought was released from the run now fell away. I stood in the world.

Just before going into my building, I paused and turned around, deciding to stop by a couple grocery stores since I needed more supplies, and it's often easier to do the shopping without the baby, even though the stroller can be quite useful for getting large packs of mineral water and milk. I wanted to fill the shelves with those kinds of things and some cat food and litter. There was a cheap shop on the way home where I could get most of that stuff. Once inside, I decided I might as well get some more vegetables and the cereal and eggs and pretty soon I had far too much stuff to carry reasonably. I checked out another city bike from the corner and put most of the items in the basket and slung the milk over one handle and the water over the other. That way I walked home the last four blocks pushing the bike, and I was in a new full sweat by the time I got it all up to the apartment. I felt particularly exhausted after the 10-mile run. It's not always possible to calculate the best method, and even then sometimes you have to go out again even if you thought you were done.

I spent a lot of time imagining what it was like for my mother after one child, and then two and then three and all the way to seven, numbers six and seven the twins, all with Mom's first husband, then three more with her brother-in-law. Ten children.

I set the groceries on the floor inside by the door and directly flopped down in the beat-up, fur-covered chair used only by the cat. It was quiet in the apartment. It felt quiet on the street until a siren roared by and then an overzealous motorcycle. Those sounds were painful. They shocked me inside and brought out the white violence feeling, something safe and protected in me suddenly being shattered. Nothing is actually safe or protected.

Chapter 6
The Blue of Night

It was 4AM when I finally lay down next to the baby. We didn't have to be at the airport until 2PM, an hour by train. We would be in San Francisco by 8PM Pacific Time. The blue of night was beginning to come in through the cracked window. Fresh and cool and spacious. The dark sky lingered outside with several brave stars breaking through the strong urban atmosphere, sending down soft flickers of distant galaxies. Silence lay thick in the air with nothing penetrating it but the baby breathing and the warm embrace of our bodies lying together on the mattress tucked under deep cover. I felt a palpable gentleness of thought as though it was holding me still, the moment still in the vibrant hum that surrounded me and protected me as I curved my body back toward my baby daughter.

Staring at her, so small and perfect, I saw the years of my life pass, all the collected experiences that defined me and that I imagined my baby living for herself, accumulating, hoping I would be able to provide her something I had never gotten or perhaps never understood. The choices that I as her mother would need to make in order to teach my daughter how to make choices herself. Suddenly, all this time backwards and forwards, all the counting and not-counting of it passing became so vivid and frightening, so imminent and substantial. *The unendurable is the beginning of the curve of joy*, wrote Djuna Barnes. In the soundless room, my heart beat softly and I heard it, and then I heard my baby's gentle heart too and all the minute sounds of life around her, the cat sleeping on the chair, the insects in the floorboards, the neighbors sleeping above and below, the water rushing through pipes and the gas held in an eternal flame in the kitchen *chaudière*. It was still dark outside. I breathed deeply and suddenly again it was completely still, no sounds from the street, nothing in the air but the soft breathing of the baby and her delicate almost translucent, closed eyelids, looking so solemn yet serene in sleep.

I gently lifted my arm from against the side of her sleeping form and reached my hand to the floor next to the mattress. I softly wrapped my fingers around Henry's forgotten alarm clock and brought it up to my chest, setting it down in the center on my t-shirt. I silently lifted my right arm up toward the middle of my body, and, holding the clock securely between both hands, I turned it over. I quietly unlatched the plastic casing on the back, taking care not to stir the baby with each minute sound, and slowly took the batteries out, sending a flat, vibrating ping into the air as the first and then second cylinder pulled away from the spring. With the cool, smooth objects against my palm, I carefully placed the batteries back into the clock this time backwards, negative to positive, negative to positive, then delicately set it back down beside the mattress on the floor, resting my arms once again on the baby. I put my head back on the pillow and waited for sleep, watching the shapes dance through the light from the window in the night air.

Katy Masuga is the author of *The Origin of Vermilion* (Spuyten Duvyil, 2016), *Henry Miller and How He Got That Way* (Edinburgh UP, 2011), *The Secret Violence of Henry Miller* (Boydell and Brewer, 2011) and numerous essays and articles as well as short stories that blur fiction and nonfiction.

www.ingramcontent.com/pod-product-compliance
Lightning Source LLC
Chambersburg PA
CBHW051636180726
48284CB00006B/1753

* 9 7 8 1 9 5 2 4 1 9 1 2 6 *